ALSO BY DICK CHENEY

Heart

In My Time

EXCEPTIONAL

Why the World Needs a Powerful America

DICK CHENEY
AND LIZ CHENEY

THRESHOLD EDITIONS

New York   London   Toronto   Sydney   New Delhi

Threshold Editions
An Imprint of Simon & Schuster, Inc.
1230 Avenue of the Americas
New York, NY 10020

First Threshold Editions hardcover edition September 2015

THRESHOLD EDITIONS and colophon
are trademarks of Simon & Schuster, Inc.

For information about special discounts for bulk purchases,
please contact Simon & Schuster Special Sales at
1-866-506-1949 or business@simonandschuster.com.

The Simon & Schuster Speakers Bureau can bring authors to your
live event. For more information or to book an event, contact
the Simon & Schuster Speakers Bureau at 1-866-248-3049
or visit our website at www.simonspeakers.com.

Manufactured in the United States of America

1   3   5   7   9   10   8   6   4   2

Library of Congress Cataloging-in-Publication Data is available.

ISBN 978-1-5011-1541-7
ISBN 978-1-5011-1544-8 (ebook)

To the men and women of the United States Armed Forces,
defenders of liberty, sustainers of freedom

CONTENTS

It is up to us in our time to choose, and choose wisely, between the hard but necessary task of preserving peace and freedom, and the temptation to ignore our duty and blindly hope for the best while the enemies of freedom grow stronger day by day.

—PRESIDENT RONALD REAGAN, MARCH 23, 1983

Yes, We Are Exceptional

*And now let us indulge an honest exultation in the conviction of the
benefit which the example of our country has produced and is likely
to produce on human freedom and human happiness. And let us endeavor to comprehend in all its magnitude and to feel in all its importance the part assigned to us in the great drama of human affairs.*
—DANIEL WEBSTER, DEDICATION OF
BUNKER HILL MONUMENT, 1825

Less than fifty years after our founding, the benefit of America's
example for the world was evident. Yet Daniel Webster could
not have begun to imagine the true magnitude of the role we would
play "in the great drama of human affairs." We have guaranteed freedom, security, and peace for a larger share of humanity than has any
other nation in all of history. There is no other like us. There never has
been. We are, as a matter of empirical fact and undeniable history, the
greatest force for good the world has ever known.

Born of the revolutionary ideal that we are "endowed by our Creator with certain inalienable rights," we were, first, an example of
freedom's possibilities. During World War II, we became freedom's
defender; at the end of the Cold War, the world's sole superpower.

We did not seek the position. It is ours because of our ideals and our power, and the power of our ideals. In the words of British historian Andrew Roberts, "In the debate over whether America was born great, achieved greatness, or had greatness thrust upon her, the only possible conclusion must be: all three."

We are, as constitutional scholar Walter Berns put it, "the one essential country." It isn't just our *involvement* in world events that has been essential for the triumph of freedom. It is our *leadership*. No other nation, international body, or community of nations can do what we do. For the better part of a century, security and freedom for millions of people around the globe have depended on America's military, economic, political, and diplomatic might. For the most part, until the administration of Barack Obama, we delivered.

Since Franklin Roosevelt proclaimed us the "Arsenal of Democracy" in 1940, Republican and Democratic presidents alike have understood the indispensable nature of American power. Presidents from Truman to Nixon, from Kennedy to Reagan have known that America's strength must be safeguarded, her supremacy maintained. In the 1940s, American power and leadership were essential to victory in World War II and the liberation of millions from the grip of fascism. In the Cold War, American strength and supremacy were key in liberating Eastern Europe, defeating Soviet totalitarianism, and ensuring the survival of freedom. In this century, our leadership and our might will once again be required for the defeat of militant Islam and the preservation of our security and liberty in the face of threats from other dedicated adversaries. Yet despite the explosive spread of terrorist ideology and organizations, the establishment of an ISIS caliphate in the heart of the Middle East, the proliferation of nuclear weapons, and increasing threats from Iran, China, North Korea, and Russia,

President Obama has departed from the bipartisan tradition going back seventy-five years of maintaining America's global supremacy and leadership.

He has abandoned Iraq, leaving a vacuum being filled by our enemies. He says he will do the same in Afghanistan. He has made dangerous cuts to America's conventional forces and reduced our nuclear arsenal in the misguided belief this will convince rogue nations to do the same. He has recalibrated America's foreign policy to avoid causing offense in Tehran. He has been so desperate to conclude a nuclear agreement Iran's leaders have no intention of honoring, that he has repeatedly misled the American people and granted dangerous concession after dangerous concession. He is gambling America's security on the veracity of the mullahs in Tehran. He is unconcerned with maintaining American supremacy because it is inconsistent with his worldview. "No world order," he tells us, "that elevates one nation or group of people over another will succeed."

President Obama has diminished American power and retreated from the field of battle, fueling rising threats against our nation. He has pursued a foreign policy built on appeasing our adversaries, abandoning our allies, and apologizing for America. "A civilization that feels guilty for everything it is and does," wrote Jean-François Revel, "will lack the energy and conviction to defend itself." For President Obama, it goes beyond lacking the "energy and conviction" to defend us. He has dedicated his presidency to restraining us, limiting our power, and diminishing us.

The touchstone of his ideology—that America is to blame and her power must be restrained—requires a willful blindness about what America has done in the world. It is fundamentally counterfactual. When President Obama's ideology has come crashing up against reality, America's security has suffered.

Don't worry, he tells us. Despite the carnage militant Islam is spreading across the Middle East, filling the vacuum left by President Obama's retreat, everything will be okay because our enemies are on the wrong side of history. "The arc of the moral universe is long," he recites, "but ultimately it bends toward justice," as though no action is required. The truth is America's enemies are on the wrong side of morality and justice, but they will be on the wrong side of history only if we put them there.

There is good news. Just as one president has left a path of destruction in his wake, one president can rescue us. The right person in the Oval Office can restore America's strength and our alliances, renew our power and leadership, defeat our enemies, and keep us safe. It will not be easy. There are difficult decisions to be made and very little time.

We have faced grave challenges before, and the right leaders have brought us through. As Charles Krauthammer has observed:

> *It is one of the enduring mysteries of American history, so near providential as to give the most hardened atheist pause—that it should have produced, at every hinge point, great men who matched the moment. A roiling, revolutionary British colony gives birth to the greatest cohort of political thinkers ever: Jefferson, Adams, Madison, Hamilton, Washington, Franklin and Jay. The crisis of the 19th century brings forth Lincoln; the 20th, FDR.*

We are living at another hinge point of history and require a president equal to this moment. We must choose wisely.

As citizens, we also have a duty to protect our ideals and our freedoms by safeguarding our history. We must ensure that our children know the truth about who we are, what we've done, and why it is uniquely America's duty to be freedom's defender.

Our children should know about the boys of Pointe du Hoc and Doolittle's Raiders, the Battles of Midway and Iwo Jima. They should learn about the courage of the young Americans who fought the Nazis at the Battle of the Bulge and the Japanese on Okinawa. They should learn why America was right to end the war by dropping the atomic bombs on Hiroshima and Nagasaki, and about the fundamental decency of a nation that established the Truman Doctrine, the Marshall Plan, the Berlin Airlift, and the North Atlantic Treaty Organization. They need to know about the horror of the Holocaust, and what it means to promise "never again."

They should know that once there was an empire so evil and bereft of truth it had to build a wall to keep its citizens in, and that the free world, led by America, defeated it. They need to know about the terrorists who attacked us on 9/11, the courage of the first responders, and the heroism of the passengers on Flight 93. They should understand what kind of world militant Islam will create if we don't defeat it.

They should learn about great men like George C. Marshall and Dwight Eisenhower and Harry Truman and Ronald Reagan. We must teach them what it took to prevail over evil in the twentieth century and what it will take in the twenty-first. We must make sure they understand that it is the brave men and women of the United States armed forces who defend our freedom and secure it for millions of others as well.

Our children need to know that they are citizens of the most powerful, good, and honorable nation in the history of mankind, *the* exceptional nation. Ordinary Americans have done heroic things to guarantee her survival. America's future, and the future of freedom for all the world, now depends on us. Speaking at Omaha Beach on the fortieth anniversary of the D-Day landings, President Reagan put it this way: "We will always remember. We will always be proud. We will always be prepared, so we may always be free."

Dick Cheney
Liz Cheney
Muy 2015
Wilson, Wyoming

PART ONE

———•◆•———

The American Century

ONE

For the Good of All Mankind

You have completed your mission with the greatest victory in the history of warfare. You have commanded with outstanding success the most powerful military force that has ever been assembled. . . . You have made history, great history, for the good of all mankind.
—GENERAL MARSHALL LETTER TO
GENERAL EISENHOWER, MAY 7, 1945

On the president's plain wooden desk were half a dozen microphones, two newly sharpened pencils, a note pad, and a pack of Camels. A small audience, including actor Clark Gable and his wife, Carole Lombard; the president's mother, Sara Roosevelt; Secretary of State Cordell Hull; and other cabinet members, had gathered. It was the sixteenth fireside chat of FDR's presidency, December 29, 1940. The mood was somber and the room was hot as the president arrived. "My friends," he began, "this is not a fireside chat on war. It is a talk on national security."

Most of Europe had fallen to Hitler. Britain stood alone. Without America's aid, she might not survive. Recalling the economic crisis of 1933, Roosevelt said the same "courage and realism" would be required to face the rising threat to America's security. "Never before since Jamestown and Plymouth Rock," Roosevelt said, "has our American civilization been in such danger as now." Declaring his intent to keep the nation out of "a last-ditch war," Roosevelt went on to describe why the security of the United States depended upon the defense of Great Britain:

> They ask for the implements of war, the planes, the tanks, the guns, the freighters, which will enable them to fight for their liberty and for our security. Emphatically we must get these weapons to them in sufficient volume and quickly enough, so that we and our children will be saved the agony and suffering of war which others have had to endure.

Referring to those who argued for appeasement, Roosevelt pointed to the experience of the past two years, and said it had proven that negotiations with Hitler were futile:

> No nation can appease the Nazis. No man can tame a tiger into a kitten by stroking it. There can be no appeasement with ruthlessness. There can be no reasoning with an incendiary bomb. We know now that a nation can have peace with the Nazis only at the price of total surrender.

To do what was required, America must discard "business as usual" and turn its full productive power toward producing the armaments needed for the defense of freedom. No strikes or lockouts, no concern about postwar surplus plant capacity or the desire for luxury goods must be allowed to stop America doing what the world required. "We must be the great arsenal of democracy. For us, this is an emergency as serious as war itself."

Roosevelt's determination to mobilize the nation was crucial to the success of the effort he knew we needed to mount. It had not been an easy or clear path getting to this point. The American people were war-weary and isolationist sentiment was strong. In the aftermath of World War I we had demobilized and retreated behind our oceans, hoping, as George Washington had advised, to avoid entangling our "peace and prosperity" in the fortunes of Europe. While we were turned inward, Adolf Hitler began his Blitzkrieg.

ON THE EVENING OF Thursday, August 31, 1939, General George C. Marshall dined at the home of Supreme Court justice Harlan Stone. Marshall was to be sworn in the next morning as Army chief of staff. The dinner guests gathered in the elegant brick home at 2340 Wyoming Avenue in Washington, D.C., during a time when one grim report from Europe followed another. Eighteen months earlier Hitler had annexed Austria. Thirteen months earlier he had taken the Sudetenland region of Czechoslovakia. Six months after that, despite the promises he'd made to British prime minister Neville Chamberlain at Munich, Hitler sent his troops into Prague and took all of Czechoslovakia. Just eight days before the Stones' dinner party, the Nazis had signed a nonaggression pact with the Soviet Union. The Molotov-Ribbentrop Pact alleviated Hitler's concern that he would have to fight on two fronts and allowed him to turn his attention to Poland.

During dinner, Marshall was called to the telephone. Hitler's troops were massing on the Polish border. Hours later, as Marshall slept in Quarters One at Fort Myer, the second call came. It was 3:00 A.M. German planes were bombing Warsaw. Turning to his wife, Marshall said, "It has come." Then he dressed and headed for his office in the Munitions Building on Constitution Avenue.

Three miles to the east, across the Potomac River, another call had come in. America's ambassador to France, William C. Bullitt, had a message for President Roosevelt from the ambassador to Poland, Anthony Biddle. The German invasion had begun. "Well, Bill," the president responded to Bullitt on hearing the news, "it has come at last. God bless us all." Then he reached for a pencil and paper and made these notes of the call:

The President received word at 2:50 am by telephone from Ambass. Biddle through Ambass. Bullitt that Germany has invaded Poland and that four cities are being bombed. The Pres. directed that all Navy ships and Army commands be notified by radio at once.

In bed
3:05 am
Sept 1, '39
FDR

The Germans had assembled a massive force of sixty divisions, more than 1.5 million troops, for the invasion of Poland. Thousands of tanks and armored cars poured across the Polish frontier as German planes bombed cities, roads, railroads, munitions depots, and columns of fleeing refugees. Warsaw fell on September 27. The last Polish force was defeated on October 6. The Poles had been able to hold out against Hitler's onslaught for only a few weeks—and Poland's army was significantly larger and better equipped than the United States Army of 1939.

When George Marshall became Army chief of staff, America's army was slightly smaller than Romania's. Demobilization in the aftermath of World War I, fueled in part by strong isolationist sentiment, had ensured America's standing army was insufficient in size, skills, equipment, and resources to adequately defend the nation. In the summer of 1939 there were only approximately 174,000 enlisted men in the Army. Not a single infantry division was near its combat strength and there were no armored divisions. There were 1,175 planes. Those who were lucky were training with 1903 Springfield rifles. Other units, lacking resources to purchase actual weapons, studied blueprints and drilled with wooden machine guns. Speaking to a joint meeting of the American Military Institute and the American Historical Association at the Mayflower Hotel in Washington, D.C., on Thursday, December 28, 1939, General Marshall announced that the Army was "probably less than 25% ready for immediate action."

Building and equipping a force capable of defending the nation would require money and time. Marshall wanted the American public to understand that expenditures on defense could not be delayed. In an interview in the *New York Times* in May 1939, he listed the items the Army needed most urgently. This included "planes, semi-automatic rifles, light machine guns, modernized artillery, anti-tank cannons, heavy-caliber guns," and gunpowder. "Every one of these items," Marshall said, "requires a year or longer to produce. A billion dollars the day the war is declared will not buy ten cents' worth of such material for quick delivery."

The situation had not improved much when, five months later, at dawn on May 10, 1940, Hitler launched an assault into Belgium, Holland, and Luxembourg, heading for France. The next morning, Saturday, May 11, General Marshall arrived for a meeting in the office of Secretary of the Treasury Henry Morgenthau. Morgenthau knew additional resources were needed for defense and he was frustrated that requests for funding were arriving on the president's desk in a one-off fashion. He wanted to see the big picture and knew Marshall was the man to draw it for him.

As Marshall detailed everything that was needed immediately, including significant increases in funding for additional men and equipment, Morgenthau encouraged him not to hold back. "I don't scare easily," he said a few hours into the meeting, "and I am not scared yet." Marshall responded that the overwhelming need "makes me dizzy." Morgenthau told him, "It makes me dizzy if we don't get it."

With Marshall at his side, Morgenthau placed a call to Colonel Edwin "Pa" Watson, Roosevelt's trusted military aide. He explained that Marshall had been asked to go up to Capitol Hill on Monday, May 13, to give "confidential figures" of what the Army needed. Morgenthau wanted Marshall to see the president first. Watson agreed to make time for them on the president's schedule. When Marshall and Morgenthau arrived at the White House on Monday morning, both knew they were about to have a make-or-break meeting.

Morgenthau began by detailing the case for the massive and urgent buildup Marshall needed. He also urged the president to establish a civilian body to oversee the industrial mobilization required to arm America and her allies. The president wasn't convinced. After unsuccessfully attempting to sway Roosevelt, Morgenthau told him, "Well, I still think you're wrong." "You've filed your protest," Roosevelt said.

Sensing that he was in serious danger of losing the argument, Morgenthau asked the president if he would at least hear directly from General Marshall. "Well, I know exactly what he would say. There is no necessity for me hearing him at all." General Marshall realized it was a desperate situation, "catastrophic in its possibilities." Years later, Marshall explained, "I felt he might be president, but I had certain knowledge which I was sure he didn't possess or which he didn't grasp."

Marshall was a formal man, with the highest regard for the chain of command and for civilian control of the military. He declined invitations to socialize with the president, not wanting to become too familiar with the commander in chief. It was only because he believed the future of the nation might be at stake that he was able to do what he did next.

As General Marshall recalled later, when Roosevelt was ending the meeting, Marshall walked over to him, "stood looking down at him and said, 'Mr. President, may I have three minutes?' " Perhaps startled by Marshall's directness, Roosevelt replied, "Of course, General Marshall, of course."

Marshall began by supporting Morgenthau's argument that the president should appoint a civilian organization to oversee the industrial side of mobilization. Roosevelt had said it was unnecessary because he was dividing the duties between Morgenthau, presidential advisor Harry Hopkins, and himself. To demonstrate the untenable nature of this plan, Marshall described the lunch he'd had with Morgenthau at the Treasury Department the previous week. Even though Morgenthau had given instructions that the two of them not be bothered, they were interrupted three times on the matter of closing the New York Stock Exchange. Morgenthau had simply been trying to "understand the enormity of our situation regarding military preparedness and he wasn't even allowed to do this," Marshall said. He told the president that "none of you are supermen and Mr. Morgenthau has no more chance of managing this thing than of flying."

Marshall then detailed the needs of the Army. At that moment, when the Germans had two million men marching through Western Europe, the United States could dedicate only 15,000 men to combat. Weapons, rations, ammunition, housing—everything was needed. Finishing his presentation, which had exceeded the three minutes he asked for, Marshall summed up the stakes, telling the president: "If you don't do something . . . and do it right away, really do it today, I don't know what's going to happen to this country." Stunned, Roosevelt told Marshall to come back the next day to discuss details of the supplemental Army appropriation he needed.

On Thursday, May 16, 1940, Roosevelt appeared before Congress and asked for $896 million, including $546 million for the Army. Marshall had gotten nearly everything he'd asked for. It was only the beginning.

Ten days later the evacuation of the British Expeditionary Force from the continent of Europe began. Deployed in an effort to defend France from the coming German onslaught, the British force, along with more than 100,000 French troops, had been driven back to the sea. A race began to try to save the lives of 335,000 men trapped near the French town of Dunkirk. On June 4, 1940, Churchill described the action to the British Parliament:

> *The Royal Air Force engaged the main strength of the German Air Force, and inflicted upon them losses of at least four to one; and the Navy, using nearly 1,000 ships of all kinds, carried 335,000 men, French and British, out of the jaws of death and shame, to their native land and to the tasks which lay immediately ahead.*

Although Churchill knew the miracle of this deliverance, he also knew this wasn't a victory. "Wars," he said, "are not won by evacuations."

Nor could this war be won without America. Demonstrating the courage and fortitude that would inspire generations for the duration of the war and beyond, Churchill told his people:

> *We shall not flag or fail. We shall go on to the end, we shall fight in France, we shall fight on the seas and the oceans, we shall fight with growing confidence and growing strength in the air, we shall defend our Island, whatever the cost may be, we shall fight on the beaches, we shall fight on the landing grounds, we shall fight in the fields and in the streets, we shall fight in the hills; we shall never surrender, and even if, which I do not for a moment believe,*

this Island or a large part of it were subjugated and starving, then our Empire beyond the seas, armed and guarded by the British Fleet, would carry on the struggle, until, in God's good time, the New World, with all its power and might, steps forth to the rescue and liberation of the old.

Although the men of the British Expeditionary Force had been successfully evacuated, their weapons, ammunition, and vehicles had been lost. Only the United States had the ability to resupply Britain's forces. Roosevelt ordered it done. Shipments of weapons and matériel began flowing across the Atlantic. Churchill, in his war memoirs, wrote of this transfer of weapons for Britain's defense: "All of this reads easily now, but at that time it was a supreme act of faith and leadership for the United States to deprive themselves of this very considerable mass of arms for the sake of a country which many deemed already beaten."

As France fell, the Battle of Britain and the Battle of the Atlantic raged on. Hitler's forces attacked England from the sky and launched assaults against Allied shipping on the seas. Britain's refusal to surrender in the face of the relentless German barrage led Ronald Reagan years later to describe this as a time when the British Isles were "incandescent with courage."

Britain fought on while her needs grew and her ability to pay dwindled. On December 9, 1940, Roosevelt was on board the USS *Tuscaloosa* in the Caribbean when he received a letter from Churchill, "one of the most important of my life," Churchill later said. It began with a survey of where the war stood as 1940 came to an end, and a description of the threat facing Britain:

The danger of Great Britain being destroyed by a swift, overwhelming blow has for the time being very greatly receded. In its place there is a long, gradually maturing danger, less sudden and less spectacular, but equally deadly. This mortal danger is the steady and increasing diminution of sea tonnage. We can endure the shattering of our dwellings and the slaughter of our civil population by indiscriminate air attacks. . . . The decision for 1941 lies upon the seas. Unless we can establish our ability to feed this Island, to import the munitions of all kinds which we need, unless we can move our armies to the various theaters where Hitler and his confederate Mussolini must be met, and maintain them there and do all this with the assurance of being able to carry it on till the spirit of the Continental Dictators is broken, we may fall by the way, and the time needed by the United States to complete her defensive preparations may not be forthcoming.

To meet this challenge, Britain would need "not less than three million tons of additional merchant shipbuilding capacity . . . Only the United States can meet this need." Churchill also sought an additional 2,000 aircraft per month and significant increases in U.S.-supplied small arms, artillery, and tanks. "When the tide of Dictatorship begins to recede," Churchill explained, "many countries trying to regain their freedom may be asking for arms, and there is no source to which they can look except the factories of the United States. I must therefore urge the importance of expanding to the utmost American productive capacity for small arms, artillery and tanks."

Finally, Churchill turned to the topic of finance. "The moment approaches," he told Roosevelt, "when we shall no longer be able to pay cash for shipping and other supplies."

By the time he arrived back in Washington a week later, FDR had devised Lend-Lease. Britain would receive loans of the equipment she needed. FDR called the press into the Oval Office on December 17 and explained the program this way:

> *Suppose my neighbor's home catches fire, and I have a length of garden hose four or five hundred feet away. If he can take my garden hose and connect it up with his hydrant, I may help him to put out his fire. Now what do I do? I don't say to him before that operation, "Neighbor, my garden hose cost me fifteen dollars; you have to pay me fifteen dollars for it." What is the transaction that goes on? I don't want fifteen dollars. I want my garden hose back after the fire is over.*

America would lend or lease equipment to the British because, as Churchill wrote, "our continued resistance to the Hitler tyranny was deemed to be of vital interest to the great Republic." This decision was, he later told Parliament, "the most unsordid act in the history of any nation."

WITH HIS "ARSENAL OF DEMOCRACY" fireside chat to the nation on December 29, 1940, President Roosevelt was building public support for Lend-Lease. Widely admired as the program would be in retrospect, many of his fellow Americans at the time sharply disagreed with it.

Aviation pioneer Charles Lindbergh, a leader of the isolationist cause, declared that he opposed Lend-Lease because arming the British would serve only to prolong the war. Speaking before the Senate Foreign Relations Committee in February 1941, he described the devastation he believed the policy would cause:

> *An English victory, if it were possible at all, would necessitate years of wars and an invasion of the Continent of Europe. I believe*

this would create prostration, famine and disease in Europe—and
probably in America—such as the whole world has never experi-
enced before.

Ignoring recent history on the continent of Europe, Lindbergh went
on to explain, "This is why I prefer a negotiated peace to a complete
victory by either side."

But those who supported the president's policy made their case,
too. In June 1940, *Life* magazine tried to dispel the notion held by
many that our oceans would protect us, by showing how distances
had shrunk in the age of airpower. *"Life* Flies the Atlantic: America
to Europe in 23 Hours by Clipper," proclaimed the opening article.
Hitler's march across Western Europe was covered extensively in reporting headlined, "German Conquest Threatens the World." In the
cover essay, columnist Walter Lippmann addressed the issue head-on:

It is manifest that in seeking to separate ourselves from the great
wars of Europe, we cannot rely on the Atlantic Ocean. . . . Oceans
are not a barrier. They are a highway. Across the oceans all the
empires of modern times have gone forth and have conquered.

One of the most eloquent statements of the case against isolationism came in the form of a poem by Edna St. Vincent Millay, published in the *New York Times* on June 14, 1940. Titled "There Are No
Islands, Any More: Lines Written in Passion and in Deep Concern for
England, France and My Own Country," Millay's poem captured the
weakness of the isolationists' assertions:

Dear Islander, I envy you:
I'm very fond of islands, too;
And few the pleasures I have known

Which equaled being left alone.
Yet matters from without intrude
At times upon my solitude

. . . .

No man, no nation, is made free
By stating it intends to be

. . . .

Oh, let us give, before too late,
To those who hold our country's fate
Along with theirs.

Millay wrote that France's and England's challenge was also ours—and that of all liberty-loving people. The question was, "Can freedom stand—must freedom fall?"

Oh, build, assemble, transport, give,
That England, France and we may live,
Before tonight, before too late,
To those who hold our country's fate
In desperate fingers, reaching out
For weapons we confer about

. . . .

Lest French and British fighters, deep
In battle, needing guns and sleep,
For lack of aid be overthrown,
And we be left to fight alone.

Neither England nor we would be left to fight alone. On March 11, 1941, President Roosevelt signed Lend-Lease into law. On December 7, 1941, the Japanese attacked Pearl Harbor. On December 11, 1941, Hitler declared war on the United States. The isolationists' position crumbled in the face of the reality of the German and Japanese killing machines.

Winston Churchill set sail for America on December 13, 1941, aboard HMS *Duke of York*. Delayed by storms at sea, Churchill's party of eighty didn't arrive at Hampton Roads, Virginia, until December 22. From there, they flew to Washington. It was night as the plane approached America's capital city. Europe's cities were under blackout orders. Churchill's aide Commander C. R. Thompson recorded the sentiment in the plane as the passengers saw the lighted city below:

> *Those in the plane were transfixed with delight to look down from the windows and see the amazing spectacle of a whole city lighted up. Washington represented something immensely precious— freedom, hope, strength. . . . My heart filled.*

Over the course of the next three weeks, the British and American chiefs of staff met twelve times to begin planning the Allied war strategy. The two most significant decisions taken during these sessions were that there must be a single commander in each theater of the war with authority over all the Allied forces in that area, and that Germany must be defeated before the Allies turned their attention to Japan. In light of the blow struck by Japan at Pearl Harbor and the demand by the American people for a response, it was no small matter for Roosevelt and his military commanders to agree to focus on defeating Germany first. British historian Andrew Roberts has called this decision "one of the greatest acts of American statesmanship of the twentieth century."

On December 26, 1941, Churchill addressed a joint session of Congress. Interest in the speech was intense. Congressmen returned to Washington from the Christmas recess. A thousand attendees filled the galleries. Five thousand more waited in the rain outside the Capitol. They weren't disappointed.

Speaking of the long road ahead, of the trials and tribulations Britain and America would face together, Churchill reminded his audience that the task in front of them was "the noblest work in the world," for it was defending "the cause of freedom in every land." And he had no doubt of the outcome:

> *Sure I am that this day, now, we are the masters of our fate. That the task which has been set us is not above our strength. That its pangs and toils are not beyond our endurance. As long as we have faith in our cause, and an unconquerable willpower, salvation will not be denied us. In the words of the Psalmist: "He shall not be afraid of evil tidings. His heart is fixed, trusting in the Lord."*

He also noted that there had been good tidings that year, and the greatest of these was that "the United States, united as never before, has drawn the sword for freedom and cast away the scabbard."

A week later, *Time* named Franklin Roosevelt Man of the Year for 1941. Of Churchill, who'd been *Time*'s Man of the Year in 1940, the editors said he was "a man of the year, of the decade, and, if his cause won, of all time." Though Roosevelt hadn't yet led his nation in combat, *Time* chose him as Man of the Year because "the use of the strength of the U.S. had become the key to the future of the war, and Franklin Roosevelt was the key to the forces of the U.S."

The day after Churchill set sail from England, another of the great men who would be indispensable to the Allied victory arrived in Washington. Colonel Dwight Eisenhower reported to General Marshall in his office in the Munitions Building on Sunday, December 14, 1941. Marshall spent twenty minutes outlining the situation the United States faced in the Pacific. Then he asked Eisenhower, "What should be our general line of action?" Eisenhower asked for some time to consider his response, went to his new desk in the War Plans division, and returned a few hours later to tell Marshall:

> *General, it will be a long time before major reinforcements can go to the Philippines, longer than the garrison can hold out with any driblet assistance, if the enemy commits major forces to their reduction. But we must do everything for them that is humanly possible. The people of China, of the Philippines, of the Dutch East Indies will be watching us. They may excuse failure but they will not excuse abandonment. Their trust and friendship are important to us. Our base must be Australia, and we must start at once to expand it and to secure our communications to it. In this last we dare not fail. We must take great risks and spend any amount of money required.*

Marshall agreed with Eisenhower's assessment and told him, "Do your best to save them."

It wasn't possible to save the Philippines in 1942, despite Eisenhower's herculean efforts to direct men and matériel to the Pacific Theater. As Japanese aims in the Pacific became clear, and as America's European allies urged that planning go forward for the "Hitler First" policy, Eisenhower increasingly recognized the importance of fighting in Europe. He wrote his thoughts on a memo pad on his desk:

> *We've got to go to Europe and fight . . . if we're to keep Russia in, save the Middle East and Burma; we've got to begin slugging with air at West Europe; to be followed by a land attack as soon as possible.*

On June 8, 1942, Marshall sent Eisenhower to Europe to command all American forces in the European Theater.

The great debate between the Allies in 1942 and 1943 concerned the timing of a cross-channel invasion of Europe. All knew it had to be done. American planners wanted it done soon. Soviet premier Joseph Stalin, whose nonaggression pact with Hitler had proven to be worth as much to him as the Munich agreement had been to the Czechs and the British, was now fighting for his nation's survival. It was crucial to the Allied cause that Stalin's forces continue to engage the Germans. It was crucial to Stalin that the Allies open a second front soon.

The British did not believe the Allies were ready for an invasion of Europe and instead urged that we fight Hitler's forces in North Africa. The American military planners saw North Africa as a diversion and wanted to move more quickly to confront Hitler in Europe. President Roosevelt sided with the British. He realized he could not overcome their reluctance, and he recognized the North Africa operation offered the best option for engaging Hitler's forces in the near term. On November 8, 1942, Operation Torch was launched when U.S. and British forces landed in Morocco and Algeria. By May 1943, after defeating the Axis forces in Tunisia, the Allies had prevailed.

As historian Rick Atkinson has noted, it was more than territory that we gained in our first campaign against the Wehrmacht:

> *Four U.S. divisions now had combat experience. . . . Troops had learned the importance of terrain, of combined arms, of aggressive patrolling, of stealth, of massed armor. They now knew what it was like to be bombed, shelled, and machine-gunned, and to fight on.*

The North Africa campaign had changed Eisenhower, as well. To the skills that made him a supremely valuable staff officer, he had now added the experience of command.

The period 1942–43 also brought victories for the Allies in the

Pacific. The most important of these occurred in June 1942 at the Battle of Midway. The Japanese sent a massive fleet, including four aircraft carriers, to attack the American base on Midway. The Americans, having broken the Japanese codes, knew of the planned attack and prepared to prevent it. Admiral Chester Nimitz deployed three American carriers—*Enterprise*, *Hornet*, and *Yorktown*—to defend the island. In a surprise attack, planes flying from these ships were able to destroy three of Japan's four carriers. A fourth Japanese carrier, *Hiryu*, was also destroyed but not before planes launched off its deck severely damaged the *Yorktown*, which was sunk the next day. The battle was a decisive victory for the Americans and inflicted severe losses on the Japanese. It changed the course of the war in the Pacific and set us on the path to defeat Japan.

IN THE SPRING OF 1944, Eisenhower had moved his headquarters from London to Portsmouth, on the southern coast of England, to be close to the main embarkation point for the Allied invasion of Europe. He had set D-Day for June 5, and had been meeting twice daily with his weather experts and his chief commanders. When the team gathered at 0400 on June 4 the weather report called for high winds, rough seas, and thick cloud cover. Eisenhower postponed the attack. Ships that had been loaded and launched had to return to port and make themselves ready to launch again in twenty-four hours.

The next day, Eisenhower's meteorologists told the assembled team that there appeared to be a small window of good weather beginning on June 6. Storms were likely to follow, raising Eisenhower's concern, as he later wrote, that the Allies might land "the first several waves successfully and then find later build-up impracticable, and so have to leave the isolated original attacking forces easy prey to German counteraction. However, the consequences of the delay justified great risk." Among the consequences Eisenhower was particularly concerned about were the safety and morale of the troops already aboard ships, "poised and ready." He gave the order to go.

Successful amphibious landings in North Africa, Sicily, and Salerno had given the Allies valuable experience, but those coastlines had been unfortified. The endeavor to land on the continent, breach Hitler's Atlantic Wall, and establish a foothold through which to supply the invading forces was unlike anything that had ever been done. In the days after the invasion, *Time* reported that "the plan had grown to a complexity of detail incomprehensible to the civilian mind." The Navy's invasion plans were 800 pages long and a full set of naval orders weighed 300 pounds. Yet the Allies' objective was clear, as were Eisenhower's orders from the combined chiefs of staff: "You will enter the continent of Europe, and, in conjunction with the other United Nations, undertake operations aimed at the heart of Germany and the destruction of her armed forces."

If the Allies had been thrown back to the sea, the consequences would have been devastating. Millions of additional lives would have been lost, and there would have been a struggle for domination in Europe between Hitler and Stalin. In an interview in 1994, historian Stephen Ambrose explained the significance of D-Day:

> *You can't exaggerate it. You can't overstate it. This was the pivot point of the twentieth century. It was the day on which the decision was made as to who was going to rule in this world in the second half of the twentieth century. Is it going to be Nazism, is it going to be communism, or are the democracies going to prevail?*

The essence of what the Allies accomplished on D-Day is captured in two photos. The first was taken from inside a Higgins boat as American GIs disembarked, laden with their backpacks and weapons, heading through the surf toward Omaha Beach. The silhouette of each soldier reminds us that it was individual men whose heroism that day saved civilization.

The second photo was taken from the heights above Omaha Beach at the end of the day on June 6, 1944. Thousands of Allied men, ships, trucks, and tanks fill the image, stretching to the horizon. The results of the massive American mobilization and production effort of the previous four years can be seen pouring onto the continent of Europe. In an oral history, John Reville, who was a lieutenant with F Company, 5th Ranger Battalion, recalled being on top of the bluff with his runner, Private Rex Low, at the end of that day of days. "Rex," Reville said, pointing out at the thousands of ships filling the English Channel, "take a look at this. You'll never see a sight like this again in your life."

June 6, 1944, was a day when America's greatness was on full display, from the unparalleled heroism of the soldiers who stormed the beaches; to the ingenuity of men like Henry Higgins, who invented the landing craft that made the invasion possible; to the courage and fortitude of the Rangers who took the cliffs at Pointe du Hoc; to the business leaders like Bill Knudsen and Henry Kaiser who had driven American industry to turn out the thousands of ships and planes necessary to win the war; to the commanders like Marshall, Eisenhower, and Omar Bradley who built the force and planned and commanded the invasion. The world had never seen anything like it.

And on that day, the eyes of all the world were on the coast of France. First news of the invasion broke overnight while most Americans slept. By 4:00 A.M. "every church was lighted and in every church people prayed," *Time* reported. As the nation awoke to the news, the mood across the land was solemn:

There was no sudden fear, as on that September morning in 1939 when the Germans marched into Poland; no sudden hate, as on Pearl Harbor day. This time, moved by a common impulse, the casual churchgoers, as well as the devout went to pray.

At 10:30 A.M., families knelt together by their radios as President Roosevelt led the nation in prayer:

Almighty, God: Our sons, pride of our Nation, this day have set upon a mighty endeavor, a struggle to preserve our Republic, our religion and our civilization, and to set free a suffering humanity. Lead them straight and true; give strength to their arms, stoutness to their hearts, steadfastness in their faith.

American GIs fighting on other fronts were gripped by the news, for they knew the way home led over the beaches of France. And in Amsterdam, one young fifteen-year-old girl tracked the movement of the Allied forces, hour by hour, through BBC broadcasts over her wireless. In her diary, she wrote:

My dearest Kitty, "This is D Day," the BBC announced at twelve. The invasion has begun! This morning at eight the British reported heavy bombing of Calais, Boulogne, Le Havre, Cherbourg, as well as Pas de Calais. . . . According to German news, British paratroopers have landed on the coast of France. . . . BBC broadcast in German, Dutch, French and other languages at ten: The invasion has begun!

Anne Frank and her family dared to hope the news meant the liberation was at hand. "A huge commotion in the Annex!" she wrote.

"Will this year, 1944, bring us victory?" No one could know, but the prospect gave them courage. "Where there is hope, there is life," Anne wrote.

Anne Frank and her family were arrested in their annex on August 4, 1944, before the liberation came. Anne and her sister, Margot, were taken to Auschwitz and then to Bergen-Belsen, where Anne died in the early spring of 1945. The British liberated the camp on April 12.

LIEUTENANT FRANCES SLANGER AND three other U.S. Army nurses waded ashore on D-Day plus four. Over the next five weeks they cared for more than three thousand wounded and dying soldiers. In her tent one night, as she thought about all she had seen, Frances wrote a letter to *Stars and Stripes* honoring the American GI:

> *To every GI wearing an American uniform—for you we have the greatest admiration and respect. . . . We have learned a great deal about our American soldier and the stuff he is made of. The wounded do not cry. Their buddies come first. They show such patience and determination. The courage and fortitude they show is awesome to behold.*

Frances did not live to see her letter published. She was killed the next night when a German shell ripped through her tent.

Born in Lodz, Poland, in 1913, Frances, together with her mother and sister, secured passage on a ship bound for America in 1920. They were Jews hoping to escape persecution and build a better life. As a young girl, Frances sold fruit on the streets of Boston with her father and dreamed of becoming a nurse. In 1937 she graduated from Boston City Hospital's School of Nursing.

Frances kept a scrapbook, as did many young girls in those days. In one of hers, she copied this:

There was a dream that men could one day speak their thoughts. There was a hope that men could stroll through the streets unafraid. There was a prayer that each could speak to his own God. That dream, that hope, that prayer became America.

FORTY YEARS AFTER D-DAY, President Reagan stood at Pointe du Hoc where American Rangers had secured the cliffs. Looking out at an audience filled with veterans of the landing, he said:

> *Behind me is a memorial that symbolizes the Ranger daggers that were thrust into the top of these cliffs. And before me are the men who put them there. These are the boys of Pointe du Hoc. These are the men who took the cliffs. These are the champions who helped free a continent. These are the heroes who helped end a war. Gentlemen, I look at you and I think of the words of Stephen Spender's poem. You are the men who in your "lives fought for life . . . and left the vivid air signed with your honor."*
>
> *The men of Normandy had faith that what they were doing was right, faith that they fought for all humanity, faith that a just God would grant them mercy on this beachhead or the next. It was the deep knowledge—and pray God we have not lost it—that there is a profound moral difference between the use of force for liberation and the use of force for conquest. You were here to liberate, not to conquer, and so you and those others did not doubt your cause. And you were right not to doubt.*

In the Normandy American Cemetery, above Omaha Beach, 9,387 Americans are buried, young men who gave all. The inscription in the central colonnade at the cemetery is a tribute to them and to all the Americans killed fighting to liberate Europe and preserve our freedom: "This embattled shore, portal of freedom, is forever hallowed by the ideals, the valor and the sacrifices of our fellow countrymen."

VICE PRESIDENT HARRY TRUMAN was presiding over the United States Senate at 4:45 P.M. on April 12, 1945, when Franklin Roosevelt died of a cerebral hemorrhage in his cottage at Warm Springs, Georgia. Unaware of Roosevelt's death, Truman recessed the Senate at five o'clock and headed through the Capitol to a meeting with Speaker of the House Sam Rayburn in his hideaway office, the "Board of Education." When Truman arrived, Rayburn told him he had a message to call the president's press secretary. Steve Early asked the vice president to come immediately to the White House. Two hours later, Truman was in the Cabinet Room being sworn in as president of the United States.

He'd been vice president for eighty-nine days, and in that time he'd met with President Roosevelt three times, once when they were being inaugurated on January 20 and twice in the Oval Office with members of the congressional leadership. Truman had no office in the West Wing and rarely used the vice president's ceremonial office in the Capitol building, preferring instead to continue working out of his Senate office in Room 240 of the Senate Office Building. Of his time as vice president, Truman said, "I enjoyed my new position as Vice-President, but it took me a while to get used to the fact that I no longer had the voting privileges I had enjoyed for ten years as a senator." Indeed, Truman had lost virtually all his power—he could no longer vote in the Senate, and he had no role in Roosevelt's White House.

The nation was in the midst of the largest war in history. America had, in Truman's words, "created military forces so enormous as to defy description." Yet there was no question but that we would have a peaceful passing of the control of this mighty force from one civilian to another. In fact, Truman noted, "When the nation's greatest leader in that war lay dead and a simple ceremony was about to acknowledge the presence of his successor in the nation's greatest office, only two uniforms were present. . . . This passed unnoticed at the time, and the very fact that no thought was given to it demonstrates convincingly how firmly the concept of the supremacy of the civil authority is accepted in our land."

Forty-six hundred miles east, the American generals commanding the Allied forces in Europe despaired. Earlier that day, Generals Eisenhower, Patton, and Bradley had come face-to-face with evil when they visited the Nazi concentration camp Ohrdruf-Nord, the first camp to be liberated by the Americans. Eisenhower wrote to General Marshall upon his return from the camp:

> *The things I saw beggar description. . . . The visual evidence and the verbal testimony of starvation, cruelty, and bestiality were overpowering. . . . I made the visit deliberately, in order to be in a position to give first-hand evidence of these things if ever, in the future, there develops a tendency to charge these allegations merely to propaganda.*

Now the three generals learned their commander in chief was dead. The man replacing him, a virtual unknown, would have responsibility for waging a global war on two fronts, a more massive military effort than any before in history. His generals did not know whether he would be up to the task.

Twelve days after Roosevelt's death, the new president learned of a project under way in the New Mexico desert that would ultimately bring an end to the war: the Manhattan Project, an effort to develop an atomic weapon. On Tuesday, April 24, Truman received a note from Secretary of War Henry Stimson: "I think it is very important that I should have a talk with you as soon as possible on a highly secret matter." The subject was of such import, Stimson wrote, "that I think you ought to know about it without further delay." At the bottom of the note, Truman wrote, "Put on list tomorrow, Wed. 25. HST."

Secretary Stimson and General Leslie R. Groves, leader of the Manhattan Project, briefed Truman at the White House at noon on April 25, 1945. Stimson had prepared a memorandum for the president that began, "Within four months we shall in all probability have completed the most terrible weapon ever known in human history, one bomb of which could destroy a whole city." Stimson wanted to ensure that Truman was fully briefed on every aspect of the program, its current status, possible implications of the use of the weapon, and safeguards for its oversight in the future. Truman agreed to his request that a committee be established to provide recommendations on these and other issues relating to an atomic bomb.

On June 1, 1945, the committee, after meeting with members of its scientific advisory panel, including Robert Oppenheimer and Enrico Fermi, issued three recommendations:

1. *The bomb should be used against Japan as soon as possible.*

2. *It should be used on a dual target—that is, a military installation or war plant surrounded by or adjacent to houses and other buildings most susceptible to damage, and*

3. *It should be used without prior warning [of the nature of the weapon].*

In the years since America dropped the atomic bombs on Hiroshima and Nagasaki, a number of arguments have been made concerning alternative courses of action. Some have said, for example, that the United States should have alerted the Japanese that we had a devastating new weapon and then conducted a test for them to see. What if we had announced a test and then it had failed? The damage to Allied morale and the consequent improvement in Japanese morale would likely have extended the war. What if we had alerted the Japanese to the location of the test and they had moved American POWs there? The Japanese had not surrendered following the massive firebombing of their cities with death tolls in the tens of thousands. Nor did they surrender after an atomic bomb was dropped on Hiroshima. The argument that a test firing would have convinced them to surrender ignores historical fact.

Others have argued that the loss of life caused by the use of the atomic bombs on Hiroshima and Nagasaki was simply too great, and, therefore, the United States was wrong to deploy this devastating new weapon. This line of thinking ignores the reality of the much greater loss of life that would have occurred had the United States not used the bombs and instead been forced to invade the Japanese home islands.

Island fighting in the Pacific had been brutal. Japanese soldiers were fighting to the death and taking thousands of our men with them. A captain in military intelligence, Charlton Ogburn Jr., recounted the fighting for historian David McCullough: "We had only too abundant evidence in those days that surrender was excluded from the Japanese ethos. Thousands of our Marines and soldiers had died rooting Japanese from their foxholes and bunkers when they were perfectly aware that their situation was hopeless." Not one Japanese unit had ever surrendered, and we weren't yet fighting on the home islands.

The experience weighing most heavily on the minds of President

Truman and General Marshall as they planned for the invasion of Japan was the battle on Okinawa. It had taken three months of heavy combat for the Americans to defeat the Japanese forces on the island. We had lost 12,000 American service members killed and 38,000 wounded or missing. On the Japanese side, the casualties were much higher, with more than 100,000 killed.

Plans for an invasion of the Japanese home islands called for an amphibious landing of 766,700 troops in the fall of 1945 on the island of Kyushu. Using casualty rates on Okinawa as a guide, planners anticipated we would lose more than 250,000 men on Kyushu alone. American planners knew that the fall of Kyushu was unlikely to lead to the surrender of Japan. In light of the fierce Japanese determination to fight on, their ongoing efforts to mobilize the entire population, and the fanatic desire of their generals to confront and defeat the U.S. force on the homeland, American planners knew that, after taking Kyushu, we would have to invade the mainland. "General Marshall told me," President Truman wrote of this prospect, "that it might cost half a million American lives to force the enemy's surrender on his home grounds."

The use of the atomic bombs saved not only American lives, but hundreds of thousands of Japanese lives, as well. Even after the devastation wrought at Hiroshima, the Japanese war council was deadlocked as to whether they should surrender. The war minister, General Korechika Anami, urged that the Japanese fight on. "Would it not be wondrous for this whole nation to be destroyed like a beautiful flower?" the general asked. Then word came that a second bomb had been dropped on Nagasaki and the war council was adjourned. The decision was left to Emperor Hirohito, who was not willing to sacrifice the nation.

At 7:35 A.M. on Friday, August 10, 1945, Radio Tokyo began broadcasting the message. *Time* reported "it was picked up by listening monitors on the Pacific Coast and teletyped to Washington."

Harry Truman was in the White House residence when he received a dispatch from the War Department. "In obedience to the gracious command of His Majesty the Emperor," the message read, ". . . the Japanese Government are ready to accept the terms enumerated at Potsdam on July 26, 1945," provided the emperor remained on his throne. Twenty-seven hours after our stations first heard the Tokyo transmission, we sent one back:

> *From the moment of surrender the authority of the Emperor and the Japanese Government to rule the state shall be subject to the supreme commander of the Allied powers, who will take such steps as he deems proper to effectuate the surrender. . . . The ultimate form of government of Japan shall, in accordance with the Potsdam declaration, be established by the freely expressed will of the Japanese people. The armed forces of the Allied powers will remain in Japan until the purposes set forth in the Potsdam Declaration are achieved.*

It took seventeen hours for the American response to reach Japan, through official diplomatic channels. And then the world waited. Finally, three days later, at 7 P.M. on Tuesday, August 14, 1945, President Truman called reporters into the Oval Office:

> *I have received this afternoon a message from the Japanese Government in reply to the message forwarded to that Government by the Secretary of State on August 11. I deem this reply a full acceptance of the Potsdam Declaration which specifies the unconditional surrender of Japan.*

The assembled White House reporters broke into cheers.

Those who argue America was wrong to use the atomic bombs

must explain how President Truman, in the aftermath of the carnage that would have resulted from an invasion of the Japanese mainland, could have explained to the American people that we had a weapon that would have ended the war and he had failed to use it. The men responsible for the development of the atomic weapons and the decision to use them were fully aware of the gravity of the choices they were making. Writing in 1947, former secretary of war Stimson explained it this way:

> *My chief purpose was to end the war in victory with the least possible cost in the lives of the men in the armies which I had helped raise. In the light of the alternatives which, on a fair estimate, were open to us, I believe that no man, in our position and subject to our responsibilities, holding in his hands a weapon of such possibilities for accomplishing this purpose and saving those lives, could have failed to use it and afterwards looked his countrymen in the face.*

ALBERT HALL IN LONDON was hung with American flags, the flags of all forty-eight states, and, over the stage, a huge portrait of Abraham Lincoln. A spotlight shone on an American eagle. It was Thanksgiving Day, 1944, months before the Allied victory, and yet the tide of the struggle had turned. The torch of leadership of the free world had passed. High representatives from the British and American governments were in the audience. American ambassador John Winant's speech was scheduled to be the last. But suddenly, *Time* reported, "a stubby, balding figure, known to all, marched down the center aisle." To roaring applause, Churchill took the stage and addressed his American allies:

It is your day of thanksgiving and when we feel the truth of the facts that are before us—that in three or four years, the peaceful, peace-loving people of the United States, with all the variety and freedom of their life, in such contrast to the iron discipline which has governed other, many other communities, that in three or four years the United States has in sober fact become the greatest military, naval and air power in the world, that—I say to you— in this time of war is in itself a subject for profound thanksgiving.

Exactly when America became the world's predominant power is the subject of some debate. On December 27, 1941, the Australian prime minister John Curtin signaled a shift when he said in an article in the *Melbourne Herald*:

Without inhibitions of any kind, I make it quite clear that Australia looks to America, free of any pangs as to our traditional links or kinship with the United Kingdom. . . . We shall exert all our energies to shaping a defense plan with the United States as its keystone.

Others point to the operations in North Africa as the key historic moment. Historian Rick Atkinson put it this way:

From a distance of sixty years, we can see that North Africa was a pivot point in American history, the place where the United States began to act like a great power—militarily, diplomatically, strategically, tactically. Along with Stalingrad and Midway, North Africa is where the Axis enemy forever lost the initiative in World War II. It is where Great Britain slipped into the role of junior

partner in the Anglo-American alliance, and where the United
States first emerged as the dominant force it would remain into
the next millennium.

William Manchester pointed to the year 1943—a year of Allied summits—as the period when "the torch of leadership passed from the British Prime Minister to the American President, and both men knew it." America, by that time, "was putting more men and matériel into the conflict and American generals . . . would be commanding the combined forces in the great battles ahead." From 1943 on, no one doubted FDR was "commander of the Allied Armies and Navies."

Historian Andrew Roberts says that, although the truth was evident sooner, the moment when America was confirmed as the "leading power of the western Alliance" came on July 1, 1944. In the aftermath of the D-Day landings, the Americans favored invading the south of France on August 15, but the British wanted to "cross the River Po, advance on Trieste and push into the Balkans in September." A deadlock ensued with Churchill finally appealing the British case to Roosevelt, who rejected it. "The baton had passed from hand to hand," Roberts wrote, "reluctantly and not without bluster, but neither was it wrenched from Britain's grasp. Churchill was to be the last British leader of the Free World."

IN NOVEMBER 1944, AS the Allied forces pushed through Europe toward Berlin, Eisenhower reminded all Americans that peace and freedom come at a price. "To get peace," he said, "we have to fight like hell." And we did.

America had deployed the greatest military force the world has ever known to secure freedom and to defeat tyranny. We had transformed ourselves, in the words of Dwight D. Eisenhower, "from a situation of appalling danger to unparalleled might in battle." The armed forces George C. Marshall built fought, as *Life* described it, "along supply lines extending 56,000 miles around 360 degrees of longitude, and from the Tropic of Capricorn to the Arctic Sea." We liberated millions and achieved the greatest victory in the history of mankind, for the good of all mankind. America—the exceptional nation—had become freedom's defender.

———•◆•———

TWO

Freedom Victorious

One of the simple but overwhelming facts of our time is this: Of all the millions of refugees we've seen in the modern world, their flight is always away from, not toward the Communist world. Today, on the NATO line, our military forces face east to prevent a possible invasion. On the other side of the line, the Soviet forces also face east—to prevent their people from leaving.
—PRESIDENT RONALD REAGAN, JUNE 8, 1982

Shortly before 10 P.M. on Tuesday, April 15, 1947, the motorcade passed under the sixteenth-century archways of the Kremlin. General George C. Marshall, architect of America's victory in World War II and the new American secretary of state, was in Moscow for meetings with his fellow foreign ministers to decide the postwar fate of Germany and Austria. Faced with economic devastation across Europe, Marshall felt a sense of urgency. He'd been in Moscow for more than a month and Soviet foreign minister Vyacheslav Molotov had stonewalled and blocked all attempts at agreement.

Marshall was taking his case directly to Stalin. As Marshall explained the dire situation to the Soviet leader, Stalin sat at his desk and slowly doodled pictures of wolves with a red pencil. When Marshall finished, Stalin responded that he really didn't share Marshall's alarm. If things weren't resolved at this conference, he said, "We may agree the next time, or if not then, the time after that." The Soviet leader was in no rush to rescue the peoples of Europe from economic despair. He knew desperation would provide a fertile ground for the spread of communist ideology. Marshall realized that the belligerence Soviet foreign minister Molotov displayed at the conference sessions was not just a reflection of Molotov's personality. It was Soviet policy.

On his flight back to the United States, Marshall contemplated Stalin's indifference to the crisis facing Europe. His advisor Charles Bohlen recalled:

> [Marshall] came to the conclusion that Stalin, looking over Europe, saw the best way to advance Soviet interests was to let matters drift. Economic conditions were bad. Europe was recovering slowly from the war. Little had been done to rebuild damaged highways, railroads, and canals. Business alliances severed by years of hostilities were still shattered. Unemployment was widespread. Millions of people were on short rations. There was a danger of epidemics. This was the kind of crisis that Communism thrived on.

In an interview in 1956, Marshall said the Moscow meeting was a turning point for him. He had believed "the Soviets could be negotiated with," he said, but "decided finally at Moscow, after the war, that they could not be." Another of Marshall's aides, Robert Murphy, put it this way: "It was the Moscow conference, I believe, that really rang down the Iron Curtain."

THE HAD BEEN EARLIER signs of trouble. On February 9, 1946, Stalin delivered a speech at the Bolshoi Theater in Moscow, in the midst of what *Time* called "the biggest most meaningless election on earth." No opposition candidates were on the ballot. Stalin wound up with 100 percent of the vote in Moscow.

In his Bolshoi speech, Stalin explained that communism and capitalism were incompatible. World War II, he claimed, was caused by capitalism and, in particular, by the unequal distribution of wealth this economic system generated. He asserted that future wars would be inevitable so long as the capitalist system survived. It was, *Time* said, "the most warlike pronouncement uttered by any top-rank statesman since V-J Day."

In Washington, State Department official Paul Nitze read the speech with care. "We interpreted it as being a delayed declaration of war against the United States," he later explained. "There wasn't any doubt about it if you read the text carefully, what he was talking about." A message was dispatched to George Kennan, the American chargé d'affaires in Moscow, asking for an analysis of Stalin's intentions and plans. Kennan sent his response in on February 22, 1946. Eight thousand words in length, the "Long Telegram" would lay the groundwork for an historic shift in American policy toward the Soviet Union.

The USSR, Kennan explained, was "a political force committed fanatically to the belief that with the U.S. there can be no permanent *modus vivendi*, that it is desirable and necessary that the internal harmony of our society be broken if Soviet power is to be secure." In other words, there could be no "permanent peaceful coexistence" between our two nations. This had nothing to do with any action taken by the United States, and there was nothing the United States could do to change the Soviet view of the situation. The United States should not expect concessions from the Soviets. What was needed was "a policy of firm containment, designed to confront the Russians with unalterable counterforce at every point where they showed signs of encroaching upon the interest of a peaceful and stable world."

On February 21, 1947, the United States had to decide whether it would put such a policy of "firm containment" into action. The first secretary at the British embassy in Washington delivered two diplomatic messages to Loy Henderson, director of the Office of Near Eastern Affairs at the U.S. State Department, notifying the United States that Britain would no longer be able to meet her obligations to provide assistance to Greece and Turkey. "The messages were shockers," said Undersecretary of State Dean Acheson. Aid to both countries would end in six weeks, on March 31, 1947.

Both nations were under threat from the Soviet Union. In Greece, a communist insurrection was under way, generating economic chaos and the potential of imminent collapse. Turkey, under pressure from Moscow to provide access to the Mediterranean for the Soviet fleet, lacked the resources to simultaneously modernize its economy and maintain the military necessary to defend against the Soviet threat. President Truman and his senior advisors quickly recognized that Greece and Turkey needed support to maintain their independence. Such assistance was something only America could provide—and it was vital for our security.

The following week, President Truman hosted a meeting of the congressional leadership to discuss possible U.S. aid to Greece and Turkey. Undersecretary of State Acheson described the situation America faced and explained what could happen if we failed to act:

> *Soviet pressure on the [Turkish] Straits, on Iran, and on northern Greece had brought the Balkans to the point where a highly possible Soviet breakthrough might open three continents to Soviet penetration. Like apples in a barrel infected by one rotten one, the corruption of Greece would infect Iran and all to the east. It would also carry infection to Africa through Asia Minor and Egypt, and to Europe through Italy and France, already threat-*

ened by the strongest domestic Communist parties in Western Europe. The Soviet Union was playing one of the greatest gambles in history at minimal cost. It did not need to win all the possibilities. Even one or two offered immense gains. We and we alone were in a position to break up the play.

On Wednesday, March 12, 1947, President Truman appeared before a joint session of Congress to request $400 million in assistance for Greece and Turkey. Speaking from the ornate white marble rostrum, with the Speaker of the House and the president pro tem of the Senate seated behind him, Truman introduced what would become known as the Truman Doctrine. "At the present moment in world history," he explained, "nearly every nation must choose between alternative ways of life. The choice is too often not a free one." He then described the difference between the principles of freedom advocated by the United States, and the methods of oppression pursued by the Soviet Union:

One way of life is based upon the will of the majority, and is distinguished by free institutions, representative government, free elections, guarantees of individual liberty, freedom of speech and religion, and freedom from political oppression. The second way of life is based upon the will of a minority forcibly imposed upon the majority. It relies upon terror and oppression, a controlled press and radio, fixed elections, and the suppression of personal freedoms.

"I believe," the president said, that "it must be the policy of the United States to support free peoples who are resisting attempted subjugation by armed minorities or by outside pressures. I believe we must assist free peoples to work out their own destinies in their own ways."

Truman closed his remarks by explaining the link between economic devastation and the rise of communism:

> *The seeds of totalitarian regimes are nurtured by misery and want.*
> *They spread and grow in the evil soil of poverty and strife. They*
> *reach their full growth when the hope of a people for a better life*
> *has died. We must keep that hope alive. The free peoples of the*
> *world look to us for support in maintaining their freedoms. If we*
> *falter in our leadership, we may endanger the peace of the world—*
> *and we shall surely endanger the welfare of our own Nation.*

Congress approved Truman's Greek-Turkish Aid Act by large majorities in both houses. Truman signed it into law on May 22, 1947.

Secretary Marshall had returned from his meetings in Moscow seized with the importance of rebuilding Europe's shattered economies. He tapped George Kennan to lead a new Policy Planning Office in the Department of State and instructed him to prepare a report outlining how America could most effectively assist the European recovery. Kennan delivered his report the day after President Truman signed the aid act. The Policy Planning staff advised, among other things, that the assistance should be based on a joint recovery plan prepared with direct involvement of the Europeans. It also suggested that the new assistance should not exclude the Soviets or Eastern Europe.

Marshall decided to use a speech during Harvard's commencement exercises to explain the necessity for America to act. He began by describing the devastation facing Europe and the damage that could be done, as a result, to America's economy. "It is logical," he said, "that the United States should do whatever it is able to do to assist in the return of normal economic health in the world, without which there can be no political stability and no assured peace." Our assistance would be open to all in Europe who needed it, including the

Soviet Union and its allied states. "Our policy," Marshall said, "is not directed against any country or doctrine but against hunger, poverty, desperation and chaos." The program he was proposing would, he said, "require a willingness on the part of our people to face up to the vast responsibility which history has clearly placed upon our country." Wanting to reaffirm how high the stakes were and how important it was for America to act, Marshall had added handwritten notes to the end of his prepared remarks. He read them now, saying that he realized America was "remote from the scene of these troubles" and it was difficult perhaps to grasp the full scale of the suffering. And yet, he said, "The whole world of the future hangs on a proper judgment. It hangs, I think, to a large extent on the realization of the American people . . . of just what can best be done and what must be done."

Marshall received a resounding ovation when he finished his twelve-minute speech, but the cheers were more likely for him than what he said. A modest man, not given to oratory, he had delivered the speech in such a matter-of-fact way that not even James Bryant Conant, president of Harvard, understood its significance. But the world would soon understand. Between 1948 and 1951, the United States would provide more than $13 billion to sixteen European countries, nearly $130 billion in 2015 dollars.

A key element of Marshall's plan was that American assistance would be provided in response to needs identified by the Europeans. British foreign minister Ernest Bevin and French foreign minister Georges Bidault reacted quickly, arranging a meeting with Soviet foreign minister Molotov in Paris shortly after Marshall's speech to outline assistance needs. The three-way talks did not last long. Molotov announced on July 2, 1947, that the Soviets were withdrawing.

On July 3, the French and British invited twenty-two other European nations to attend a planning conference in Paris. The ministers of the government of Czechoslovakia were planning to participate—

until Stalin summoned the Czech prime minister and foreign minister to Moscow and ordered them not to attend. The Czech foreign minister, Jan Masaryk, said, "I went to Moscow as a minister of a free state and I am returning as Stalin's slave."

Cabinet ministers in Soviet Bloc countries were not the only ones Stalin was enslaving. Drawing upon newly released documents in the Soviet and East European archives, historian Anne Applebaum has methodically detailed the Soviet strategy to quash dissent, eliminate opposition, and establish totalitarian rule across Eastern Europe in the late 1940s and early 1950s. Totalitarian rule meant, as one of Mussolini's opponents first described it, "Everything within the state, nothing outside the state, nothing against the state."

In every nation occupied by the Red Army at the end of the war, the Soviets carried out a four-part program to impose their rule. They created local secret police forces modeled after Stalin's NKVD. They took over the radio stations. They carried out policies of ethnic cleansing. And they banned or took over the youth groups. Young people were a special target. "Even before they banned independent political parties for adults, and even before they outlawed church organizations and independent trade unions," Applebaum writes, "they put young people's organizations under the strictest possible observation and restraint." The slogan of the German Young Pioneers explains the philosophy of their Soviet masters: "Those who own the youth own the future."

To these methods of suppression and persecution, the Soviets added a military blockade of West Berlin in June 1948. In the aftermath of World War II, the Allies had divided Germany into four occupation zones, overseen by the Americans, the British, the French, and the Soviet Union. Berlin was inside Soviet-occupied East Germany, but the city itself was also divided into four sectors. All overland routes into Berlin went through East Germany.

In the spring of 1948, the Soviets began imposing restrictions on travel into West Berlin. Initially they denied entry to trains loaded with coal. The restrictions grew more severe and on June 24 the Soviets imposed a full blockade. Their objective was to drive the Allies out of Berlin, in contravention of the agreement reached after World War II.

Determined not to abandon the people of West Berlin, the United States and Britain, with some assistance from France, began to airlift food, coal, and other needed items into the blockaded city. Over the next eleven months, the Allies flew 278,228 flights into West Berlin, delivering 2,326,406 tons of food, coal, and other supplies. The Berlin Airlift went on until May 1949, when Stalin, realizing he could not bring the city to her knees, lifted the blockade.

In these post–World War II years the United States undertook an effort never before seen in history—to restore economic vitality and political freedom across Europe, including to her former enemy Germany. A similar program to establish democracy and free markets was under way in Japan. The economic and political freedom enjoyed today by peoples of Germany and Japan is a testament to the success of these efforts. In the words of historian Andrew Roberts, "To have helped raise their former deadliest foes to such a place is a tribute to the magnanimity of the English-speaking peoples in not going down the path of mass-despoliation that Stalin envisioned for both countries, and which he carried out against much of the industrialized plant of East Germany."

Economic support for the rebuilding of Europe was crucial, but it was increasingly clear that the nations of Western Europe also required support to resist Soviet expansionism. "Something needed to be done," according to President Truman, "to counteract the fear of the peoples of Europe that their countries would be overrun by the Soviet Army before effective help could arrive. Only an inclusive security system could dispel these fears."

As discussions were under way to design this new security alliance, the British outlined some of the risks involved. The biggest risk they identified was one that is still raised in nearly all discussions of European security arrangements and Russia today. President Truman explained:

> *The principal risk involved, Bevin said, was that the Russians might be so provoked by the formation of a defense organization that they would resort to rash measures and plunge the world into war. . . . On the other hand, if a collective security system could be built up effectively, it was more than likely that the Russians might restudy the situation and become more cooperative.*

Recognizing that leaving individual European nations to defend themselves would be the ultimate provocation, the United States and eleven other nations agreed to form the North Atlantic Treaty Organization. The North Atlantic Treaty was signed in Washington on April 4, 1949, and ratified by the Senate on July 21. It would become the most successful military alliance in history.

For forty years, from the signing of the NATO treaty in 1949 to the fall of the Berlin Wall in 1989, the alliance was crucial in deterring Soviet aggression and keeping the peace. Without NATO and the commitment of the United States to maintain large numbers of forces in Germany and elsewhere on the continent, there can be no doubt that the Soviets would have moved to expand the territory under their control. The security guarantee provided by NATO was crucial to Western Europe's ability to rebuild thriving economies, free from the constant threat of Soviet adventurism.

The twelve original NATO member nations were Belgium, Canada, Denmark, France, Britain, Iceland, Italy, Luxembourg, the Netherlands, Norway, Portugal, and the United States. In 1952, Greece and Turkey joined, and in 1955, West Germany became a member. In 1966, the French, who were seeking improved relations with the Soviets and had doubts about America's willingness to make good on its extended deterrence commitments to Europe, announced they were pulling out of NATO's military structure and requested the removal of NATO bases from French territory. When told of French president Charles de Gaulle's decision, President Lyndon Johnson famously instructed Secretary of State Dean Rusk to ask De Gaulle, "Does your order include the bodies of American soldiers in France's cemeteries?"

Spain joined NATO in 1980, and, as the Cold War came to an end, NATO began to offer membership to former Warsaw Pact nations. Hungary, Poland, and the Czech Republic joined in 1999, and Lithuania, Estonia, Latvia, Bulgaria, Romania, Slovakia, and Slovenia joined in 2004.

The heart of NATO's defense pact is found in Article 5, which embodies the concept of collective self-defense. It holds that "an armed attack on one or more [members] shall be considered an armed attack on all." Less than twenty-four hours after the attacks of September 11, 2001, Article 5 was invoked for the first time in the fifty-year history of the alliance.

AT 4:00 P.M. ON May 14, 1948, David Ben-Gurion stepped out of a car at No. 16 Rothschild Boulevard in Tel Aviv. The white-haired Ben-Gurion entered the city's art museum, where at 5:00 P.M. he declared the establishment of the state of Israel. Eleven minutes later, the United States recognized the new country. President Truman had been committed to the cause of the creation of a Jewish state. He recognized Israel despite the fact that, as he described it, "[t]he Department of State's specialists on the Near East were, almost without exception, unfriendly to the idea of a Jewish state."

On May 15, British forces, stationed in Palestine for the previous thirty years, pulled out. Five Arab armies invaded the newly created state. Born in war, Israel has survived and thrived in one of the world's most dangerous regions to become one of America's strongest and most important allies—until the Obama administration.

ON JANUARY 12, 1950, at the National Press Club in Washington, D.C., Secretary of State Dean Acheson explained American policy in Asia. He described an American "defensive perimeter" that, most unfortunately, did not include South Korea. North Korea's leader, Kim Il Sung, had been seeking Stalin's approval to send his forces across the 38th parallel and invade the South. Following Acheson's speech, he got it. Stalin also prodded Ho Chi Minh to be more aggressive in Indochina.

President Harry Truman was in the library of his home in Independence, Missouri, when Acheson called him on Saturday, June 24, 1950. "Mr. President," he said, "I have very serious news. The North Koreans have invaded South Korea." By the next morning, the UN Security Council had been called into emergency session and President Truman was headed back to Washington. While he was airborne, the UN unanimously passed a resolution declaring that the North Korean action was "a breach of the peace" and demanding that the North withdraw its forces immediately. Fortuitously, the Soviet delegate was not in attendance, having begun a boycott previously over the UN's refusal to seat a delegate from Communist China.

Truman called his secretaries of defense and state, along with the Joint Chiefs of Staff and the three service secretaries, together for a dinner meeting. The interior of the White House was being gutted and rebuilt, so they dined at Blair House, where Truman lived for much of his presidency. Dean Acheson read reports from the U.S. ambassador in South Korea to the assembled group. Then Acheson laid out his recommendations, which included sending the Seventh Fleet into the Formosa Strait to prevent the conflict spreading, and providing ammunition and supplies to the South Korean army.

Each of the attendees at the meeting was asked for his views on Acheson's recommendations. Truman wrote later that there was "complete almost unspoken acceptance on the part of everyone that whatever had to be done to meet this aggression had to be done. There was no suggestion from anyone that either the United States or the United Nations could back away from it." Truman also firmly believed that North Korean aggression had to be countered without expanding the war to worldwide dimensions. This concern was shared by America's European allies, who feared that a broader land war in Asia could make it difficult for America to keep its commitments to NATO, thereby leaving Western Europe vulnerable to Soviet coercion or attack.

Truman named five-star general Douglas MacArthur to command the international force called for by the United Nations. The effort to resist the North Korean invasion started badly. The Korean People's Army, well supplied by the Soviets, forced the American-led coalition back to Pusan, on the southern tip of the Korean peninsula. The war might well have been lost had it not been for MacArthur's daring landing at Inchon. Seventy thousand troops from the Army's X Corps, led by the 1st Marine Division, conducted the surprise amphibious assault and took Seoul on September 26, 1950. The American-led coalition crossed the 38th parallel into North Korea and took the North Korean capital, Pyongyang, on October 20.

The war seemed won as American forces ate Thanksgiving dinner on November 25, but the next day the Chinese entered the war, sending 300,000 troops crashing across the Yalu River into North Korea. General MacArthur sought approval to cross the Yalu, and urged attacks on Chinese cities. He clearly did not share Truman's view that the war must be won without expanding it. In April 1951, Truman relieved him of command.

The Chinese army fighting the Americans on the Korean peninsula was officially known as the Chinese People's Volunteer Army. It was under the supreme command of Chairman Mao Zedong, who had defeated the Chinese nationalists and declared a new, communist China on October 1, 1949. Mao came to power promising to create a prosperous, egalitarian society. Instead, according to *The Black Book of Communism*, Mao's policies resulted in the death of 65 million Chinese, through political persecution, mass imprisonment, and starvation.

The war in Korea raged on until July 1953, when an armistice was declared, leaving both sides once again facing each other across the 38th parallel. The United States had prevented a communist takeover of South Korea, but at a tremendous cost: 36,564 Americans died in combat.

THE SUCCESSFUL TESTING OF the first atomic bomb at the Trinity Site in New Mexico in 1945 had made the United States the world's only nuclear power. As President Ronald Reagan once noted, we did not use this monopoly to expand our territory or threaten other nations. "Historians looking back at our time," he said, "will note the consistent restraint and peaceful intentions of the West." How different the world would have been, he said, if the nuclear monopoly had been in the hands of the Soviets. America's nuclear monopoly ended on August 29, 1949, when the Soviets detonated an atomic bomb at a remote site in Kazakhstan.

A few months later, in November 1949, President Truman established a special committee of the National Security Council to advise him on whether the United States should move forward with development of an even more devastating technology—a hydrogen or thermonuclear bomb. Paul Nitze, a State Department representative who participated in the committee discussions, later described the factors they had to consider. According to physicist Edward Teller,

Nitze wrote, "Such a weapon [was] technically feasible," and according to Ernest Lawrence, director of the University of California's Radiation Laboratory, "The Soviets possessed capacity similar to ours." Thus, the only conclusion to be reached, wrote Nitze, was "that the Russians were already working on an H-bomb."

The committee met with the president on January 31, 1950, to present its recommendation that research and development go forward. When Truman had finished reading the committee's report, Secretary of State Dean Acheson turned to Atomic Energy Commission chairman David Lilienthal, who had agreed that the research go forward but had concerns he wanted to address directly to the president.

Truman cut the presentation short. "Can the Russians do it?" he asked. Assured they could, he signed off on the group's recommendation. The meeting lasted less than ten minutes. It was the right decision. We now know the Soviets were well along in their efforts. They tested their own thermonuclear weapon within nine months of America's first hydrogen bomb test.

The new world created by the first Soviet atomic test and the possibility of these new "super" weapons meant that the United States faced an entirely new strategic circumstance. Truman instructed the secretaries of state and defense to produce a new national security strategy crafted for the growing threats. That strategy was laid out in NSC-68, one of the most important documents of the Cold War era.

NSC-68 put the lie to the idea, more treasured in the decades since than it was at the time, that there was any moral equivalence between the Soviet Union and the United States:

> The fundamental purpose of the United States is laid down in the
> Preamble to the Constitution: ". . . to form a more perfect Union,
> establish justice, insure domestic tranquility, provide for the com-

*mon defense, promote the general welfare, and secure the blessings
of liberty to ourselves and our posterity." In essence, the fundamental purpose is to assure the integrity and vitality of our free society,
which is founded upon the dignity and worth of the individual.*

By contrast:

*The fundamental design of those who control the Soviet Union
and the international communist movement is to retain and so-
lidify their absolute power, first in the Soviet Union and second
in the areas now under their control. In the minds of the Soviet
leaders, however, achievement of this design requires the dynamic
extension of their authority and the ultimate elimination of any
effective opposition to their authority.*

And what were the consequences of the Kremlin's objectives?
NSC-68 put it this way:

*The design . . . calls for the complete subversion or forcible destruc-
tion of the machinery of government and structure of society in
the countries of the non-Soviet world and their replacement by
an apparatus and structure subservient to and controlled from
the Kremlin. To that end Soviet efforts are now directed toward the
domination of the Eurasian land mass. The United States, as the
principal center of power in the non-Soviet world and the bulwark
of opposition to Soviet expansion, is the principal enemy whose integrity and vitality must be subverted or destroyed by one means or
another if the Kremlin is to achieve its fundamental design.*

To defend against the expanded Soviet threat, NSC-68 called for
the rapid buildup by the United States and its allies of the "politi-

cal, economic, and military strength" of the free world. Though some argued that America should retreat into isolation, Secretary of State Acheson memorably pointed out the flaw in this thinking:

> *We should not pull down the blinds and sit in the parlor with a loaded shotgun, waiting. Isolation was not a realistic course of action. It did not work and it had not been cheap. Appeasement of Soviet ambitions was, in fact, only an alternative form of isolation. It would lead to a final struggle for survival with both our moral and our military position weakened.*

Put another way, in cautionary words from the document itself that seem particularly relevant sixty-five years later, "No people in history have preserved their freedom who thought that by not being strong enough to protect themselves they might prove inoffensive to their enemies."

IN THE POWER STRUGGLE that followed Soviet premier Stalin's 1953 death, Nikita Khrushchev emerged victorious, becoming first secretary of the Communist Party and, in 1958, premier of the Soviet Union. In 1956 Khrushchev took the unprecedented step of condemning Stalin and some of his harshest tactics in a secret speech at the Twentieth Congress of the Communist Party of the Soviet Union.

Despite this, Khrushchev remained an unrepentant Marxist-Leninist and was certainly no friend to the United States. He did not bother to hide his bellicosity. In November 1956 at a cocktail party at the Polish embassy in Moscow, "red-faced and gesticulating," he famously told the assembled Western diplomats, "We will bury you . . . whether you like it or not, history is on our side. We will bury you."

His threats became more specific as he bragged about the progress Moscow was making in the area of missile technology. President

Eisenhower, who took office in 1953, had doubled the rate of B-52 bomber production. Khrushchev knew his bomber force could not match America's, so he changed the subject. "Bombers are useless," he said, "compared to rockets."

Time reported: "Every day of every week, Moscow rolls out pronouncements about the successes of its experiments with intercontinental ballistic missiles." The magazine quoted Khrushchev saying, "In the day of the missile, Europe might become 'a veritable cemetery,' and the US is just as vulnerable."

Khrushchev's threats did not appear to be idle. In May 1957, the Soviets launched the world's first intercontinental ballistic missile and, in October of that year, the world's first satellite, Sputnik. Because the Soviet Union was a closed society, the West could not be sure just how large Khrushchev's arsenal was. Nor could they know the economic deprivation the Soviet government was willing to force on its people in order to free up money to spend on defense.

On a visit to Moscow in July 1959, Vice President Richard Nixon met with Khrushchev, and together they toured the first-ever American trade exhibit in the Soviet Union. Beginning in a model of an American kitchen and then carrying on into a modern television studio, Khrushchev and Nixon conducted a spontaneous debate about the merits of communism versus capitalism. It was an extraordinary event, portions of it captured on film, all of it conducted with the press corps hanging on every word. The two men sparred about everything from standards of living to kitchen appliances to missiles.

In response to Khrushchev's assertion that the Soviet Union met the needs of all of its citizens, Nixon explained the merits of freedom and choice. "Diversity, the right to choose, the fact that we have 1,000 builders building 1,000 different houses is the most important thing. We don't have one decision made at the top by one government official." Khrushchev argued that the American exhibit really wasn't that impressive. "It's clear to me," he said, "that the construction workers didn't manage to finish their work." It didn't matter, though, because, Khrushchev explained, the Soviets would soon be passing the Americans by in every way.

In response, Nixon echoed a theme to which he returned throughout the day, the importance of people communicating freely: "I can only say that if this competition which you have described so effectively, in which you plan to outstrip us, particularly in the production of consumer goods . . . If this competition is to do the best for both of our peoples and for people everywhere, there must be a free exchange of ideas." There were some areas where the Soviets were ahead of the United States and others where the situation was reversed, said Nixon. As Khrushchev interrupted to assert Soviet predominance in rocket technology, Nixon smiled, put his hand on Khrushchev's shoulder, and said, "You must not be afraid of ideas."

IN HIS FAREWELL ADDRESS to the nation on January 17, 1961, President Eisenhower issued a warning about the "military-industrial complex." His warning has sometimes been distorted by those claiming he opposed the establishment of such a complex. A full reading of his remarks reveals something quite different. "A vital element in keeping the peace," Eisenhower said, "is our military establishment. Our arms must be mighty, ready for instant action, so that no potential aggressor may be tempted to risk his own destruction." The threat America faced was so great that "we can no longer risk emergency improvisation of national defense." It had become necessary, he said, to create "a permanent armaments industry of vast proportions. Added to this, three and a half million men and women are directly engaged in the defense establishment." In other words, the military-industrial complex was created of necessity for the defense of the nation.

"We recognize the imperative need for this development," Eisenhower continued. "Yet we must not fail to comprehend its grave implications." These included the possibility of undue influence on our government. Eisenhower warned:

> *In the councils of government, we must guard against the acquisition of unwarranted influence, whether sought or unsought, by the military-industrial complex. . . . We must never let the weight of this combination endanger our liberties or democratic processes. We should take nothing for granted. Only an alert and knowledgeable citizenry can compel the proper meshing of the huge industrial and military machinery of defense with our peaceful methods and goals, so that security and liberty may prosper together.*

Every president since has had to grapple with this fundamental issue. Without our armed forces, there would be no liberty. They are the ultimate guarantor and protector of our freedoms. But as our civilian leaders adopt policies to provide for our security, they must also keep in mind their sacred duty to safeguard the civil liberties of the American people.

IN JANUARY 1961 A new American president took the oath of office. The first president born in the twentieth century, John F. Kennedy carried an aura of glamour, vigor, intellect, and energy. A handsome war hero, he had prevailed in 1960 in part by portraying the Eisenhower-Nixon administration as weak on communism. Throughout the campaign he criticized the "missile gap," the superiority in missiles that Eisenhower had purportedly allowed the Soviets to achieve.

Expectations for the new president were high, but the first months did not go well. Kennedy approved a plan, inherited from the Eisenhower administration, to use Cuban exiles to spark an uprising aimed at ousting Cuba's communist dictator, Fidel Castro. At the last minute, however, Kennedy canceled the U.S. air support the exiles were counting on. The invasion failed, the CIA-backed guerrillas were captured, and the Bay of Pigs operation went down in history as a fiasco.

In Moscow, Khrushchev followed events closely. He was sizing up America's new president, and he wasn't impressed. This seemed to be a man he could get the better of, and he planned to do just that at their upcoming summit in Vienna.

Documents in the Soviet archives released since the collapse of the Soviet Union detail Khrushchev's plan. In a meeting with the Presidium of the Supreme Soviet on May 26, 1961, Khrushchev laid out his scheme for isolating West Berlin and shutting off the flow of refugees from the East. He did not believe the Americans or any of the other Western powers would stop him, and as he saw it the situation was dire: thousands of East German citizens were fleeing the Soviet Bloc through West Berlin. Khrushchev planned to notify Kennedy that the Soviets and the East Germans would sign a treaty by the end of the year closing all corridors of access to West Berlin, with or without U.S. approval.

Kennedy and Khrushchev met in Vienna June 3–4, 1961. The two-day meeting was tense throughout, but it was over the issue of Berlin that Khrushchev's bullying reached its peak. Kennedy explained to Khrushchev that America would not accept the loss of access to West Berlin. In the aftermath of World War II, the Allies had agreed on arrangements for the governing of Berlin, and Kennedy told Khrushchev that the Soviets could not unilaterally change that agreement by denying access to the other powers. Khrushchev threatened that if the Americans attempted to exercise those rights after the treaty with East Germany had been signed, the Soviets would respond militarily.

New York Times reporter James "Scotty" Reston had an interview scheduled with Kennedy at the end of the second day of meetings. Reston reported that the president entered the room, sank down on a couch, and sighed. Reston said to him, "Pretty rough?" Kennedy replied, "Roughest thing in my life." Reston wrote:

> *Kennedy said just enough in that room to convince me of the following:*
>
> > *Khrushchev had studied the events of the Bay of Pigs; he would have understood if Kennedy had left Castro alone or destroyed him; but when Kennedy was rash enough to strike at Cuba and not bold enough to finish the job, Khrushchev decided he was dealing with an inexperienced young leader who could be intimidated and blackmailed.*

Khrushchev left Vienna and went to East Berlin, where he announced a treaty would be concluded by December 31. As the pace of the exodus from the East increased that summer—16,500 refugees fled into West Berlin in the first eleven days of August alone—Khrushchev decided more immediate action was needed. In the early morning hours of August 13, 1961, *Time* reported, East Berliners were awakened by "the scream of sirens and the clank of steel on cobblestones" as military convoys spread across their portion of the city, sealing off all access points to the West:

> *As the troops arrived at scores of border points, cargo trucks were already unloading rolls of barbed wire, concrete posts, wooden horses, stone blocks, picks and shovels. When dawn came four hours later, a wall divided East Berlin from the West.*

Would Khrushchev have risked the wall if Eisenhower had still been in office? It seems unlikely. Khrushchev had issued threats to shut off Western access to Berlin in 1958 and then backed down after meeting with Eisenhower in the United States. Khrushchev's assessment of Kennedy as weak and inexperienced clearly played into his decision making.

It is also true that the building of the Berlin Wall was an admission of the failure of the communist system. There is nothing one can say in defense of a system of government that can keep its people within its borders only by what *Time* described as "bullets, bayonets, and barricades." Those aspects of communist systems—the secret police, the persecution, the murder, the oppression, the absence of freedom—that required a wall across the heart of Berlin to imprison its people would also be the characteristics that brought about communism's ultimate collapse thirty years later.

ONCE THE WALL WENT up, the world wondered what the Soviets would do next. Would Khrushchev back down or would he provoke a larger crisis between the two nuclear-armed nations by carrying out his pledge to prevent Western access to the entire city?

Kennedy decided to call Khrushchev's bluff. Since taking office, Kennedy had learned that the missile gap on which he had campaigned did not exist. In fact, U.S. satellite images had confirmed the Soviets' arsenal was smaller than America's. Kennedy decided to send a clear message to Khrushchev about America's strategic superiority, as a warning against escalation of the Berlin crisis.

He authorized his deputy secretary of defense, Roswell Gilpatric, to give a speech detailing America's military advantage. After listing the immediate steps America had taken in response to Soviet actions in Berlin, Gilpatric continued, "But our real strength in Berlin—and at any other point in the perimeter of the free world's defenses that might tempt Communist probes—is much more broadly based." America was confident in its ability to deter communist action because of "a sober appreciation of the relative military power of the two sides." Despite the Soviet bluster about their superiority, Gilpatric said he suspected they actually knew the truth. He wanted to be sure they knew that we knew it, too:

> While the Soviets use rigid security as a military weapon, their Iron Curtain is not so impenetrable as to force us to accept at face value the Kremlin's boasts. The fact is that this nation has a nuclear retaliatory force of such lethal power that an enemy move which brought it into play would be an act of self-destruction on his part.

Describing the land-, air-, and sea-based platforms that constituted America's nuclear triad, Gilpatric explained, "The total number of our nuclear delivery vehicles, tactical as well as strategic, is in the tens of thousands; and, of course, we have more than one warhead for each vehicle." Summing up, Gilpatric said, "In short, we have a second strike capability which is at least as extensive as what the Soviets can deliver by striking first. Therefore, we are confident that the Soviets will not provoke a major nuclear conflict." In closing, Gilpatric issued one more clear warning to Khrushchev:

> Those who would impose a totalitarian world order and deny men and nations the right to pursue their own destinies should understand one point very clearly. The United States does not seek to resolve disputes by violence. But if forceful interference with our rights and obligations should lead to violent conflict—as it well might—the United States does not intend to be defeated.

Khrushchev decided not to escalate the crisis in Berlin. He would, however, test American resolve a year later when he installed SS-4 and

SS-5 ballistic missiles on the island of Cuba. Missile sites in Cuba gave him the ability to directly threaten the United States. He was also interested in expanding the Soviet sphere of influence and supporting Castro's Marxist-Leninist regime. As Khrushchev claimed later, "The fate of Cuba and the maintenance of Soviet prestige in that part of the world pre-occupied me. We had to think of some way of confronting America with more than words. . . . The logical answer was missiles."

Khrushchev likely assumed he could take advantage of a president he had judged to be weak, but he was wrong. Speaking to the nation on October 22, 1962, Kennedy reminded his audience, "The 1930s taught us a clear lesson: aggressive conduct, if allowed to go unchecked and unchallenged, ultimately leads to war." Therefore, America had to secure "the withdrawal or elimination" of the Soviet missiles. He announced he would impose a quarantine on shipments of all offensive military equipment to Cuba. He ordered the armed forces to "prepare for any eventualities," and he made clear he would hold the Soviets responsible: "It shall be the policy of this nation to regard any nuclear missile launched from Cuba against any nation in the Western hemisphere as an attack by the Soviet Union on the United States, requiring a full retaliatory response upon the Soviet Union."

Kennedy addressed Premier Khrushchev and said he now had an opportunity to "move the world back from the abyss of destruction" by removing the missiles. Over the next few days, the crisis built. On October 24, twenty Russian ships looked set to challenge the quarantine. Instead, they turned around.

On October 26, Khrushchev transmitted a long letter to Kennedy. If Kennedy promised not to invade Cuba, Khrushchev would remove the missiles. While the Americans were preparing a response, a second letter arrived. This one added a new condition. Kennedy must also agree to remove NATO missiles from Turkey. The Americans decided to publicly ignore the second letter and respond to the first. At the same time, Attorney General Robert Kennedy met secretly with the Soviet ambassador and agreed to withdraw the missiles from Turkey within six months. The next day, Radio Moscow announced that the order had been given to dismantle and remove the missiles from Cuba. Because the Turkish agreement was secret, Khrushchev appeared to have been the one who blinked.

The Cuban Missile Crisis reminded officials and citizens alike of the reality of the nuclear threat. In its aftermath the United States and the Soviet Union signed the Nuclear Test Ban Treaty, prohibiting atmospheric testing of nuclear weapons. A new doctrine was developed that would govern America's nuclear policy for the next twenty years, mutual assured destruction, or MAD, which meant that our own nuclear arsenal had to be of sufficient size and quality that the Soviets would know, were they ever to strike first, that we would survive the attack and strike back with devastating force. In their first strike on us, they would be sowing the seeds of their own annihilation.

IN BERLIN IN 1953, Hungary in 1956, and Czechoslovakia in 1968, the Soviets used military force to crush opposition movements within the Soviet Bloc. They were simultaneously providing military and economic support for insurgents and guerrilla movements in noncommunist countries around the globe, including for the Viet Cong guerrillas, who were attempting a communist takeover of South Vietnam. In response, in 1961, President Kennedy sent 500 U.S. military advisors to train the South Vietnamese. By the end of 1963, there were more than 16,000 American military advisors in Vietnam. At the height of the war, in 1968, President Lyndon Johnson had deployed 563,000 American troops to Vietnam.

The objective of preventing a communist takeover of South Vietnam was a worthy one. There were many errors in the way America pursued this objective, about which much has been written elsewhere. Perhaps the most significant obstacle to our success was that our policy was never aimed at defeating the enemy. Secretary of Defense Robert McNamara captured the essence of U.S. policy in Vietnam when he famously asked General William Westmoreland in 1965, "How many additional American and Allied troops would be required to convince the enemy he would be unable to win?" The American strategy wasn't to win. It was to convince the enemy he couldn't.

Former secretary of state and national security advisor Henry Kissinger explained it another way:

> *The strategic goal was not to lose in order to give South Vietnam time to create democratic institutions and social programs that would win the war for the hearts and minds of the population. . . . What is certain is that the process required a time span of stalemated war beyond the psychological endurance of the American public.*

President Nixon, elected in 1968, began to bring America's troops home from Vietnam and formally ended the war in January 1973 with the Treaty of Paris. America's combat troops came home, and the United States promised to provide economic assistance and renewed military support to the South if the North Vietnamese violated the treaty. Despite these promises, when the North reinvaded the south in early 1975, the U.S. Congress refused to provide funding for the assistance we had promised. Saigon fell to the North Vietnamese in April 1975.

The way the war ended was tragic. We had abandoned millions of South Vietnamese, leaving them to the mercy of the communists. Kissinger explained:

The United States devoted two decades of blood and treasure to help a group of newly independent fledgling societies avoid conquest by their merciless and militarily more powerful communist neighbor in North Vietnam. Yet, when the precarious peace wrought by the Paris Agreement was challenged, the United States, in the throes of physical and psychological abdication, cut off military and economic assistance to people whom we had given every encouragement to count on our protection. This consigned those we had made our wards to an implacable—and, in Cambodia, genocidal—communist conqueror.

On April 23, 1975, President Gerald Ford spoke at Tulane University and declared the war "finished as far as America is concerned." Even those who had supported the war felt a sense of relief at its end.

Long after the conclusion of the war, there was a view among many of our nation's top military leaders that the political leadership had failed our men and women in uniform. And in many ways this is true. President George H. W. Bush and his team were very aware of this when the United States deployed forces to liberate Kuwait in 1990. President Bush was committed to deploying a force large enough to win and providing them with all the resources they needed to do the job the country had asked them to do.

WHEN RICHARD NIXON BECAME America's thirty-seventh president in 1969, he inherited an array of international challenges, including America's ongoing war in Vietnam and the nuclear arms race with the Soviets. Henry Kissinger described the priorities of Nixon's first-term foreign policy strategy:

(1) to extricate from Vietnam under honorable conditions; (2) to confine the dissent of the protest movement to Indochina; (3) to

seize the high ground of the peace issue by a strategy that dem-
onstrated to the American public that, even while pursuing the
Cold War, we would do our utmost to control its dangers and
gradually overcome it; (4) to broaden the diplomatic chessboard
by including China in the international system; (5) to strengthen
our alliances; (6) and, from that platform, to go on the diplomatic
offensive, especially in the Middle East.

It is a well-informed summing up that contrasts markedly with President Obama's description of his foreign policy strategy: "Don't do stupid stuff."

It was clear from Nixon's first days in office that there were tensions between the Soviet Union and China. The president decided to exploit those tensions and drive a wedge between the world's two most powerful communist nations. On Monday, February 21, 1972, as a Chinese military band played "The Star-Spangled Banner," Nixon became the first American president to visit China while in office. Strategically the trip accomplished what he had hoped by reestablishing relations between the United States and China, inserting an irritant into the conduct of foreign policy for the Soviet Union and demonstrating that America's national security policy was larger than the war in Vietnam. "On the way back from Beijing," Kissinger said later, "I knew we'd made history."

Nixon and Kissinger also made history when they established the controversial policy of détente, which was intended to reduce the tensions between the United States and the Soviet Union, and to lessen the crises between the two powers that dominated the first two decades of the Cold War. The Strategic Arms Limitation Talks (SALT), an agreement to limit the number of ballistic missiles in the arsenal of each superpower, was one of the products of détente.

Critics of the policy point out that it essentially solidified the status quo and ensured that America would not confront Soviet oppression or question the Soviets' right to exert their rule throughout the Soviet Bloc. Critics of the policy also point out that it was only when Ronald Reagan discarded détente and confronted the Soviets across all fronts that the Berlin Wall came down and the Soviet Union itself ceased to exist.

It is not clear that Reagan's approach would have been as effective in the 1970s as it was in the 1980s. Strategies (or tactical approaches, for that matter) have to be tied to concrete circumstances. The art of statesmanship is understanding the environment correctly and choosing the most effective ways and means to secure national objectives. It is also true that another of the hallmarks of détente, the Helsinki Accords, sowed the seeds of the destruction of the Soviet empire.

IN AUGUST 1974, PRESIDENT Nixon resigned over his role in the Watergate break-in and cover-up. That evening, even before Vice President Gerald Ford took the oath of office to become America's thirty-eighth president, he met the press in front of his home in Alexandria, Virginia. His first order of business was to reassure the world that America's national security and foreign policy was in experienced hands and would remain unchanged. Henry Kissinger would be staying on. "Let me say without any hesitation or reservation," Ford said, "that the policy that has achieved peace . . . will be continued as far as I'm concerned as President of the United States."

One of President Ford's first acts was to pardon Richard Nixon, a decision highly controversial at the time, but widely praised today. Ford rightly judged that in the aftermath of everything the nation had been through, it was time to begin to heal and to move on.

IN JULY 1974, ALEKSANDR Solzhenitsyn, a prominent Soviet dissident who had been imprisoned in Stalin's prison camps, visited

Washington. He had been stripped of his Soviet citizenship after the publication of *The Gulag Archipelago*, his devastating account of life in the camps. There was a debate inside the White House about whether President Ford should meet with Solzhenitsyn. Henry Kissinger and his deputy, Brent Scowcroft, advised against it. Arguing for the meeting was one of the authors of this book, Dick Cheney, who wrote in a memo:

My own strong feeling is that the President should see Solzhenitsyn. . . . I think the decision not to see him is based on a misreading of Détente. Détente means nothing more and nothing less than a lessening of tension. Over the last several years it has been sold as a much broader concept to the American people. At most, détente should consist of agreements wherever possible to reduce the possibility of conflict, but it does not mean that all of a sudden our relationship with the Soviets is all sweetness and light. . . .

I can't think of a better way to demonstrate for the American people and for the world that Détente with the Soviet Union . . . in no way means that we've given up our fundamental principles concerning individual liberty and democracy. Solzhenitsyn, as the symbol of resistance to oppression in the Soviet Union, whatever else he may be, can help us communicate that message simply by having him in to see the President. Seeing him is a nice counterbalance to all of the publicity and coverage that's given to meetings between American presidents and Soviet leaders. Meetings with Soviet leaders are very important, but it is also important that we not contribute any more to the illusion that all of a sudden we're bosom-buddies with the Russians.

[The Soviets] have been perfectly free to criticize us for our actions and policies in Southeast Asia over the years, to call us imperialists, war-mongers, and various and sundry other endearing

terms, and I can't believe they don't understand why the President might want to see Solzhenitsyn.

Cheney lost the argument, and Ford's refusal to see Solzhenitsyn became a key element in the conservative foreign policy case against Ford.

Henry Kissinger would later write, "In retrospect, I believe we would have been wise to . . . schedule a meeting with the President . . . in as unobtrusive and dignified a manner as possible." The trepidation some in the Ford administration felt about shining a light on human rights abuses inside the Soviet Bloc would be overcome with the signing of the Helsinki Accords.

The Conference on Security and Co-operation in Europe opened on July 30, 1975, in Helsinki, Finland. Former secretary of state Kissinger has written of the conference and the accords that followed, "Turning points often pass unrecognized by contemporaries." Both sides had incentives to participate and sign the accords, and, it is fair to say, neither side recognized the dramatic impact the agreement would ultimately have on the collapse of communism and the downfall of the Soviet Union.

The accords included provisions that affirmed the postwar division of Europe, which the Soviets wanted. The accords also, and more important as it turned out, included language recognizing "the universal significance of human rights and fundamental freedoms . . . in conformity with the purposes and principles of the Charter of the United Nations and with the Universal Declaration of Human Rights."

Former ambassador to the United States Anatoly Dobrynin described the reaction of Soviet Politburo members when they read the text. He said they had no objections to the first parts of the treaty, but when they read the article guaranteeing human rights, "their hair stood on end." Foreign Minister Andrei Gromyko tried to reassure them, arguing that the significant thing about the Helsinki treaty was that it recognized the postwar borders of Europe. "That's what we shed our blood for in the great patriotic war," Gromyko said. "All thirty-five signatory states are now saying—these are the borders of Europe." As for the sections about human rights, Gromyko declared, "We are the masters of this house, and each time, it will be up to us to decide how to act. Who can force us?"

As President Ford saw it, "The Soviet Union and the Warsaw Pact nations did not recognize that the human rights provision was a time bomb. We, the United States believed that if we could get the Soviet Union and the Warsaw Pact nations to respect human rights, that was worth whatever else was agreed to in the Helsinki Accords."

The Soviet leadership believed they could explain the agreement to their people by stressing the final settlement of the postwar boundaries and essentially ignoring the human rights provisions, but according to Ambassador Dobrynin, when the full text of the accords was published in the official Soviet Communist Party paper, *Pravda*, it had "the weight of an official document." Thus, in Dobrynin's words, "It gradually became a manifesto of the dissident and liberal movement, a development totally beyond the imagination of the Soviet leadership."

Within months of the treaty's signing, "Helsinki Groups" began forming in countries behind the Iron Curtain. What had once been forbidden—demanding respect for fundamental rights from Soviet Bloc governments—was now, in essence, officially sanctioned. The Soviet government had, after all, signed a treaty committing to observance of those rights and published the treaty for all to see.

On January 1, 1977, a group of intellectuals in Prague signed the "Charter 77" manifesto urging the government of Czechoslovakia to live up to its obligations under the human rights provisions of the Helsinki Accords. A number of the signatories were imprisoned, including playwright Vaclav Havel. While Havel was in prison and later under house arrest, his influence grew as he continued to write essays and plays about human rights and human freedom. Twelve years later, he would become the first president of liberated Czechoslovakia.

PRESIDENT FORD LOST THE 1976 election to Jimmy Carter. The Nixon pardon had cost him politically. There was also a moment during the October 6 presidential debate from which it was very hard to recover. A question from Max Frankel of the *New York Times* implied that the Helsinki Accords meant the United States accepted Soviet domination of Eastern Europe. President Ford responded by saying, "There is no Soviet domination of Eastern Europe and there never will be under a Ford administration."

Frankel was perplexed and followed up: "I'm sorry? Did I understand you to say, sir, that the Russians are not using Eastern Europe as their own sphere of influence and occupying most of the countries there and making sure with their troops that it's a communist zone?" Ford doubled down, explaining that the people of Yugoslavia, Romania, and Poland did not consider themselves to be dominated by the Soviet Union. The national press and the Carter campaign had a field day. The next day President Ford clarified his statement, but the damage had been done.

ON JANUARY 12, 1977, eight days before he was sworn in as president of the United States, Jimmy Carter met at Blair House with General George Brown, chairman of the Joint Chiefs of Staff, and members of Carter's national security team. According to a report by Rowland Evans and Robert Novak in the next day's *Washington Post*, Carter and his top advisors were receiving a briefing on the Single

Integrated Operational Plan, which covered "the President's awesome responsibilities in the event of a Soviet attack." Carter shocked the assembled group by instructing General Brown to begin studies of the possibility of cutting the U.S. strategic nuclear arsenal significantly to only 200–250 intercontinental ballistic missiles. General Brown, reported Evans and Novak, was "stunned speechless."

Two months later, Carter sent Secretary of State Cyrus Vance on a mission to Moscow. In late 1974, President Ford and Soviet premier Leonid Brezhnev had agreed in principle on nuclear arms limitations that would extend the terms of the SALT I Treaty. Vance arrived in Moscow with a plan for far deeper cuts in each side's arsenal. Brezhnev flatly rejected it. Les Gelb, who served in the Carter State Department and traveled to Moscow with Vance, explained later that the mission's failure was interpreted as a sign that "the Carter team was inept." The impact of this misstep was, in Gelb's view, "a deep stab wound."

In May, President Carter explained his aims for strategic arms reductions in a commencement address at the University of Notre Dame, calling for a freeze on modernization and weapons production, along with "continued substantial reductions." He also said, "The great democracies are not free because we are strong and prosperous. I believe we are strong and prosperous because we are free." It was an odd turn of phrase given that it was precisely America's strength that guaranteed our freedom. As for the other "great democracies" to which Carter referred, in the aftermath of World War II, they, too, were free because America was strong.

In June 1977, President Carter canceled America's B-1 bomber program. The B-1 was to have replaced the aging B-52s. Carter secured nothing in return from the Soviets. In April 1978, Carter announced he was stopping the development of America's neutron bomb program, again without securing anything in return from the

Soviets. Even members of his own party were concerned. "I'm dismayed and puzzled. I don't understand," said Georgia Democratic senator Sam Nunn. "They're not on a very clear course."

The appearance of American weakness was compounded by a sense of diplomatic incompetence. On March 6, 1980, for example, the American ambassador to the United Nations voted to condemn Israel's building of settlements on the West Bank. Arab states hailed the vote. Israel, which had expected an abstention from the United States, was shocked. The following Monday, the White House was forced to issue a statement in Carter's name explaining that the vote had been, in fact, a "mistake." It was, according to the White House spokesman, a "foul-up" in communications between the State Department and the White House.

The most significant and long-lasting damage to American interests during President Carter's administration came with the takeover of Iran by the militant Islamist regime of Ayatollah Khomeini. The shah of Iran, Reza Pahlavi, who was deposed in January 1979, had been one of America's most important allies in the Middle East. Less than a year after he was deposed, an Iranian mob stormed the U.S. embassy in Tehran and took sixty-six Americans and forty others hostage. The Iranians would ultimately hold fifty-two Americans hostage for 444 days.

When the shah fell, the government of Saudi Arabia asked the United States for a demonstration of our continued commitment to our other allies in the region. President Carter sent a squadron of F-15s. When the planes were airborne, he announced they were unarmed.

Until 2009, Jimmy Carter's was the least competent presidency of the postwar era. His misguided actions extended beyond his time in the White House. When the United States was attempting to gain UN support to liberate Kuwait in 1990, we learned that former president Carter had contacted heads of government with seats on the Security Council and urged them to vote against the American position. By then his influence was not what it had been when he was in office, and he failed.

Governor Ronald Reagan of California summed up the concern millions of Americans felt about President Carter's mishandling of our national security policy. Accepting the Republican presidential nomination on July 17, 1980, Reagan asked:

> *Who does not feel a growing sense of unease as our allies, facing repeated instances of an amateurish and confused administration, reluctantly conclude that America is unwilling or unable to fulfill its obligations as leader of the free world? Who does not feel rising alarm when the question in any discussion of foreign policy is no longer, "Should we do something?" but "Do we have the capacity to do anything?"*

Six months later, on January 20, 1981, Ronald Reagan began to restore America's strength, confidence, and capacity to lead. He'd been elected in a landslide—489 electoral votes to Carter's 49. Shortly after Reagan took the oath at noon, the Iranians released the American hostages.

ON OCTOBER 16, 1978, the papal conclave elected Polish cardinal Karol Wojtyla to be bishop of Rome. History would know him as Pope John Paul II.

On hearing of Wojtyla's election, Yuri Andropov, who was then head of the KGB, angrily inquired of the KGB chief in Warsaw, "How could you possibly allow the election of a citizen of a socialist country as pope?" The Soviets were right to be afraid. Shortly after becoming pope, John Paul II made clear the role he intended to play. The church behind the Iron Curtain was "not a church of silence anymore," he said, "because it speaks with my voice."

Pope John Paul II made a pilgrimage to his homeland in June 1979. Millions of Poles turned out to greet him as he made his way across the country. On June 2, his first day in Poland, he was received at the Polish White House by President Henryk Jablonski and Communist Party leader Edward Gierek. In his public remarks at the occasion, the pope spoke of the importance of freedom for the church in Poland. He reminded his hosts that they would be responsible for their treatment of people of faith "before history and before your own conscience." He also told them that he would continue to care as deeply about the well-being of the Polish church as he had when he was archbishop of Kraków.

In sermon after sermon in this nation where communists had outlawed religion, John Paul II spoke of the "thousand-year-right of citizenship" of the Christian church in Poland. He said, "Christ cannot be kept out of the history of man in any part of the globe, at any longitude or latitude." And he said, "Without Christ it is impossible to understand the history of Poland." Not only was Christ the past, the pope declared, he was "our Polish future." Millions of voices lifted in response chanting, "We want God!"

Communist Party signs posted on walls across the country read "The Party is for the people." During the pope's visit a handwritten addendum appeared on thousands of the signs: "But the people want the Pope."

John Paul II's last stop was his hometown of Kraków. He stayed in his old room at the archbishop's residence. For each of the three nights he was there, thousands of young people gathered in the streets and on the roofs of adjacent buildings, cheering and singing. When the pope appeared on the residence's small balcony, the chants rose up, *Sto lat! Sto lat!* ("May you live a hundred years!") Instead of delivering a sermon, the pope sang, each night, with the Polish students and workers gathered outside his window.

His final mass was on June 10 on the Kraków Commons. The largest crowd in Polish history gathered to hear him. There in the fields of Kraków, the pope proclaimed:

> *As a bishop does in the sacrament of Confirmation so do I today extend my hands in that apostolic gesture over all who are gathered here today, my compatriots. And so I speak for Christ himself: "Receive the Holy Spirit!"*

He spoke of "this Kraków in which every stone and every brick is dear to me," and he urged his fellow Poles to be strong:

> *You must be strong, dear brothers and sisters. . . . You must be strong with the strength of faith. . . . Today, more than in any other age you need this strength. You must be strong with love, which is stronger than death. . . . When we are strong with the Spirit of God, we are also strong with the faith of man. . . . There is therefore no need to fear.*
>
> *So I beg you: never lose your trust, do not be defeated, do not be discouraged. . . . Always seek spiritual power from Him from whom countless generations of our fathers and mothers have found it. Never detach yourselves from Him. Never lose your spiritual freedom.*

Poland's communist authorities were helpless against the power of this pope, a son of Poland, delivering God's blessings to millions of his fellow countrymen. In a nation where faith was outlawed, every time John Paul II spoke, urging his people not to lose their "spiritual freedom," not to detach themselves from God, not to be defeated or discouraged, he was committing the most radical—yet completely unobjectionable—act. The very foundations of Poland's communist regime began to crumble.

Thirteen million Poles saw John Paul II in person during those nine days in June. His biographer George Weigel explained the lasting impact of his visit: "By giving his people an experience of their individual dignity and collective authority, John Paul II had already won a major victory from which there could be no retreat. He had begun to exorcise the fear . . . and the sense of hopelessness." In an interview with journalist Peggy Noonan years later, Solidarity leader Lech Walesa said, "We knew . . . Communism could not be reformed. But we knew the minute he touched the foundations of Communism it would collapse." In 1980, when Walesa signed the charter creating Solidarity, the first labor union in a communist country, he did it with a pen bearing John Paul II's picture.

In December 1981, the Soviets had had enough. They ordered Polish general Wojciech Jaruzelski to impose martial law and arrest the leaders of Solidarity. When they came for Walesa, he told his captors, "This is the moment of your defeat. These are the last nails in the coffin of Communism."

IN THE UNITED STATES, Ronald Reagan was providing the hammer. Reagan had ended the policy of détente and replaced it with a determination to confront and defeat communism. In a speech to the British Parliament on June 8, 1982, Reagan spoke directly about the "failure" and "decay" of the Soviet system:

> *It is the Soviet Union that runs against the tide of history by denying human freedom and human dignity to its citizens. It also is in deep economic difficulty. . . . The dimensions of this failure are*

*astounding: A country which employs one-fifth of its population
in agriculture is unable to feed its own people.*

President Reagan spoke of "the march of freedom and democracy,"
which would "leave Marxism-Leninism on the ash-heap of history."

A few months later, Reagan addressed those who argued that there
was a moral equivalence between the United States and the Soviet
Union. In a speech to the National Association of Evangelicals on
March 8, 1983, the president reminded his audience that totalitarian
leaders who "preach the supremacy of the state, declare its omnipo-
tence over individual man, and predict its eventual domination of all
peoples on the Earth . . . are the focus of evil in the modern world."
He warned against ignorance where the nature of our enemy was concerned. "If history teaches anything, it teaches that simple-minded
appeasement or wishful thinking about our adversaries is folly. It
means the betrayal of our past, the squandering of our freedom."

Finally, knowing that religious leaders had been active in the nuclear freeze movement, Reagan cautioned:

*I urge you to beware the temptation of pride—the temptation of
blithely declaring yourselves above it all and label[ing] both sides
equally at fault. [It is an error] to ignore the facts of history and
the aggressive impulses of an evil empire, to simply call the arms
race a giant misunderstanding and thereby remove yourself from
the struggle between right and wrong and good and evil.*

President Reagan matched his words with actions. He restored
the B-1 bomber President Carter had canceled, significantly increased
U.S. defense spending, deployed Pershing missiles to Europe in response to Soviet deployment of SS-20s, and authorized the Strategic
Defense Initiative, to develop missile defense technology to defend

the nation from attack. The Soviets complained that SDI was destabilizing since it would make the doctrine of mutual assured destruction obsolete, and that Reagan's increases in defense spending "disrupted the parity" in arms created over many years. His expenditures forced the Soviets to keep spending.

In a speech to the nation on March 23, 1983, Reagan explained why SDI was needed and provided a tutorial in defense budgeting. It shouldn't be done, he explained, by "deciding to spend a certain number of dollars." Rather, it had to be based on necessity, on a determination of what was needed to defend against all threats to the nation. Then, once a strategy to meet those threats was developed, a cost could be determined for carrying out the strategy. He explained how America's spending on many of its critical defense programs had stalled or been cut over the years, while the Soviets had maintained a constant increase.

It was critical to America's security that we not return to the days of slashed defense budgets. "It is up to us, in our time," he said, "to choose and choose wisely between the hard but necessary task of preserving peace and freedom, and the temptation to ignore our duty and blindly hope for the best while the enemies of freedom grow stronger day by day."

Then he turned to SDI. "What if free people could live secure in the knowledge that their security did not rest upon the threat of instant U.S. retaliation to deter a Soviet attack, that we could intercept and destroy strategic ballistic missiles before they reached our own soil or that of our allies?" Even though it was a formidable task, he explained, it was necessary, and he had instructed his administration to pursue the possibility offered by "defensive technologies."

In 1985, a new Soviet leader came to power. Ronald Reagan and Mikhail Gorbachev met in Geneva in November that year. Reagan believed so strongly in the necessity of developing a defensive system that he told Gorbachev the United States would share the technology with the Soviets once it had been developed. Breaking with convention, Reagan and Gorbachev met alone for several hours without their advisors, and although they continued to disagree about SDI, they agreed to work toward significant arms reductions.

The two leaders met again in Reykjavik, Iceland, in October 1986. Proposals for sweeping arms control reductions, including the elimination of all ballistic missiles and a 50 percent reduction in each side's strategic arsenal, were on the table. Gorbachev continued to demand, however, that Reagan essentially give up SDI by confining it to laboratory testing. Reagan would not agree. In an exercise of diplomacy that should be studied by all future policy makers, Reagan knew what lines he would not cross. He was never desperate for an agreement, and he was unwilling to give up America's right to missile defense in order to appease the Soviets.

One year later Gorbachev visited the United States. He had by this time dropped his demand that Reagan abandon missile defense. On December 8, 1987, the two leaders signed the Intermediate-Range Nuclear Forces, or INF, Treaty agreeing to eliminate their intermediate-range ballistic and cruise missiles.

Inside the Soviet Union, Gorbachev had undertaken new policies to restructure and reform the government and economic system (*perestroika*) and to allow greater public discussion and dissemination of information (*glasnost*). Whether his reforms were real or would be successful was a subject of much debate in the West.

President Reagan traveled to Berlin in June 1987. Standing in front of the Brandenburg Gate, Reagan talked about Gorbachev's reforms:

And now the Soviets themselves may, in a limited way, be coming to understand the importance of freedom. We hear much from

Moscow about a new policy of reform and openness. Some politi-
cal prisoners have been released. Certain foreign news broadcasts
are no longer being jammed. Some economic enterprises have
been permitted to operate with greater freedom from state con-
trol.

But how could the West know whether these were "the beginnings of profound change" or simply "token gestures"? Reagan answered his own question and issued a direct challenge to Gorbachev:

General Secretary Gorbachev, if you seek peace, if you seek pros-
perity for the Soviet Union and Eastern Europe, if you seek liber-
alization: Come here to this gate. Mr. Gorbachev, open this gate!
Mr. Gorbachev, tear down this wall!

IN JUNE 1989, HUNGARIAN prime minister Miklos Nemeth cut off funds for the upkeep of the barbed-wire portion of the Iron Curtain along the Hungarian frontier. Shortly after that, he ordered the dismantling of the fence on the border between Austria and Hungary. In a clear sign that Moscow's relations with its satellite states were dramatically changing, Gorbachev did not object.

In Poland, the once-banned Solidarity was allowed to contest open elections. Their campaign posters featured a picture of American actor Gary Cooper from the movie *High Noon* and the name Solidarność (Solidarity) in bold red print. Solidarity won 99 of 100 seats in the Polish parliament. Poland had a noncommunist prime minister for the first time in its postwar history.

Pressure across the rest of Eastern Europe built in the summer of 1989. East Germans began to attempt to escape to the West through Hungary's partially open border, and they besieged the West German embassy in Budapest. In September 1989, the Hungarian government announced it would allow the refugees to go "to a country of their choice." When the East German government curbed travel to Hungary, thousands of refugees overran the West German embassy in Prague. Within East Germany, citizens began demanding the types of reforms they knew Gorbachev was adopting inside the Soviet Union.

In November, in response to mass demonstrations in Berlin, the government of East Germany decided to lift some of the travel restrictions on its citizens. The regime had not intended to open the wall immediately, but on November 9, 1989, as Politburo member Gunter Schabowski was briefing the press on the new rules, he stunned reporters by announcing that citizens could leave "through any of the border crossings." When the journalists asked when the new rules would go into effect, Schabowski paused, looked through his papers, and said, "According to my information, from today—onwards, immediately."

Thousands of East Germans appeared at border crossings. The guards, lacking any formal instructions, opened the gates. To cheers, singing, applause, and tears, East Germans rushed through—free at last. West Germans met East Germans on top of the wall with picks and hammers and they began to chisel away at the wall itself. In October 1990, East and West Germany were reunified and invited to join NATO.

It was one thing for Gorbachev to allow greater freedom for Poles or Hungarians or Czechs, but completely another when those demanding their independence were in parts of the Soviet Union, like Latvia, Lithuania, and Estonia. Gorbachev had not planned to oversee the breakup of the U.S.S.R. Historian Tony Judt noted that "Gorbachev was letting Communism fall in Eastern Europe in order to save it in Russia itself." It was a miscalculation. Two years after the Berlin Wall came down, the Soviet Union itself would collapse.

The unraveling began with a coup against Gorbachev conducted by hard-liners who believed his reforms were moving too quickly. In August 1991, the coup plotters managed to put Gorbachev under house arrest at his vacation dacha in the Crimea. The coup unraveled within a few days, but Gorbachev never regained full power. Boris Yeltsin, who'd stood atop a tank outside the Russian White House to face down the coup, emerged as the hero of an independent Russia. Gorbachev resigned as general secretary of the Communist Party on August 24, 1991. Four months later, the Soviet Union was dissolved and the Cold War came to an end.

COMMUNISM, SOME SAY, WAS doomed to fail. A system that attempted to extinguish the human spirit, innovation, freedom, and individualism could not survive. A governing theory that required force to keep its citizens under its control would eventually crumble. But history tells us otherwise. The Soviet Union and its totalitarian satellites did survive for decades, using force against their own people and others. According to the Council of Europe, during the period of the Cold War, communism was responsible for the deaths of 94.5 million people. It was not preordained that the Soviet system would implode. It was certainly not preordained that it would do so relatively peacefully.

The history of the Cold War is many things. It is the story of the triumph of freedom over tyranny, of the courage of millions who fought the oppression of Soviet dictatorship around the globe, and of the importance of achieving peace through strength. It is the story of individual leaders. Men and women like Ronald Reagan, George H. W. Bush, Margaret Thatcher, John Paul II, Vaclav Havel, Lech Walesa, Miklos Nemeth, and Mikhail Gorbachev played critical roles in ensuring that tyranny would not prevail. Ultimately, the story of the Cold War is the story of American leadership. The free peoples of the world would not have prevailed without us. Through Republican and Democratic administrations, some more successful than others, over the course of forty-five years, we contained the Soviets and then defeated them.

———•◆•———

THREE

Dawn of the Age of Terror

Just as surely as the Nazis during World War II, and the Soviets during the Cold War, the enemy we face today is bent on our destruction. As in other times, we are in a war we did not start and have no choice but to win.

—VICE PRESIDENT DICK CHENEY, SEPTEMBER 1, 2004

A s the Cold War ended, some declared that the era of the super-power was over, and predicted we would see the rise of a new multipolar global power structure. That didn't happen. Instead, America emerged as the world's only superpower. Our preeminence became evident in August 1990, even before the final disintegration of the Soviet Union, when Saddam Hussein invaded Kuwait.

The Soviets had been Saddam's main arms supplier. When he sent his forces into Kuwait, the Soviets had a decision to make. On their last legs as a world empire, would they support the aggression of their client state?

At the time of the invasion, Secretary of State James Baker was in Mongolia. He flew immediately to Moscow and held a press briefing with Soviet foreign minister Eduard Shevardnadze in Moscow's

Vnukovo-2 airport. Standing shoulder to shoulder, Baker and Shevardnadze issued a joint statement condemning "the brutal and illegal invasion of Kuwait" and calling for an arms embargo on Iraq. "That was the day, for me, when the Cold War ended," Baker said later.

As Dick Cheney, one of the authors of this book, recalls:

I realized how much had changed when I visited the Soviet Union in October 1990 as secretary of defense. I toured Soviet military installations, including the Moscow Air Defense Center—the heavily fortified bunker from which the Soviets would have coordinated portions of their operations if there had been a nuclear war between our two nations. No American had seen it before. When I met with the Soviet minister of defense and with Soviet leader Gorbachev, we discussed Soviet efforts at military and economic reform. I had another agenda item, as well. We needed to find out, as we prepared to take military action to liberate Kuwait, whether the Soviets had provided Saddam with any weapons we didn't know about. A few years earlier, we could not have dreamed of having such a conversation with our Cold War adversary, but now Gorbachev, Shevardnadze, and defense minister Dmitri Yazov were open with me, and assured me we wouldn't be surprised.

Once Operation Desert Storm was under way a few months later, the Soviets attempted unsuccessfully to negotiate a cease-fire that would have paused the fighting based on a promise from Saddam to withdraw from Kuwait. We did not accept it. We knew Saddam's "promises" were meaningless, and we made clear Saddam had actually to withdraw. The Soviets, who had lost much of their influence in the Middle East beginning when Anwar Sadat expelled Soviet advisors from Egypt in 1972, were still trying to be relevant in the region and on the world stage. I suspect they also were trying to avoid an embarrassing military defeat for their client state, Iraq.

President Bush launched the air war on January 16, 1991. A few weeks later, on February 23, 1991, the ground war began. Within one hundred hours, U.S. forces had defeated the Iraqis. In the years since, the decision to stop the fighting and not to go all the way to Baghdad has been a target of criticism. Some say if the United States had toppled Saddam in 1991, we would not have had to go back to Iraq in 2003. On the other hand, some argue that we were right not to remove him in 1991, and we shouldn't have removed him in 2003, either. The truth is that our mission in 1991 was to liberate Kuwait. We had built an extensive coalition, including with other Arab states, to do that. The coalition would not have held together had we pushed on to Baghdad.

In 2003, the world was a very different place. Terrorists had killed three thousand people in the worst attack on our homeland in history. We had evidence that al Qaeda was planning additional attacks and that they were seeking the world's deadliest weapons. We knew, for example, that they were trying to manufacture anthrax and that Osama bin Laden had met with Pakistani nuclear scientists in an effort to procure nuclear weapons. We had to do everything necessary to ensure al Qaeda was unable to launch another, far more lethal attack.

Saddam's Iraq was the most likely nexus between the terrorists and the devastating weapons they sought. Twelve years, sixteen UN Security Council resolutions, international sanctions, and no-fly zones had failed to diminish the threat Saddam posed. As the sanctions regime began to crumble, the calculation about the nature of Iraq's threat to the United States and the need for military action to defeat Saddam was very different in 2003 than it was in 1991. We did the right thing in 1991 and in 2003.

————————

THROUGHOUT THE COLD WAR, the size and structure of America's military had largely been determined by the need to defend the United States and our allies against the Soviet Union. For example, we had to maintain the ability to deploy ten divisions to Europe within ten days of a decision to mobilize in response to a Soviet conventional invasion of Western Europe. As the Cold War came to an end, that requirement and others like it were no longer relevant. Planners in the Defense Department began thinking through what kind of force posture was needed now that the nation's most significant enemy had essentially imploded.

The United States was able to make significant reductions in our conventional forces in Europe as well as in our strategic nuclear forces. But it was clear that the dissolution of the Soviet Union did not mean the end of global threats to the United States. We needed to ensure our force was structured and sized based on our new security needs and strategy. As the George H. W. Bush administration came to an end in January 1993, the Defense Department published the Regional Defense Strategy, laying out what the United States must do to maintain the victory we had won. The strategy identified four key goals for America's defense efforts:

- to deter or defeat any attack against the United States and to honor our historic and treaty commitments;
- to strengthen and extend mutual defense alliances;
- to preclude any hostile power from dominating a region critical to our interests; and
- to preclude conflict by reducing sources of regional instability and to limit the violence should conflict occur.

With respect to the Middle East, this meant:

We must be prepared to act decisively in the Middle East/Persian Gulf region as we did in Operations Desert Shield and Desert Storm if our vital interests are threatened anew. We must also be prepared to counter the terrorism, insurgency, and subversion that adversaries may use to threaten governments supportive of U.S. security interests. . . . To discourage the rise of a challenger hostile to our interests in the region, we must maintain a level of forward military presence adequate to reassure our friends and deter aggressors and present a credible crisis response capability.

The guidance made clear there should be no diminution of American strength, power, or involvement in the world. "Only a nation that is strong enough to act decisively," the strategy document said, "can provide the leadership needed to encourage others to resist aggression." Weakness and indecisiveness on the part of the United States have always been, and will always be, provocative to our adversaries.

ON FRIDAY, FEBRUARY 26, 1993, Islamic terrorists drove a van containing a 1,400-pound bomb into the garage of the North Tower of the World Trade Center in New York City. They detonated the explosive shortly after noon, blowing a crater six stories deep. The attack killed six people and injured more than a thousand. In response to this act of war, the U.S. government issued an indictment. One of the lead prosecutors on the case, Andrew McCarthy, put it this way: "Our response was to call in not the Marines, but the prosecutors." While the enemy continued to plot, plan, and launch attacks over the next few years, McCarthy notes, our strategy didn't change:

The enemy's declaration of war would be complemented by a campaign of murder and mayhem, culminating in the same place, eight years later when the first strike would be dwarfed. In the interim, the United States would respond with the law. And so, while the enemy prosecuted the war, we prosecuted the enemy—er, the defendants.

Undeterred by the criminal charges we were filing against them, the terrorists continued to attack. On November 13, 1995, Islamic terrorists detonated a truck bomb outside a Saudi National Guard building in Riyadh used by the United States, killing five Americans. On June 25, 1996, another truck bomb was detonated at the U.S. military barracks at Khobar Towers near Dhahran, Saudi Arabia, killing nineteen U.S. servicemen and wounding hundreds more.

On August 23, 1996, Osama bin Laden issued his first fatwa declaring war on the United States. He mocked America's response to the attacks in Riyadh and at Khobar Towers, and to previous attacks, as well:

A few days ago the news agencies communicated a declaration issued by the American Defense Secretary, a crusader and an occupier, in which he said he had learned only one lesson from the bombings in Riyadh and Khobar: not to retreat before the cowardly terrorists. Well, we would like to tell the secretary that his words are funny enough to make even a mother grieving for the loss of her child burst out laughing, because they show the fear that grips him. Where was this supposed bravery in Beirut, after the attack of [1983]? . . . Where was this bravery in Aden, which you fled twenty-four hours after two attacks had taken place?

He saved his greatest scorn for America's withdrawal from Somalia. On October 3, 1993, two American Black Hawk helicopters on a mission to capture Somali warlord Mohammed Aidid and his key lieutenants were shot down in Mogadishu. A massive firefight ensued in which the U.S. Army Rangers and American special operators displayed tremendous heroism and courage. Eighteen Americans were killed and seventy-five were wounded. Pictures flashed across the world of Somalis dragging the body of a dead American through the streets.

U.S. commanders on the ground had requested tanks and AC-130 gunships for the mission. AC-130s are devastatingly accurate and have massive firepower. American commanders in Somalia reported the AC-130 had been very effective in earlier missions. Low-flying and armed with a powerful array of weapons, they struck fear into the hearts of the Somali militias.

According to a Senate Armed Services Committee report compiled after the Mogadishu operation, General Wayne Downing, commander of the U.S. Special Forces Command, requested the AC-130s for the battle in Mogadishu in a discussion with Joint Chiefs of Staff chairman General Colin Powell and U.S. Central Command (CENTCOM) commander General Joseph Hoar. "I advised that we'd like to have the AC-130s. General Powell advised that we needed to keep the numbers down," General Downing said. Powell told the committee he didn't recall the conversation, but the damage done by the planes in earlier operations, he said, "wasn't the greatest imagery on CNN." The AC-130s were not deployed. The request for the tanks was also denied, in an apparent effort not to increase America's presence in Somalia. As a result, our forces on the ground did not have the weapons they needed.

On October 7, 1993, four days after the battle, President Bill Clinton announced that all American troops would leave Somalia by March 31, 1994. In his 1996 declaration of war on the United States, bin Laden pointed to the withdrawal as the ultimate sign of American weakness:

Your most disgraceful case was Somalia, where, after vigorous
propaganda about the power of the USA and its post Cold War
leadership of the new world order you moved [American soldiers
in]. However when tens of your soldiers were killed in battle . . .
you left the area carrying disappointment, humiliation, defeat
and your dead with you. Clinton appeared in front of the whole
world threatening and promising revenge, but these threats were
merely a preparation for withdrawal. You were disgraced by Allah
and you withdrew; the extent of your impotence and weaknesses
became very clear.

Bin Laden used the stories of America's retreat to encourage his followers. His message was that the United States was not as strong as
it seemed, or claimed. He had watched our responses in the wake
of attacks in Beirut, Riyadh, and Somalia and took one deadly lesson from this history: when attacked, America didn't strike back, she
retreated.

On Friday, August 7, 1998, simultaneous truck bombs were detonated at the American embassies in Nairobi, Kenya, and Dar es Sa-
laam, Tanzania. Two hundred twenty-four people, including twelve
Americans, were killed. More than five thousand were wounded in
this al Qaeda operation. In response, the CIA and the Department
of Defense drew up a list of targets connected to Osama bin Laden
and al Qaeda. The list included al Qaeda training camps in Khost,
Afghanistan, and a pharmaceutical factory in Sudan. U.S. intelligence showed the pharmaceutical factory, al Shifa, to be the site of
a chemical weapons program with which Osama bin Laden was involved. American intelligence also suspected Iraqi involvement with
the plant's chemical weapons program.

A soil sample collected clandestinely at the plant showed high
levels of a precursor for VX nerve gas known as EMPTA. Journalist

Stephen Hayes has reported that a senior intelligence official briefing reporters said at the time, "Iraq is the only country we're aware of" that made VX using EMPTA. Intelligence also showed top Iraqi chemical weapons specialists had attended the plant's opening. In addition, the National Security Agency had intercepted phone calls between the plant's general manager and Iraqi chemical weapons experts.

The cruise missile strikes ordered by President Clinton destroyed the pharmaceutical plant but had no discernible impact on al Qaeda operations. In subsequent years, debate arose in the intelligence community about the accuracy of the reports on the pharmaceutical plant. Reports that bin Laden himself might be in the Khost terrorist training camps turned out not to be true.

Once again, the Clinton administration turned to the legal system. In November 1998, the Justice Department indicted Osama bin Laden for the bombings of the American embassies in Kenya and Tanzania, and for conspiring to kill Americans overseas. Less than two years later bin Laden struck again. On October 12, 2000, a small boat loaded with explosives rammed into the side of the USS *Cole* in the harbor of Aden, Yemen. Seventeen American sailors were killed. Although it was clear al Qaeda was responsible for the attack, President Clinton took no action in response.

Throughout the 1990s, the United States tended to treat attacks as law enforcement problems, with the result that neither the terrorists responsible for the attacks nor the countries that provided them sanctuary paid a price. Striking us appeared to be a way for the terrorists to achieve their objectives since the attacks were often followed by the withdrawal of U.S. forces, as in Beirut and Somalia.

Al Qaeda launched its most devastating attack on the morning of September 11, 2001, killing nearly 3,000 people. Two terrorist-hijacked planes flew into the World Trade Center in New York. Less than an hour later, a third plane was flown into the Pentagon. Passengers on a fourth hijacked plane, United Airlines Flight 93, heard that other planes had been used as weapons and decided to take action. With tremendous courage, they stormed the cockpit and overwhelmed the hijackers. Flight 93 crashed in a field outside Shanksville, Pennsylvania, killing all those on board. Based on its flight path, it is clear Flight 93 was headed for Washington, likely with the intention of targeting either the U.S. Capitol or the White House. The actions of the brave passengers on board saved many others.

The attacks on that day changed everything. This was a clear act of war, deadlier than Pearl Harbor, targeting civilians in the economic and political centers of American power.

On the night of 9/11, our family was evacuated to an undisclosed location—Camp David—where we would spend many days and nights over the months to come. "I spent much of that night thinking about what needed to be done," recalls Dick Cheney:

We had to go after those who attacked us and killed three thousand of our fellow citizens. We had to defeat any further attempts to launch mass casualty attacks against the United States, which meant, first and foremost, recognizing that we were at war and beginning to operate accordingly. Having just suffered the most devastating attack in our history, we had a duty to use all the means at our command to go after and destroy al Qaeda.

In an interview with Tim Russert the Sunday after the attacks, I said we would have to "work the dark side," using intelligence to learn all we could about the enemy, who they were, how there were organized and financed, so we could disrupt any plans for future attacks. I was also convinced by the events of that day that we had to focus our efforts on those who sponsored terrorism and provided safe harbor to the terrorists.

Holding state sponsors of terror accountable was a key element of what would become known as the Bush Doctrine. Another important component was the principle of preemption. The United States could not wait for the terrorists to launch an attack and then respond. We had to disrupt and prevent attacks before they occurred. As President Bush explained in March 2003, "Terrorists and terror states do not reveal these threats with fair notice, in formal declarations—and responding only to such enemies after they have struck first is not self-defense, it's suicide." This was particularly true because of the devastating possibility of a terrorist attack on the homeland involving chemical, biological, or nuclear weapons.

This possibility was a subject that one of the authors of this book, Dick Cheney, then vice president, discussed in an interview in April 2001:

> *I think we have to be more concerned than we ever have about so-called homeland defense, the vulnerability of our system to different kinds of attacks. Some . . . homegrown, like Oklahoma City. Some inspired by terrorists external to the United States— the World Trade Towers bombing, in New York. The threat of a terrorist attack against the U.S., eventually, potentially with weapons of mass destruction—bugs or gas, biological or chemical agents, potentially even, someday, nuclear weapons.*

To reduce the likelihood of one of these threats materializing, the United States needed a robust intelligence capability, one that enabled us to uncover the threats and thwart the terrorists' plans. Intelligence had to be our first line of defense.

Nine days after the attacks of 9/11, in a speech to a joint session of Congress, President Bush delivered an ultimatum to the Taliban regime in Afghanistan that was harboring Osama bin Laden:

Deliver to the United States authorities all the leaders of al Qaeda who hide in your land. Release all foreign nationals, including American citizens you have unjustly imprisoned. Protect foreign journalists, diplomats, and aid workers in your country. Close immediately and permanently, every terrorist training camp in Afghanistan and hand over every terrorist, and every person in their support structure, to appropriate authorities. Give the United States full access to terrorist training camps, so we can make sure they are no longer operating. These demands are not open to negotiation or discussion. The Taliban must act, and act immediately. They will hand over the terrorists or they will share their fate.

President Bush also explained to the American people the challenge of the war in which we were now engaged:

This will not be like the war against Iraq a decade ago, with a decisive liberation of territory and a swift conclusion. . . . Americans should not expect one battle, but a lengthy campaign, unlike any we have ever seen. It may include dramatic strikes, visible on TV, and covert operations, secret even in success.

At 2:45 P.M. on September 26, 2001, the first team of CIA officers arrived in Afghanistan. They flew into the Panjshir Valley through a 14,500-foot pass in the Hindu Kush mountains, on a Russian military helicopter the CIA had purchased and upgraded. They made contact with the Northern Alliance, a tribal group whose leader, Ahmed Shah Massoud, had been assassinated by al Qaeda two days before the 9/11 attacks, and they began coordinating efforts to take down the Taliban.

A few weeks later, the first twelve-man special operations team went in near Mazar-e-Sharif in northern Afghanistan and another team seized the compound belonging to Mullah Omar, leader of the

Afghan Taliban. Two hundred Army Rangers seized an airfield near Kandahar. Linked up with the Northern Alliance by the CIA team, the special operators began fighting side by side with them, sometimes on horseback, calling in air strikes on Taliban positions.

Mazar-e-Sharif fell on November 9, 2001. Herat fell to the Northern Alliance on November 11, Kabul on November 13, and Jalalabad on November 14. Kandahar, the last Taliban stronghold, fell on December 7.

Hamid Karzai, a Pashtun, was selected as Afghanistan's interim leader at a United Nations conference in December 2001, and inaugurated as chairman of the Afghan Interim Authority on December 22, 2001. In a little over three months, the United States, working with our Afghan allies, had overthrown the Taliban, liberated 25 million people, and begun the difficult work of denying al Qaeda the bases from which to train and plan attacks against us.

In Afghanistan the United States has continued to face a deadly and determined enemy, one who is fighting to this day to take back territory and reestablish sanctuaries for our enemies. Our security depends upon ensuring that terrorists can never again establish bases in Afghanistan from which to launch attacks against America.

The lessons of America's involvement in Afghanistan should by now be clear. We turned our backs on the country once before, to devastating effect, after the Soviets left in the 1980s. Walking away again would be the height of recklessness.

WHILE THE UNITED STATES was undertaking military operations in Afghanistan, work was also under way to strengthen our defenses and our intelligence capabilities. General Mike Hayden, director of the National Security Agency, explained that the NSA could do more if they could get additional authorizations from the president.

President Bush readily agreed but imposed tight conditions to ensure that these new and necessary security programs did not violate the civil liberties or constitutional rights of citizens. One of the new conditions was that the president would personally reauthorize the program every thirty to forty-five days. His reauthorization would be based on assessments by the director of the CIA, the secretary of defense, and the U.S. attorney general that each extension was necessary, based on the most current intelligence. The president also instructed that the existence of the program be very close-hold, and he wanted to personally sign off on granting access to the program to anyone outside the NSA. It was one of the most highly sensitive and effective intelligence efforts in the history of the National Security Agency.

The purpose of this program was to collect information on phone calls from suspicious numbers outside the United States to numbers inside the U.S. The data collected focused on the fact of a call, not the content. If a suspicious call were intercepted, there were procedures for referring the calls to the FBI and or to the Foreign Intelligence Surveillance Act (FISA) court for the necessary approval to collect the content of the call.

In 2004, despite the fact that Attorney General John Ashcroft had approved the program at least twenty-three times, his new deputy attorney general, James Comey, raised concerns. Even after General Hayden and lawyers from the NSA explained the national security importance of the program and the safeguards in place to protect civil liberties, Comey refused to authorize the twenty-fourth extension.

When these new concerns arose, Vice President Cheney and General Hayden convened a meeting in the Situation Room in the basement of the West Wing of the White House to brief an expanded group of members of Congress and to consult with them about whether, in light of the new concerns, the administration should seek additional congressional authorization for the program. The Republican and Democratic leadership from the House and Senate were in attendance, along with the Republican and Democratic leaders of the House and Senate intelligence committees.

General Hayden briefed the lawmakers on the program and its results. Cheney then asked the leaders if they thought the program should continue. There was unanimous agreement that it should. Cheney then asked if the congressional leaders believed the administration should seek additional legislative authority for the program. Again they were unanimous. They advised that the administration not seek additional authorization, out of concern that the details and existence of this sensitive and highly effective program would be exposed.

In 2005, the *New York Times* published leaked details about the program. President Bush had asked the publisher and editor of the paper not to print the information because it would damage our security, aid our enemies, and make it more difficult to prevent future attacks. The *Times* published it anyway.

The next day, the president spoke about the importance of the program in his weekly radio address. He reminded the American people that the 9/11 hijackers had been in the United States communicating with terrorists overseas prior to the attacks. "Two of the terrorist hijackers who flew a jet into the Pentagon, Nawaf al Hamzi and Khalid al Mihdhar, communicated while they were in the United States to other members of al Qaeda who were overseas," the president explained. "But we didn't know they were here, until it was too late."

As we write this today, Congress has diminished the authorities of the NSA to track terrorist phone calls. Some members have launched campaigns to end the program entirely. Military historian Max Boot has suggested that those who advocate shutting down the NSA program would do well to tour the 9/11 Memorial & Museum at the site of the World Trade Center. It is a powerful reminder of the enemy we face and of the importance of doing all we can to stop them. The NSA program is a crucial tool in that effort. "Had this program been in effect prior to 9/11," General Hayden has explained, "it is my professional judgment that we would have detected some of the 9/11 al Qaeda operatives in the United States and we would have identified them as such."

Those who oppose this program will be accountable for explaining to the American people why they fought to make it more difficult for the United States government to effectively track the communications—and therefore the plans—of terrorists inside the United States.

THE NEED FOR A policy concerning the detention of terrorists— and a place to detain them—became clear early in the war in Afghanistan. As the United States captured enemy combatants, it was essential to ensure they did not return to the field of battle to kill more Americans. To meet this need, the Department of Defense established a detention facility at the U.S. naval base at Guantánamo Bay, Cuba.

The facility at Guantánamo was and remains safe, secure, humane, and necessary. Nevertheless, there have been years of attempts to close it, though doing so requires releasing the detainees. In efforts led by the State Department, some detainees were released during the George W. Bush administration. President Obama has accelerated releases, even though by the time he took office, the detainees left in Guantánamo were the worst of the worst, men whose own home countries often refused to take them back. There are now years of evidence that many of the detainees who have been released are returning to the field of battle. According to the annual report issued by the director of national intelligence in 2014, nearly one-third of those released are back in the fight.

Today, for example, the lead recruiter for ISIS in Afghanistan and parts of Pakistan is former Guantánamo detainee Abdul Rahim Muslim Dost. Two days after Abu Bakr al-Baghdadi declared himself caliph of the Islamic State in June 2014, Dost pledged his allegiance. He now spends his days recruiting jihadists to send to Syria and Iraq to fight for ISIS.

Dost is a particularly useful reminder of the propaganda about Guantánamo and detainees that has appeared in the leftist European press. In an article in the *Guardian* newspaper in April 2006, Dost was described as "a softly spoken Afghan" whose only desire was that the U.S. military return to him the poetry he had written while at Guantánamo. "Those words are very precious to me," the "Poet of Guantánamo" wrote the *Guardian* reporter.

IN 2002 THE UNITED States captured Abu Zubaydah, a senior al Qaeda operations expert, in Pakistan. After his capture, he initially provided some information and then stopped cooperating. The CIA was confident he knew more, and ordinary interrogation methods, such as those described in the Army Field Manual, had proven ineffective.

Drawing on techniques used to train our own people in the Survival, Evade, Resistance, and Escape, or SERE, program, the CIA developed a series of techniques they proposed to use on Abu Zubaydah. They sought the approval of the president, the National Security Council, and the Justice Department before proceeding. They wanted to ensure that none of the techniques was in violation of the law or any of the treaty obligations of the United States. The Justice Department provided legal opinions outlining the limits of lawful interrogation and detailing the techniques that could be used.

Other safeguards were put in place, such as requiring the approval of the director of the CIA before any detainee could be questioned using these methods. The National Security Council approved the program.

And it worked. After being subjected to the techniques, Abu Zubaydah provided information that led to Ramzi bin al-Shibh. He was captured on September 11, 2002, as he was plotting a terrorist attack on London using commercial airplanes. Information from bin al-Shibh and Abu Zubaydah led us to Khalid Sheikh Mohammed, the mastermind of 9/11.

In 2014, six former directors and deputy directors of the CIA wrote that, despite claims to the contrary made by the program's opponents, the program was "invaluable in three critical ways":

- *It led to the capture of senior al Qaeda operatives, thereby removing them from the battlefield.*
- *It led to the disruption of terrorist plots and prevented mass-casualty attacks, saving American and allied lives.*
- *It added enormously to what we knew about al Qaeda as an organization and therefore informed our approaches on how best to attack.*

A 2004 CIA report provided specific details about the extensive information we obtained from one of the detainees, Khaled Sheikh Mohammed, after he was waterboarded. Titled "Khaled Sheikh Mohamed: Pre-Eminent Source on al Qaeda," the report stated:

Debriefings since his detention have yielded . . . reports that have shed light on the plots, capabilities, the identity and location of al-Qaeda operatives and affiliated terrorist organizations and networks. He has provided information on al Qaeda's strategic doctrine, probable targets, the impact of striking each target set, and likely methods of attacks inside the United States.

We now also know it was information from this program that led us directly to Osama bin Laden. According to Leon Panetta, director of the CIA and secretary of defense under President Obama:

The real story was that in order to put the puzzle of intelligence together that led us to bin Laden, there were a lot of pieces out there that were a part of that puzzle. Yes, some of it came from some of the tactics that were used at that time . . . interrogation tactics that were used.

As we pieced together intelligence about al Qaeda in the aftermath of the 9/11 attacks, the enhanced interrogation program was one of the most effective tools we had. It saved lives and prevented attacks.

LEAVING SADDAM HUSSEIN IN power in Iraq after 9/11, in light of the threat he posed, would have been, as former British prime minister Tony Blair has noted, an act of political cowardice. This is not to say that Saddam was responsible for 9/11. It is to observe that in the aftermath of 9/11, when thousands of Americans had been slaughtered by terrorists armed with airline tickets and box cutters, we had an obligation to do everything possible to prevent terrorists from gaining access to much worse weapons. Saddam's Iraq was the most likely place for terrorists to gain access to and knowledge of such weapons.

On October 10, 2002, the House of Representatives passed the resolution authorizing the use of force in Iraq by a vote of 296–113, forty-six more votes in favor than had been the case for Operation

Desert Storm in 1991. Shortly after midnight the Senate approved the resolution 77–23, a much larger margin than for the Gulf War.

The United Nations Security Council, on November 8, 2002, unanimously approved Security Council resolution 1441. It gave Iraq a final opportunity to disarm, demanded immediate and unrestricted access for UN inspectors, and required that Iraq provide a "complete declaration of all aspects" of its weapons of mass destruction programs and delivery systems. Iraq failed to comply. On March 17, 2003, President Bush addressed the nation and gave Saddam Hussein forty-eight hours to leave Iraq. Two days later President Bush gave the order launching Operation Iraqi Freedom.

Our forces performed magnificently, and within weeks Saddam Hussein had fallen and we had taken Baghdad. As U.S. troops swept through Iraqi cities, they were, in fact, greeted as liberators. The headline in the *Washington Post* on April 9, for example, reported, "U.S. Forces Move Triumphantly Through Capital Streets, Cheered by Crowds Jubilant at End of Repressive Regime." Iraqi dissident Kanan Makiya visited the White House that night. Makiya's books *Republic of Fear* and *Cruelty and Silence* documented the atrocities Saddam had committed for years against his own people. Coming at the end of the day that Saddam's regime had been toppled, it was an emotional meeting. "Thank you," Makiya said, "for our liberation."

As we now know, Saddam did not have stockpiles of weapons of mass destruction. However, it requires a willing suspension of disbelief and a desire to put politics above safety to assert that the absence of stockpiles meant the absence of a threat to the United States. David Kay, who led the international Iraq Survey Group, tasked with finding Saddam's stockpiles, said, "I actually think that what we learned during the inspections made Iraq a more dangerous place, potentially, than in fact we had thought before the war." Kay and his successor Charles Duelfer made clear that Saddam retained the intent, knowledge, and dual-purpose infrastructure to restart WMD programs once the international sanctions regime collapsed. Citing Iraqi diplomat Tariq Aziz, Duelfer wrote that Saddam would likely have restarted his nuclear program first. He had purposely kept at hand the men and women with the skill and knowledge to do so.

Between 2003 and 2006, coalition forces in Iraq, led by the United States, accomplished a great deal. They deposed a horrific dictator with ties to terrorists and plans to reconstitute his WMD program. They provided security for the Iraqi people as they went to the polls in the first truly democratic elections in their history. They liberated the country and handed responsibility for the government back to the Iraqis.

But al Qaeda in Iraq, led by Abu Musab al-Zarqawi, was determined to sow destruction. We know from correspondence captured by American troops that Zarqawi was intent on fomenting a sectarian war inside Iraq. For more than two years, despite horrific attacks by Sunni terrorists, the Shi'a largely resisted being drawn in, but on February 6, 2006, Zarqawi's terrorists blew up one of the holiest Shi'ite sites—the Golden Dome Mosque in Samarra. Shi'a militias, in many instances backed by Iran, took up the task of killing Sunnis.

As the violence increased, there were some who argued we should walk away and "leave Iraq to the Iraqis." But America's security depended then, as it does now, on ensuring that Iraq does not become a safe haven for terrorists. President Bush rightly decided we could not abandon Iraq.

On January 10, 2007, the president announced that he was committing five additional brigades—more than twenty thousand additional troops—to the war in Iraq. The additional troops, he said, would be accompanied by a new strategy, a counterinsurgency effort to provide security for local populations, particularly in Baghdad. He faced significant opposition from Republicans and Democrats, including Senators Barack Obama and Hillary Clinton. Secretary Clinton later admitted, according to former secretary of defense Robert Gates, that her opposition to the surge in troops was political since she was, at that time, competing against Senator Obama in the Iowa caucuses.

President Bush did the right and courageous thing. The surge and the adoption of a new counterinsurgency strategy worked. With the additional troops and the new strategy, we were able to provide security for the Iraqis and demonstrate that we were not going to abandon them. A Sunni force, the Sons of Iraq, rose up to fight the insurgency and al Qaeda with us. Together, we largely defeated al Qaeda and the Shi'ite militia groups and enabled the Iraqis to begin to build a new country.

HISTORY WILL BE THE ultimate judge of our decision to liberate Iraq. It will be debated long after we are gone, and it is important for future decision makers that those debates be based on fact.

Those who say the invasion of Iraq in 2003 was a mistake are essentially saying we would be better off if Saddam Hussein were still in power. That's a difficult position to sustain. Saddam had deep, long-standing, far-reaching relationships with terrorist organizations, including al Qaeda and its affiliates. These relationships have been repeatedly confirmed in documents captured after the war. Saddam's Iraq was a state based on terror, overseeing a coordinated program to support global jihadist terrorist organizations. Ansar al Islam, an al Qaeda–linked organization, operated training camps in northern Iraq before the invasion. Zarqawi, the future leader of al Qaeda in Iraq, funneled weapons and fighters into these camps, before the invasion, from his location in Baghdad. We also know, again confirmed in documents captured after the war, that Saddam provided funding, training, and other support to numerous terrorist organizations and individuals over decades, including to Ayman al-Zawahiri, the man who leads al Qaeda today.

We also know that Saddam Hussein had the technology, equipment, facilities, and scientists in place to construct the world's worst weapons. We know he intended to reconstitute these programs as soon as the international sanctions regime collapsed. He had an advanced nuclear program in place prior to Operation Desert Storm. The International Atomic Energy Agency (IAEA) reported that had his efforts not been derailed by Desert Storm, he could have had a nuclear device by 1992.

In 1998, Saddam kicked the international weapons inspectors out of Iraq. He violated every one of the seventeen UN Security Council resolutions passed against him.

Critics of the liberation of Iraq would do well to read about his 1988 chemical weapons attack on Halabja, particularly the accounts telling of the babies and children who died slow, painful deaths in bomb shelters where they had sought refuge with their families. The shelters became, as Saddam knew they would, gas chambers. The lesson of Halabja and perhaps two hundred other villages and towns that Saddam attacked with chemical weapons is that Saddam had no compunction, no moral compass, no hesitation to *use* the world's worst weapons, even against his own people.

Saddam's was a reign of terror characterized by torture, rape rooms, the murder of parents in front of their children and children in front of their parents, and the oppression of the Kurds, Marsh Arabs, and Shi'ites. George W. Bush captured it well when he wrote that Saddam was "a homicidal dictator pursuing WMD and supporting terror at the heart of the Middle East."

Against the weight of historical evidence, some critics claim that the Bush administration manufactured or exaggerated the intelligence about Saddam's weapons programs. The charge doesn't stand up against the facts. Both the Senate Select Committee on Intelligence and the Robb-Silberman Commission issued bipartisan reports concluding there was no politicization of the intelligence or pressure on analysts to change their judgments about Iraq's WMD. In fact, intelligence assessments about Saddam's weapons programs stretched back at least a decade:

- A 1993 National Intelligence Estimate found that international support for sanctions was eroding but judged that even if they remained in place, Saddam Hussein would "continue reconstituting Iraq's conventional military forces" and "will take steps to re-establish Iraq's WMD programs."

- A 1994 Joint Atomic Energy Intelligence Committee report assessed that "the Iraqi government is determined to covertly reconstitute its nuclear weapons program."

- In 2000, a National Intelligence Estimate judged, "Despite a decade-long international effort to disarm Iraq, new information suggests that Baghdad has continued and expanded its offensive BW [biological weapons] program by establishing large scale, redundant and concealed BW agent production capability. We judge that Iraq maintains the capability to produce previously declared agents and probably is pursuing development of additional bacterial and toxin agents. Moreover, we judge that Iraq has BW delivery systems available that could be used to threaten U.S. and Allied forces in the Persian Gulf region."

- In late 2000, one of the first intelligence reports that the newly elected president and vice president received was titled "Iraq: Steadily Pursuing WMD Capabilities."

The Bush administration wasn't alone in reading the intelligence reports. Others who did, going back to 1998, recognized the danger Saddam posed and urged action—though they later changed their views when it seemed politically expedient to do so. Some of these individuals include:

JOHN KERRY: "When I vote to give the President of the United States the authority to use force, if necessary, to disarm Saddam Hussein, it is because I believe that a deadly arsenal of weapons of mass destruction in his hands is a threat, and a grave threat to our security."

HILLARY CLINTON: "Saddam Hussein is a tyrant who has tortured and killed his own people" and "used chemical weapons on Iraqi Kurds and Iranians. . . . Intelligence reports show that Saddam Hussein has worked to rebuild his chemical and biological weapons stock, his missile delivery capability, and his nuclear program." Saddam "has also given aid, comfort, and sanctuary to terrorists, including al Qaeda members."

JOE BIDEN: "Ultimately, as long as Saddam Hussein is at the helm, no inspectors can guarantee that they have rooted out the entirety of [his] weapons program," and "the only way to remove Saddam is a massive military effort led by the United States."

JAY ROCKEFELLER: There is "unmistakeable evidence that Saddam Hussein is working aggressively to develop nuclear weapons and will likely have nuclear weapons within the next five years. . . . Saddam's government has contact with many international terrorist organizations that likely have cells here in the United States. . . . September 11 changed our world forever. We may not like it, but it is the world in which we live. When there is a grave threat to Americans' lives, we have a responsibility to take action to prevent it."

NANCY PELOSI: "Saddam Hussein has been engaged in the development of weapons of mass destruction technology which is a threat to countries in the region," and "he has made a mockery of the weapons inspections process."

BILL CLINTON: "Heavy as they are, the costs of action must be weighed against the price of inaction. If Saddam defies the world, and we fail to respond, we will face a far greater threat in the future. . . . Mark my words, he will develop weapons of mass destruction. He will deploy them, and he will use them."

In 1998, Congress had passed and Bill Clinton had signed into law the "Iraq Liberation Act," making regime change in Iraq the policy of the United States. A few months later, President Clinton had launched air strikes against Saddam's WMD capabilities.

Saddam's support for terrorists; his willingness to use the world's worst weapons; his intent to reconstitute his own programs, including nuclear ones, using scientists, technology, equipment, and facilities that he kept on hand; and his thwarting of the international community for more than a decade by repeatedly defying UN Security Council resolutions all combined to form the toxic mix that made Saddam a grave threat to the United States. We were right to invade and remove him from power.

America's liberation of Iraq also sent a clear message to others in the region that we would take military action if necessary. Within a few days of our capture of Saddam, Libyan leader Muammar Qaddafi announced he would like to turn over his nuclear program. He feared he would suffer the same fate as Saddam. Shortly after that, we were able to dismantle the nuclear proliferation network established by A. Q. Khan, Qaddafi's supplier of nuclear technology. Khan was put out of business and placed under house arrest in Pakistan. Those who say we should not have taken action in Iraq should spend a moment contemplating what the so-called Arab Spring might have looked like with a nuclear-armed Qaddafi in power in Tripoli, or what we might be facing today if Libya's weapons were in the hands of militant Islamists.

The war to liberate Iraq was indisputably difficult. It included tragedy and challenges we did not foresee. Every war does, but these tragedies and challenges do not detract from the rightness of our cause. The question is what to do in the face of setbacks. History has proved that President Bush's decision to surge forces into Iraq and adopt a counterinsurgency strategy under the command of Generals David Petraeus and Ray Odierno worked.

Success in Iraq was also secured by the skill of people like Ambassador Ryan Crocker and General Stanley McChrystal. The methods McChrystal and our special operators developed in Iraq—taking down a terrorist target, exploiting the information found at the site, moving immediately to act on the leads and take down other terrorists— were honed over a number of years. In April 2004, McChrystal has written, special operators ran a total of ten operations in Iraq. That August they conducted eighteen. By 2006, his teams had improved their methods to the point where they could average more than three hundred operations per month, "against a faster, smarter enemy and with greater precision and intelligence yield."

Such operations, a critical tool in the war on terror, stand in stark contrast to the Obama administration's actions in Benghazi, Libya, for example. The administration did not move quickly in the aftermath of the attack on our facility and the murder of our people to uncover critical intelligence and capture or kill those responsible. Instead they spent eighteen months building a legal case before they moved to capture Ahmed Abu Khattala. Once they had him in hand, they read him the Miranda warnings.

When President Obama took office in January 2009, al Qaeda in Iraq had been defeated. Iraq was a stable nation moving toward true democracy, allied with America in the heart of the Middle East. The real proof that things were in good shape as President Obama took over is that his administration immediately set about trying to claim credit for the situation. Vice President Joe Biden memorably predicted in 2010 that Iraq "will be one of the great achievements of this administration." President Obama repeatedly claimed, "We are leaving behind a sovereign, stable, self-reliant Iraq," as he set about withdrawing all U.S. forces.

President Obama failed to understand that Iraq's security, sovereignty, and stability were fragile. It is a tragedy that he abandoned Iraq, sacrificing the gains secured by American blood and treasure. We have not yet begun to see the full cost of that decision.

AT THE DAWN OF the age of terror, the United States was once again faced with an enemy committed to the destruction of freedom and the worldwide spread of a deadly ideology. We dedicated ourselves, for seven and a half years after the attacks of 9/11, to preventing further attacks on the homeland. We built up our defenses, improved our intelligence capabilities, put programs in place to detain and effectively interrogate the enemy, and took the fight to them. The United States recognized that this was not a fight that could be won on defense.

Few suggested, in the days when the attack was fresh in our minds, that we would be safe if we just withdrew from the conflicts of the world. The feebleness of that line of thinking was obvious against the backdrop of the smoldering ruins of the twin towers, the smoke rising from the Pentagon, and the burning wreckage in a field in Pennsylvania. Comforting as isolationism might seem to some now, all these years later, it is no more serious an option than it was then. Neither America, nor our allies, nor the cause of freedom will be safe if we retreat within our borders, ignore rising threats, and hope for the best.

Nine days after the attacks, when President George W. Bush addressed a joint session of Congress, he talked of the grief and loss we all felt, and the memories we would forever carry with us of that September day. He said, "Even grief recedes with time and grace. But our resolve must not pass." In words as true now as they were then, he described our obligation:

> *Freedom and fear are at war. The advance of human freedom—the great achievement of our time, and the great hope of every time—now depends on us. Our nation—this generation—will lift a dark threat of violence from our people and our future. We will rally the world to this cause by our efforts, by our courage. We will not tire, we will not falter, and we will not fail.*

PART TWO

———◆———

The Era of Obama

The Apology Tour

*I am absolutely certain that generations from now, we will be able to
look back and tell our children that this was the moment when we
began to provide care for the sick and good jobs to the jobless; this was
the moment when the rise of the oceans began to slow and our planet
began to heal; this was the moment when we ended a war and secured
our nation.*

—SENATOR BARACK OBAMA, JUNE 3, 2008

The claims made by Senator Obama the night he declared victory
in the Democratic presidential primary were extraordinary. His
election as president would not only end a war and ensure the nation's
security, it would affect the rise of the oceans and the health of the
planet. The new nominee's level of self-regard was apparent, as was
his underlying belief that America had played a malign role in the
world. If the election of a new American president could alleviate all
these problems, then America must have been largely responsible for
creating them.

In Senator Obama's view, America's sins were both of omission
and commission. Explaining the rise of radical Islam, for example, he
said in an interview on July 13, 2008, "There has been a shift in Islam

that I believe is connected to the failures of governments and the failures of the West to work with many of these countries in order to make sure opportunities are there, that there's bottom-up economic growth."

Previously, in his 2006 book, *The Audacity of Hope*, Senator Obama had taken a longer look back. He assessed the last fifty years of American foreign policy through the lens of Indonesia, a nation he called "the land of my childhood." With a nod to "our role in liberating former colonies" and establishing international institutions to "help manage the post World War II order," the broad outline of America's effect on the world consisted, he said, of

> [o]ur tendency to view nations and conflicts through the prism of the Cold War; our tireless promotion of American-style capitalism and multinational corporations; the tolerance and occasional encouragement of tyranny, corruption, and environmental degradation when it served our interests; our optimism once the Cold War ended that Big Macs and the Internet would lead to the end of historical conflicts; the growing economic power of Asia and the growing resentment of the United States as the world's sole superpower.

Where some see an exceptional nation, unmatched in the history of the world in our goodness and our greatness, in our contributions to global freedom, justice, and peace, Barack Obama sees a nation with at best a "mixed" record. Yes, there was a successful outcome to the Cold War, but it brought us, he writes, "the distortions of politics, the sins of hubris, the corrupting effects of fear," not to mention "an enormous military buildup" that has, in his view, warped the way U.S. leaders view the world. That buildup, of course, was essential to our winning the Cold War.

In the early months of the Obama administration, the president embarked upon a world tour, during which he made sure that people in foreign capitals knew he believed that much was wrong with America. In Strasbourg, France, on April 3, 2009, he said, "America has shown arrogance and been dismissive, even derisive." Noting that generations of Americans and Frenchmen had "fought and bled to uphold [our] values," President Obama then explained that the detention facility at Guantánamo was a "sacrifice of [our values] for expedience sake" and announced that that was his reason for closing it. Returning to the topic later at the same event, Obama said:

> *In dealing with terrorism, we can't lose sight of our values and who we are. That's why I closed Guantánamo. That's why I made very clear that we will not engage in certain interrogation practices. . . . When you start sacrificing your values, when you lose yourself, then over the long term that will make you less secure. When we saw what happened at Abu Ghraib, that wasn't good for our security—that was a recruitment tool for terrorism. Humiliating people is never a good strategy to battle terrorism.*

As he issued a call to avoid humiliating terrorists who slaughter innocents, President Obama also perpetuated a falsehood that America's critics were peddling—that what happened at Abu Ghraib prison outside Baghdad represented official policy, that it had something to do with or was related to America's enhanced interrogation program. His eliding these things together was utterly irresponsible, particularly since he did it on foreign soil.

During the Q&A session following his remarks, President Obama also explained his view that if America would just cut the size of its nuclear arsenal, Iran and North Korea would be convinced to abandon their nuclear ambitions. "I would like to be able to say that as a consequence of my work," he explained, "we drastically lessened the threat of not only terrorism, but of nuclear terrorism." This meant that America needed to "take serious steps to actually reduce our stockpiles." Doing so "would give us greater moral authority to say to Iran, don't develop a nuclear weapon; to say to North Korea, don't proliferate nuclear weapons." The obstacle to effective diplomacy with rogue states, In President Obama's view, was that America's nuclear arsenal was too big.

The next day in a press conference following a NATO meeting on Afghanistan, President Obama was asked "whether you subscribe, as many of your predecessors have, to the school of American exceptionalism that sees America as uniquely qualified to lead the world, or do you have a slightly different philosophy?" Obama said, "I believe in American exceptionalism, just as I suspect the Brits believe in British exceptionalism and the Greeks believe in Greek exceptionalism."

President Obama's next stop was Prague, where he focused his remarks on nuclear proliferation. Once again the first step in his plan toward seeking a "world without nuclear weapons" was to reduce America's nuclear arsenal. "To put an end to Cold War thinking," he said, "we will reduce the role of nuclear weapons in our national security strategy, and urge others to do the same."

With respect to Iran, the world's chief state sponsor of terror, ruled by a regime with American blood on its hands, Obama explained that he would "seek engagement with Iran based on mutual interests and mutual respect." This engagement would facilitate Iran taking "its rightful place in the community of nations, politically and economically." Although never mentioning Iran's support for terrorism, the president did say that Iranian nuclear and ballistic missile activity posed a real threat. "The Czech Republic and Poland have been courageous in agreeing to host a defense against these missiles," he said.

Five months later, President Obama abruptly canceled the very missile defense system he had praised in Prague's Hradčany Square. Russia objected to the system, and the administration canceled it a week before Obama was scheduled to meet Russian president Dmitry Medvedev. The announcement also came on the seventieth anniversary of the Soviet invasion of Poland, adding insult to injury to our European allies.

On April 17, 2009, President Obama attended the Summit of the Americas in Trinidad and Tobago. He sat silently in the ballroom of the Hyatt Regency while Nicaraguan president Daniel Ortega delivered a fifty-minute diatribe about the evil America had done in the world. When it was his turn to speak, President Obama didn't dispute the lies, or ignore them; he made a joke that affirmed them. "I'm grateful," he said, "that President Ortega didn't blame me for things that happened when I was three months old."

President Obama traveled to Cairo in June 2009 for a speech "to the Muslim world." Acknowledging a strain between the United States and the Muslim world, he explained that the tension had been "fed by colonialism that denied rights and opportunities to many Muslims and a Cold War in which Muslim-majority countries were too often treated as proxies without regard to their own aspirations."

He provided his perspective on world order, saying that "human history has often been a record of nations and tribes subjugating one another to serve their own interests." This could not continue:

> In this new age, such attitudes are self-defeating. Given our interdependence, any world order that elevates one nation or group of people over another will inevitably fail. Our problems must be dealt with through partnership; progress must be shared.

These were astonishing assertions for an American president to make. In this new global order where nations do not pursue their interests, there would be no place for the United States to seek its own security. In this new global order, in which no nation is to be elevated over another, the United States, the most powerful nation in the world, would have to abdicate much of its power.

The president of the United States then proceeded to compare the attacks of 9/11 to the policies put in place afterward to keep us safe:

> *And finally, just as America can never tolerate violence by extremists, we must never alter our principles. 9/11 was an enormous trauma to our country. The fear and anger it provoked was understandable, but in some cases, it led us to act contrary to our ideals. We are taking concrete actions to change course. I have unequivocally prohibited the use of torture by the United States, and I have ordered the prison at Guantánamo Bay closed by next year.*

On that June day in the heart of the Arab world, in the city that was home to 9/11 lead hijacker Mohammed Atta and al Qaeda's future leader Ayman al-Zawahiri, President Obama suggested that the murderous, evil attacks that al Qaeda had launched on our country were in a category with the lawful actions that the United States undertook afterward in the name of protecting our country.

By September, President Obama was issuing his apology for America and his call for a coequal community of nations at the United Nations General Assembly:

> *No one nation can or should try to dominate another nation . . . no balance of power among nations will hold. The traditional divisions between the South and the North make no sense in an interconnected world; nor do alignments of nations rooted in the cleavages of a long-gone Cold War.*

His proclamation was of a piece with the new global order he had advocated in Cairo, but more detailed. Now alliances such as NATO were illegitimate.

The 2009 apology tour finally came to an end in Japan. Two months before President Obama's November visit, the U.S. ambassador sent a cable to Washington reporting that the Japanese vice foreign minister had informed him "the idea of President Obama visiting Hiroshima to apologize for the atomic bombing during World War II is 'a non-starter.' " When the cable became public, the White House disavowed the plan. President Obama had to settle for bowing deeply to the somewhat surprised Japanese emperor, one more unprecedented act in the annals of American presidential diplomacy.

———————◆•◆———————

FOUR

Ending Wars

I will end this war in Iraq responsibly, and finish the fight against al Qaeda and the Taliban in Afghanistan.
—SENATOR BARACK OBAMA, ACCEPTANCE SPEECH,
DEMOCRATIC NATIONAL CONVENTION, AUGUST 28, 2008

You don't end a war by withdrawing from the battlefield. You just give the ground to your enemies—IS[IS] and Iran.
—RYAN CROCKER, U.S. AMBASSADOR TO IRAQ, 2007–2009

President Obama was determined to take America off its war footing. On his first full day in office, at his first National Security Council meeting, he instructed his military commanders to provide timetables for withdrawing U.S. forces from Iraq. Twenty-four hours later, he signed an executive order requiring the closing of the prison facility at Guantánamo Bay and a second order ending the enhanced interrogation program, thereby curtailing America's ability to detain or interrogate terrorists effectively.

According to former CIA director General Mike Hayden, more than half of what America knew about al Qaeda in the years after 9/11 came from detainees in the enhanced interrogation program.

Hayden was appointed by President Bush, but members of President Obama's intelligence team have expressed similar views:

> LEON PANETTA, FORMER CIA DIRECTOR: "At bottom, we know we got important, even critical intelligence from individuals subjected to these enhanced interrogation techniques."
>
> JOHN BRENNAN, CIA DIRECTOR: "[I]nterrogations of detainees on whom EITs were used did produce intelligence that helped thwart attack plans, capture terrorists, and save lives. The intelligence gained from the program was critical to our understanding of al-Qa'ida and continues to inform our counterterrorism efforts to this day."
>
> DENNIS BLAIR, FORMER DIRECTOR OF NATIONAL INTELLIGENCE: "High value information came from interrogations in which those methods were used and provided a deeper understanding of the al Qaeda organization that was attacking this country."

Despite the weight of the evidence about the importance of this program to our national security, the new president canceled it on his second full day in office. Three months later, in April 2009, President Obama decided to publicly release the Justice Department memos describing the enhanced interrogation methods in detail. CIA directors going back to 1995 urged the president not to take this step. President Obama's own CIA director, Leon Panetta, was so concerned with the damage the memo release could do to our intelligence capabilities that he rushed to the White House with the leading officers from the CIA's Clandestine Service and Counterterrorism Center in an attempt to stop the president. Sitting in the Oval Office, every one of these individuals argued against the release of the memos. Men and women who spent their days on the front lines of the war on terror argued vehemently that making these memos public would do extensive damage to our intelligence capabilities.

Release of the memos meant al Qaeda would now know every one of our methods and the limits to which we could legally go in questioning terrorists. The president would be tying the hands of every future president by revealing techniques that would no longer be effective if needed, including in situations where thousands of American lives were on the line. Revealing this information publicly also put at risk our relationships with other intelligence services and countries that had cooperated with us in this program. Finally, in the middle of a war, releasing these memos would be devastating to the morale of the men and women in America's intelligence community on whom we depend to keep us safe. Their work had been authorized by the president and every member of his National Security Council and approved by the Department of Justice, but now a new president was rescinding the authorization and accusing them publicly of abandoning American values.

Barack Obama was undeterred. He released the memos the next day.

On April 20, he visited the CIA in the wake of the memos' release. "Don't be discouraged," he told hundreds of agency professionals gathered in the lobby. "Don't be discouraged that we have to acknowledge, potentially, that we've made some mistakes. That's how we learn." One wonders exactly what lessons the men and women in our intelligence community, whose work had saved lives and prevented attacks, were supposed to learn from a commander in chief who was saying they had failed "to uphold our values and ideals" and who had just released information that made it harder to fight and win the war.

One of the authors of this book, Dick Cheney, recalls when he decided to speak out:

By May 2009, I had had enough. I fully understood the preroga-
tive of President Obama to put his own policies in place and to
change course from policies we had pursued, even though I dis-
agreed fundamentally with the decisions he was making. It was
altogether different, however, when he began spreading untruths
about our programs and slandering the people who ran them.
I was not going to sit by and let him attack men and women
whose actions had been approved by us and had saved thousands
of American lives. Nor was I going to head for the hills, as so many
politicians do when a policy they once supported becomes unpopu-
lar. When Attorney General [Eric] Holder suggested he would in-
vestigate and potentially prosecute intelligence officials for doing
their jobs, my view was he would have to start with those of us on
the National Security Council who had approved this program in
the first place. I wanted the American people to know the truth
about the program.

I scheduled a speech for Thursday, May 21, 2009, at the
American Enterprise Institute in Washington, D.C., to set the rec-
ord straight. Shortly after the day and time for my speech were
announced, the White House announced the president would be
making a speech that same day. The two sets of remarks set out a
stark contrast between President Obama's beliefs and my own.

Speaking from the National Archives, President Obama ac-
cused those of us in the previous administration of "walking away
from the sacred principles enshrined in this building." He said we
had "failed to use our values as our compass" and had, through
the establishment of Guantánamo and the use of enhanced inter-
rogation, implemented policies that "are not who we are, and they
are not America." In a speech in which he made national secu-
rity a wedge issue, challenged the patriotism of his opponents, and

claimed we had abandoned America's most sacred values, he closed by insisting we should not make national security a wedge issue.

When the president had finished, I laid out the truth about all we had done. The enhanced interrogation program "was used on hardened terrorists after other efforts failed." It was legal, essential, justified, successful, honorable, and right. It saved lives, prevented attacks, and, we now know, helped lead us to Osama bin Laden. "The intelligence officers who questioned the terrorists," I said, "can be proud of their work and proud of the results, because they prevented the violent deaths of thousands, if not hundreds of thousands, of innocent people."

To call enhanced interrogation a program of torture, as President Obama has so many times, is to libel the dedicated professionals who saved American lives, and to cast terrorists and murderers as innocent victims. On the topic of America's most sacred values, I believe strongly, as I said that day, "No moral value held dear by the American people obliges public servants ever to sacrifice innocent lives to spare a captured terrorist from unpleasant things." Furthermore, when our nation is targeted by terrorists bent on our destruction, "Nothing is more consistent with American values than to stop them."

Ending programs that kept us safe, revealing the details about those programs to the terrorists, and spreading untruths about our policies was misguided, unjust, and highly irresponsible. It was recklessness cloaked in righteousness. It was my view then and remains so today, that President Obama, having so consistently distorted the truth about the enhanced interrogation program and the brave Americans who carried it out, is in no position to lecture anyone about American values.

———

ON CHRISTMAS DAY 2009, Umar Farouk Abdulmutallab smuggled a bomb in his underwear aboard Northwest Airlines Flight 253 from Amsterdam to Detroit. There were nearly three hundred people on board. As the plane began its descent, passengers reported hearing what sounded like firecrackers. Abdulmutallab's bomb failed to explode but it started a fire. The other passengers overpowered him. Abdulmutallab was arrested and questioned for only fifty minutes before FBI agents read him his Miranda warnings.

Abdulmutallab had spent four months training with al Qaeda in Yemen. He had ties to radical cleric Anwar al-Awlaki. The National Counterterrorism Center had amassed intelligence on Abdulmutallab, none of which was used in his interrogation. None of the nation's top counterterrorism officials was consulted by the FBI leadership or the agents on the scene.

In congressional hearings on Wednesday, January 20, 2010, Director of National Intelligence Dennis Blair admitted that it hadn't occurred to the administration to activate the new High-Value Detainee Interrogation Group, or HIG, the interagency office that was supposed to handle terrorist interrogation, to question Abdulmutallab:

> *Frankly, we were thinking more of overseas people and duh!* [*Blair slaps his forehead*] *we didn't put it then. That's what we'll do now. And so we need to make those decisions more carefully. I was not consulted and the decision was made on the scene. It seemed logical to the people there but it should have been taken using this HIG format at a higher level.*

In a clarification issued after the hearing, Blair explained that what he meant to say was that the FBI received important intelligence from Abdulmutallab and that intelligence "will be available in the HIG *once it is fully operational.*" In other words, eleven months after President Obama had ended the enhanced interrogation program, there was no operational program to interrogate terrorists.

Three days later, when he made his first statement about the attack, President Obama seemed unaware of the intelligence linking Abdulmutallab to al Qaeda. Despite the fact that Abdulmutallab had been trained, armed, and sent by al Qaeda to down an American civilian airliner, Obama referred to him as "an isolated extremist." This was one of many instances in which the Obama administration seemed either not to know about, or was unwilling to acknowledge, the threat we were facing.

In a briefing with the press on January 7, 2010, President Obama's counterterrorism advisor, and future director of the CIA, John Brennan, explained that he had been "surprised" that al Qaeda in the Arabian Peninsula was capable of attacking the United States. In the same briefing, Secretary of Homeland Security Janet Napolitano said she was surprised by al Qaeda's "determination" to attack the United States and their tactic of "using an individual to foment the attack."

This lack of familiarity with the threat of terror attacks on the United States by two of our top counterterrorism officials was troubling. It was part of a larger pattern—and seemed often to be by design. From its earliest days in office, the Obama administration downplayed the threat of terrorism and the strength of al Qaeda. Wars would no longer be wars; they would be "overseas contingency operations." Terrorist attacks would now be "man-caused disasters." Al Qaeda–trained terrorists weren't part of any larger network; they were "isolated extremists" and "lone wolves." The terrorist attack on the U.S. Army base at Fort Hood was just "workplace violence."

It is a fair question why a president would choose to downplay the threat of terror attacks on the nation. President Obama came into office with bold plans to transform the nation, to expand the size of the federal government, nationalize one-sixth of the economy, and massively increase government spending on domestic programs. In order to do this, he needed to make major cuts in defense spending, which required, in part, that we stop fighting costly wars. That, in turn, required convincing the American people that the threat from al Qaeda was fading and that the nation no longer needed to be on a war footing.

After all, if al Qaeda were still a threat, how could an American president justify leaving the field of battle and diminishing our ability to defeat our enemies?

IRAQ

The cornerstone of President Obama's 2008 campaign for the presidency was his opposition to the Iraq War. One would be hard-pressed to find a single day during the campaign when Barack Obama did not promise to "end the war in Iraq." He went so far as to detail how he would carry out these plans. "On my first day in office," he repeatedly promised, "I will bring the Joint Chiefs of Staff in, and I will give them a new mission, and that is to end this war responsibly and deliberately, but decisively." The war would have to end, he said, within the next sixteen months.

At his first National Security Council (NSC) meeting on January 21, 2009, President Obama instructed his military commanders to provide him with three options for withdrawal, at least one of which had to be along the sixteen-month timetable on which he had campaigned.

America's ambassador to Iraq, Ryan Crocker, was getting ready to retire after more than thirty-seven years in the foreign service. He'd served as American ambassador in Lebanon, Kuwait, Syria, and

Pakistan before being posted to Iraq in 2007. He gave his final press briefing as ambassador the day after the NSC meeting on the Iraq withdrawal. In it he issued a clear warning about the danger of a "precipitous" American departure from Iraq. "Al Qaeda is incredibly tenacious," he said. "They will have to be killed or captured, and as long as they hang on, they are looking for opportunity to regenerate." He continued, "If we were to decide suddenly, 'we're done,' they would certainly work to use space that opened up to do just that. I think it would encourage neighbors with less than benign intentions to carry them out, and perhaps most importantly I think it would have a chilling effect on Iraqis."

Ambassador Crocker had been indispensable in bringing about the relative stability in Iraq that greeted President Obama as he took office. In his final press conference, Crocker reflected on his tenure. "Taking a look back at when I arrived here in March 2007 and how it looked and felt then, [there's been] a really remarkable transition within Iraq itself," he said. "Neither the Iraqis nor we can take our eye off that ball, because as we tragically have seen, there are still elements out there, particularly al Qaeda, capable of delivering devastating attacks." Crocker went on to note that while the Iraqi security forces had made "enormous" progress over the last two years, they still needed U.S. support.

Despite the White House focus on timetables and numbers in early 2009, American military officials in Iraq knew the challenge was much tougher. One put it this way: "It is more than just a question of how fast and how low; it includes calculating how much risk you are willing to take in Iraq." The risk was that a withdrawal based on U.S. political timetables instead of on conditions on the ground would leave Iraq unable to provide for her own security. Such a policy would sacrifice the gains for which so many Americans had fought and died, and leave a vacuum that al Qaeda and Iran would rush to fill.

In response to President Obama's request for drawdown time-tables, Ambassador Crocker and General Ray Odierno, the commander of U.S. forces in Iraq, recommended a period of twenty-three months before the formal end of America's combat operations. This would allow the maximum number of U.S. forces to remain in Iraq through the upcoming Iraqi presidential elections and enable the United States to maintain the maximum pressure on "extremist networks" that threatened the security of Iraq. Crocker and Odierno included a list of ten reasons why the twenty-three-month time frame was the most responsible approach. Among these, it "maintains the greater security presence through the window of greatest risk" and it provides "most effective pressure vs. AQI [al Qaeda in Iraq] and balances Iranian influence in Iraq, to best deny extremist organizations the ability to regenerate organizational capacities."

In addition to the twenty-three-month timetable supported by Odierno and Crocker, the president considered two other options: the Obama campaign time frame of a sixteen-month drawdown and a compromise of nineteen months suggested by Secretary Gates, though neither of the shorter schedules had a military rationale. The president would also decide how many American troops to leave in place after the end of combat operations. General Odierno believed a residual American force of 50,000–55,000 troops would be necessary through the end of December 2011, when the existing Status of Forces Agreement expired. After that, the expectation was that a new SOFA would be negotiated to enable the United States to leave a stay-behind force in Iraq.

General Odierno and Ambassador Crocker also made the point that adopting a twenty-three-month drawdown schedule would enable the president to shift to either of the faster timetables if conditions on the ground warranted. There was no military necessity to make announcements about timetables at this point at all.

President Obama rejected the twenty-three-month timetable, the residual force of 50,000–55,000 through the end of 2011, and the advice that no immediate announcement on a timetable was militarily necessary.

On February 27, 2009, at Camp Lejeune, President Obama lauded the "relative peace" and substantial reduction in violence in Iraq brought about by the surge, though he did not credit the surge, likely because he had opposed it. He also said that al Qaeda had "been dealt a serious blow." Therefore, he announced, he would be removing all American combat brigades from Iraq over the next eighteen months. "Let me say this as plainly as I can, by August 31, 2010, our combat mission in Iraq will end." Having decided on a faster drawdown than the one recommended by his commander in the field, the president then announced that after the combat brigades were withdrawn, he would leave 35,000–50,000 troops in Iraq until the end of 2011. At that point, he explained, "I intend to remove all U.S. troops from Iraq by the end of 2011."

President Obama also announced at Camp Lejeune that he was appointing Chris Hill to be America's new ambassador to Iraq. It was a perplexing choice. In Hill's last diplomatic assignment, he had been responsible for the disastrous nuclear negotiations with North Korea, which the North Koreans used to buy time as they developed their massive uranium enrichment program. Hill had no experience working in the Middle East and no apparent understanding of the importance of actively engaging with the Iraqis to ensure a stable government would be left behind once American forces withdrew. He informed General Odierno that from here on Iraq would be treated like any other sovereign country, and America's diplomats and military leaders should not attempt to try to shape its future. By early 2010, things had deteriorated to the point that America's military leaders believed Hill was spending more time tracking which Iraqis the military met with than actually meeting with Iraqis himself.

Sixteen months later Hill left Iraq. "The most merciful comment I can make," said Mowaffak al-Rubaie, the former Iraqi national security advisor, "is that Chris Hill's legacy in his time here was uneventful, from the American government's side, while Iraq was full of events. He was a traditional diplomat with no experience in the Middle East, the Islamic world or Iraq. . . ." Hill did accomplish one thing. According to Emma Sky, a British advisor to General Odierno, Hill was reportedly determined to ensure that the U.S. embassy compound in Baghdad had grass. "Great rolls of lawn turf were brought in . . . and took root," wrote Sky. "There was now grass on which the ambassador could play lacrosse."

As the Obama administration began its withdrawal and shifted its focus elsewhere, Iraqi officials expressed concern about America's dwindling commitment to Iraq. The concerns ranged from who would fill the vacuum if American forces withdrew completely, to worries that President Obama's renewed engagement with Iran would come at Iraq's expense. In May 2009, Iraqi vice president Tariq al-Hashemi told visiting U.S. diplomats that he was worried about the "pervasive Iranian influence in both the security and political arenas" in Iraq, and he said he "hoped that the US Government was not sacrificing its interest in Iraq for its growing interest in Iran." Hashemi's chief of staff noted that Iraq was not yet a sovereign state, but a "collection of competing interests in a state-like environment." He said, "Iran understands this and is in Iraq for the long-term, whereas the U.S. is only here for the short term."

As the meeting concluded, the Iraqi vice president asked once again what would fill the vacuum when American troops left. Undersecretary Bill Burns, according to the embassy's report of the meeting, "reiterated that the U.S. is determined to keep its commitments to Iraq, build strong political and security institutions, and will not exchange Iraq's security as part of discussions with Iran." Sadly, President Obama would walk away from just those commitments over the next few years.

On August 12, 2010, the Iraqi Army chief of staff was even more direct about what the security of his country required. Lieutenant General Babakir Zebari told a London newspaper that the Iraqi Army would not be ready to protect the nation until 2020 and that they would need support from U.S. troops until then.

In a speech from the Oval Office on August 31, 2010, President Obama announced the end of American combat operations in Iraq. It was time, he said, for us to turn our attention to problems at home and to the war in Afghanistan, where, he said, "al Qaeda continues to plot against us, and its leadership remains anchored in the border regions of Afghanistan and Pakistan. We will disrupt, dismantle and defeat al Qaeda, while preventing Afghanistan from serving as a base for terrorists." But, as important as the war in Afghanistan was, we were going to fight it only for the next year. "Next August," he explained, "we will begin a transition to Afghan responsibility."

In case America's withdrawal from the field of battle looked to the world like a defeat, President Obama offered this: "In an age without surrender ceremonies, we must earn victory through the success of our partners and the strength of our own nation." He could hardly have been more wrong. In an age of terror, America must earn victory by defeating the terrorists, not by ceding them large swaths of territory and resources.

As 2011 opened, President Obama had to determine what size residual force the United States would leave in Iraq after the current Status of Forces Agreement expired in December. America's new commander in Iraq, General Lloyd Austin, recommended a force of between 20,000 and 24,000. The White House said that was too large. General Austin then recommended 19,000, with two other options for 16,000 troops with different glide paths for withdrawal. Again, the White House said no. The president decided, based on no military rationale, that he was prepared to leave behind no more than 3,500 troops. In addition, the United States would insist that any new Status of Forces Agreement would have to be approved by the Iraqi parliament. In light of the political atmosphere in Baghdad at the time, this was essentially a poison pill.

Iraqi prime minister Nouri al-Maliki suggested a memorandum of understanding or an executive agreement that would not require the politically impossible step on which Obama was insisting. The White House said no. In the end, the number of troops President Obama was willing to consider in a stay-behind force was too small to protect America's interests or Iraq's security. Maliki was being asked to take a big political risk—seeking parliamentary approval—for minimal security gain. The deal fell apart.

America's commitment to Iraq's security was now being replaced by something else. In a joint press conference with Maliki on December 12, 2011, Obama said America and Iraq would be "partnering for our shared security." This did not mean "stationing American troops there or with U.S. bases in Iraq," President Obama was quick to add. "Those days are over." What America would be doing, among other things, would be establishing "a new formal channel of communication between our national security advisors." In addition, America and Iraq would be "partnering for regional security." The president didn't offer any details, but he did issue an edict. "Just as Iraq has pledged not to interfere in other nations," he said, "other nations must not interfere in Iraq. Iraq's sovereignty must be respected."

President Obama still seemed not to understand that words divorced from action cannot defeat a determined enemy.

On December 14, 2011, the president visited Fort Bragg to commemorate the end of the war in Iraq. America's withdrawal was "a moment of success," he said.

> *Now, Iraq is not a perfect place. It has many challenges ahead. But we're leaving behind a sovereign, stable, and self-reliant Iraq, with a representative government that was elected by its people. We're building a new partnership between our nations. And we are ending a war not with a final battle but with a final march toward home.*

When President Obama arrived in office, Iraq was stable, largely because of the surge of forces and the adoption of a counterinsurgency strategy ordered by George W. Bush, but that stability would not last long. On December 17, 2011, at 0230 hours, the last American ground convoy left Iraq.

A senior Obama administration official interviewed by Michael Gordon and General Bernard Trainor for their book *The Endgame* explained:

> *[W]e came to the conclusion that achieving the goal of a security partnership with Iraq was not dependent on the size of our footprint in country, and that stability in Iraq did not depend on the presence of the U.S. forces.*

It was a convenient conclusion, and it was wrong. Though the Iraqis themselves certainly bear a portion of the responsibility for the failure to secure a new Status of Forces Agreement, it is clear President Obama did not want to leave any American forces in Iraq.

He has since tried to deny this—as terror and destruction spread across Iraq in the wake of America's complete withdrawal. President

Obama has tried to assert that the troop withdrawal wasn't his plan after all. Most memorably, in an appearance on the South Lawn of the White House in August 2014, the president was asked whether, in light of the rise of ISIS and the violence spreading across Iraq and Syria, it might not have been better to have left some U.S. troops in Iraq. "You know," he said, "the thing I find interesting about this, is that people are acting as though It were my decision."

The president seemed to have forgotten his repeated claims of credit for the removal of all U.S. forces from Iraq, beginning with his announcement of the end of combat operations in a speech from the Oval Office in October 2011. "After taking office," he explained, "I announced a new strategy that would end our combat mission in Iraq and remove all of our troops by the end of 2011. . . . So, today, I can report that, as promised, the rest of our troops in Iraq will come home by the end of the year."

Obama similarly took credit for removing all U.S. forces nearly every day of the 2012 presidential election campaign. During a debate with his Republican opponent, former governor Mitt Romney, on October 22, 2012, President Obama criticized him for asserting that America should have left a stay-behind force. "Now you just gave a speech in which you said we should still have troops in Iraq. That's not a recipe for making sure we are taking advantage of the opportunity and meeting the challenges of the Middle East."

In his State of the Union address on January 24, 2012, President Obama heralded all he had done to end war, and explained what this new era would mean for America:

> Ending the war in Iraq has allowed us to strike decisive blows against our enemies. From Pakistan to Yemen, the al Qaeda operatives who remain are scrambling, knowing they can't escape the reach of the United States of America.

He wrapped our exit from Iraq in a glossy metaphor:

> *As the tide of war recedes, a wave of change has washed across the*
> *Middle East and North Africa, from Tunis to Cairo; from Sana'a*
> *to Tripoli.*

There was indeed a wave of change washing across the Arab world. Tragically, it would be led by thousands of militant Islamist terrorists marching under the black banners of al Qaeda and ISIS.

AFGHANISTAN

In 2008, candidate Barack Obama left no uncertainty as to his position on the war in Afghanistan. In a speech before the Veterans of Foreign Wars that August, he said:

> *This is the central front in the war on terrorism. This is where the*
> *Taliban is gaining strength and launching new attacks. . . . This*
> *is a war we have to win. And as commander in chief, I will have*
> *no greater priority than taking out these terrorists who threaten*
> *America, and finishing the job against the Taliban.*

At about that time, work was under way in the Bush White House from which President Obama and his team would benefit. In the fall of 2008, President Bush ordered "a quiet surge" of additional U.S. forces to Afghanistan. At the same time, he instructed the National Security Council to conduct a review of Afghan policy and provide recommendations for the road ahead. Simultaneous reviews were under way at the State Department, Defense Department, and U.S. Central Command (CENTCOM).

President-elect Obama and his national security team were briefed on the findings and recommendations of these reviews early in the transition process. The incoming national security advisor, General Jim Jones, asked that the Bush administration not announce the findings of their policy review publicly and President Bush agreed. He wanted to give the incoming team every opportunity to succeed.

In March 2009, when President Obama launched his new Afghanistan strategy, which included additional troops and a focus on counterinsurgency, it bore a striking resemblance to the review and findings the Bush team had provided. In a speech from the Eisenhower Executive Office Building, the president told the American people what was at stake:

> *We are in Afghanistan to confront a common enemy that threatens the United States, our friends and our allies, and the people of Afghanistan and Pakistan who have suffered the most at the hands of violent extremists. So I want the American people to understand that we have a clear and focused goal: to disrupt, dismantle and defeat al Qaeda in Pakistan and Afghanistan, and to prevent their return to either country in the future. That's the goal that must be achieved.*

To complete this mission, President Obama had ordered the deployment of an additional 17,000 U.S. troops to Afghanistan. In May 2009, he appointed General Stanley McChrystal to take over command of U.S. forces and the International Security Assistance Force in Afghanistan. Secretary Gates instructed McChrystal to undertake a sixty-day assessment of the situation on the ground before making any requests or recommendations for resources.

General McChrystal submitted his findings on August 30. He urged immediate action. "Failure to gain the initiative and reverse insurgent momentum in the near term (next 12 months)—while Afghan security capacity matures," he wrote, "risks an outcome where defeating the insurgency is no longer possible." It was also crucial that the president dedicate the necessary resources to the fight. "Failure to provide adequate resources," McChrystal's report concluded, "also risks a longer conflict, greater casualties, higher overall costs, and ultimately, a critical loss of political support. Any of these risks, in turn, are likely to result in mission failure." General McChrystal assessed he would need an additional 40,000 troops to accomplish the mission President Obama had given the military. McChrystal wrote later that he viewed the troop calculation not as a "request" but as providing his "best military advice to the commander in chief."

Having told the American people for the last two years that he was dedicated to doing everything it took to win in Afghanistan, and having already established the mission in March 2009, the Obama administration nonetheless took months debating McChrystal's assessment and troop request. As Secretary of Defense Gates described it, "Over and over again we would rehash the issues and get further into the weeds—details beyond what was needed or appropriate."

Ultimately, the president decided to send 30,000 additional troops. At least one of the reasons he did not grant the full troop request was political. During one of the meetings to discuss the troop levels, according to former secretary of defense Gates, the president had said, "On Afghanistan, my poll numbers will be stronger if I take issue with the military over Afghanistan policy."

President Obama announced his decision in a speech on December 1, 2009, at West Point. He explained all that was at stake. America's security, "the security of our allies, and the common security of the world," he said, depended upon denying al Qaeda a safe haven and reversing the Taliban's momentum. And then, in what may be the most ambivalent presidential call to arms in history, he said, "As commander in chief, I have determined that it is in our national interest to send an additional 30,000 troops to Afghanistan. After 18 months, our troops will begin to come home." In case the Taliban or al Qaeda or our allies didn't catch this first reference to a timetable, a few paragraphs later the president said we would "begin the transfer of our forces out of Afghanistan in July of 2011." After telling the world that this was a war of necessity, not a war of choice, Barack Obama was now announcing he would be fighting it only for the next eighteen months.

Much of what the president said about Afghanistan in 2009 was true. American security did depend upon defeating al Qaeda and denying them a safe haven. Those things were still true two years later when the president chose to withdraw the majority of American forces from the field of battle.

By the spring of 2011, the president had lost the will to fight and win the war in Afghanistan. Secretary of Defense Gates has written about the deep concern he felt sitting in an NSC meeting in March 2011, listening to the president describe his determination to draw down American troops:

> As I sat there, I thought: The president doesn't trust his commander, can't stand Karzai, doesn't believe in his own strategy, and doesn't consider the war to be his. For him, it's all about getting out.

On June 22, 2011, President Obama announced that U.S. forces in Afghanistan would begin coming home in July, and that all of the surge forces he had announced in the December 2009 West Point address would be home by the summer of 2012.

It was a timetable with no military justification. In fact, it hampered the mission the president had established because the requirement to bring all the surge forces home by the end of the summer in

2012 meant they would have to begin withdrawing before the spring 2012 fighting season. They would lack the time necessary to accomplish their objectives in eastern Afghanistan—fully clearing out the Taliban and going after the Haqqani Network between Kabul and the Pakistani border. The timeline did ensure, however, that the surge forces would be home before the 2012 reelection campaign. The president could then campaign on the notion that "the tide of war is receding."

Six days after the president's announcement of the timetable for withdrawing the surge forces, Marine Lieutenant General John Allen, who had been nominated as the new commander of coalition forces in Afghanistan, was testifying under oath in front of the Senate Armed Services Committee. Senator Lindsey Graham asked him whether the withdrawal pace chosen by the president was "one of the options presented to the president," by General Petraeus, who had taken over command in Afghanistan in June 2010. This exchange ensued:

ALLEN: It is a more aggressive option than that which was presented.

GRAHAM: My question is, was that an option which was presented?

ALLEN: It was not.

General Petraeus and Chairman of the Joint Chiefs Mike Mullen both also testified that the drawdown plan announced by Obama was "more aggressive" than they had hoped. Petraeus went on to say that the time frame was the result of "broader considerations" beyond military ones.

In the years since, the president has continued to draw down our forces regardless of conditions on the ground. As we write this, nearly

10,000 American troops remain in Afghanistan. Despite a decision by the president to slow the rate of withdrawal, he has remained determined that all American forces will be out by the end of 2016, leaving only "an embassy presence by the end of next year," he said, "just as we've done in Iraq."

In February 2015, General John Campbell, commander of the U.S. and NATO forces in Afghanistan, testified that as the United States continues to draw down, Taliban, al Qaeda, and al Qaeda affiliates will "undoubtedly attempt to reestablish their authority and prominence in Afghanistan," and "present a formidable challenge" to the Afghan National Security Force (ANSF). Campbell explained that as the United States withdraws from its base in Kandahar Province, the Taliban's historic stronghold, the departure of coalition forces "would provide the Taliban momentum" to expand offensive operations throughout the country.

The first months of 2015 have seen an increase in Taliban violence in key regions across the country and in Kabul. This has occurred even in regions like the south, where the ANSF has attempted to undertake operations to clear the Taliban. According to the Institute for the Study of War, the current security situation in Afghanistan has "begun to reflect the strategic landscape before the 2010 surge. ANSF units are increasingly confined to their bases and security checkpoints, unable or unwilling to go out on patrol in the community."

ISIS has also expanded its operations in Afghanistan and Pakistan, through the establishment of the "Wilayat of Khorasan." A *wilayat* is an ISIS administrative unit through which operations are conducted in a particular geographic area. As of this writing, ISIS has a presence in at least eight of Afghanistan's thirty-four provinces, and the group is actively recruiting fighters from Afghanistan to travel to Iraq and Syria.

Despite the resurgence of America's enemies, President Obama continues to insist on taking our forces off the field of battle. He is no longer interested in prevailing in what he once said was the necessary war. He is interested only in leaving. What has caused this change? Vali Nasr, dean of the School of Advanced International Studies at Johns Hopkins University and a former advisor on Afghanistan for President Obama, offers this explanation:

> *It was to court public opinion that Obama first embraced the war in Afghanistan. And when public opinion changed, he was quick to declare victory and call the troops back home. His actions from start to finish were guided by politics and they played well at home. But abroad, the stories we tell to justify our on again, off again approach to this war do not ring true to friend or foe. They know the truth: that we are leaving Afghanistan to its own fate. Leaving even as the demons of regional chaos that first beckoned us there are once again rising to threaten our security.*

THE 2012 PRESIDENTIAL ELECTION

In a complex and heroic operation, members of SEAL Team Six launched into Pakistan from Afghanistan on May 1, 2011, and killed Osama bin Laden. They performed brilliantly. President Obama deserves credit for ordering the raid. Members of our military and intelligence community, including interrogators in the enhanced interrogation program, deserve credit for finding bin Laden. It was just and right that the man responsible for the attacks of 9/11 met his demise at the hands of the United States armed forces.

In the aftermath of the successful raid in Abbottabad, the Obama administration increasingly claimed al Qaeda was in decline or had been defeated. In hundreds of speeches during the 2012 presidential campaign, President Obama said some version of "The war in Iraq is

over, the war in Afghanistan is winding down, al Qaeda has been dec-
imated, Osama bin Laden is dead." The message was clear. President
Obama's actions had diminished the threat of a terrorist attack, and al
Qaeda was on the ropes. The reality was somewhat different—while
Obama was proclaiming al Qaeda's demise, it and other militant Is-
lamic terrorist groups were resurgent across the globe.

Lieutenant General Michael Flynn, director of the Defense Intelligence Agency from 2012 to 2014, offered this view as he was leaving
his post:

> When asked if the terrorists were on the run, we couldn't respond
> with any answer but "no." When asked if the terrorists were de-
> feated, we had to say "no." Anyone who answers yes to either of
> those questions either doesn't know what they are talking about,
> they are misinformed, or they are flat out lying.

A RAND Corporation study published in 2014 confirmed what
General Flynn was saying. It found, for example:

> Beginning in 2010, there was a rise in the number of Salafi-
> jihadist groups and fighters, particularly in Syria and North
> Africa. There was also an increase in the number of attacks perpe-
> trated by al Qaeda and its affiliates.

Between 2010 and 2013, according to the study, there was a 58 percent increase in the number of Salafi-jihadist groups. And more
groups meant more attacks:

> There was a significant increase in attacks by al Qa'ida-affiliated
> groups between 2007 and 2013, with most of the violence

in 2013 perpetrated by the Islamic State of Iraq and al-Sham (43 percent)... al Shabaab (25 percent); Jabhat al-Nusrah (21 percent); and al-Qa'ida in the Arabian Peninsula (10 percent).

The study also addressed the status of "core al Qaeda," the group President Obama has claimed repeatedly to have defeated. Noting that the "broader Salafi-Jihadist movement has become more decentralized," the report explained, "using the state of core al Qa'ida in Pakistan as a gauge of the movement's strengths (or weaknesses) is increasingly anachronistic for such a heterogeneous mixture of groups."

We now know, in addition, as a result of the documents captured in the bin Laden raid, that Obama's claims about the condition of "core al Qaeda" were untrue. Stephen F. Hayes and Thomas Joscelyn reported:

At precisely the time Mr. Obama was campaigning on the imminent death of al Qaeda, those with access to the bin Laden documents were seeing, in bin Laden's own words, that the opposite was true. Says Lt. Gen. Flynn: "By that time, they probably had grown by about—I'd say close to doubling by that time. And we knew that."

On September 6, 2012, as he accepted the Democratic Party's presidential nomination, the president said this:

Four years ago, I promised to end the war in Iraq. We did. I promised to focus on the terrorists who actually attacked us on 9/11, and we have. We've blunted the Taliban's momentum in Afghanistan, and in 2014, our longest war will be over. A new tower rises

*above the New York skyline, al Qaeda is on the path to defeat, and
Osama bin Laden is dead.*

Five days later, on September 11, 2012, an al Qaeda–affiliated
group attacked two American facilities in Benghazi, Libya, killing
Ambassador Chris Stevens, Sean Smith, Tyrone Woods, and Glen
Doherty. Not only was al Qaeda not on the path to defeat, it was resurgent across the Middle East and had just carried out a brutal and well-
planned attack against the United States, on the anniversary of 9/11.

In the days and weeks following the attacks, President Obama,
Secretary of State Clinton, U.S. ambassador to the UN Susan Rice,
and other administration officials misled the American people about
what had happened, attempting to cast the attacks as spontaneous
uprisings in response to an anti-Islamic Internet video, though there
was no evidence for such a claim. Here is a sampling of what they
said:

SECRETARY CLINTON: "We've seen rage and violence directed
at American Embassies over an awful Internet video that we
had nothing to do with. It is hard for the American people
to make sense of that because it is senseless, and it is unacceptable." (September 15, 2012)

AMBASSADOR RICE: "The information, the best information
and the best assessment we have today is that in fact this was
not a preplanned, premeditated attack. That what happened
initially was that it was a spontaneous reaction to what had
transpired in Cairo as a consequence of the video. People
gathered outside the embassy and then it grew very violent."
(September 16, 2012)

PRESIDENT OBAMA: "That is what we saw play out in the last
two weeks, as a crude and disgusting video sparked out-

rage throughout the Muslim world. Now I have made it clear that the United States government had nothing to do with this video and I believe its message must be rejected by all who respect our common humanity." (September 25, 2012)

They made these claims despite evidence to the contrary, including:

- The State Department Operations Center had reported on September 11, 2012, at 6:08 P.M., while the attacks were still under way, that an al Qaeda–linked group had already claimed credit.
- The CIA station chief in Libya reported on September 12 that the U.S. facilities in Benghazi had been the target of a terrorist attack by Islamic militants.
- The assistant secretary of state for Near Eastern affairs had informed the Libyan government on September 12, 2012, that an al Qaeda–affiliated group had been involved in the attack.
- There was no protest or demonstration or gathering of people angry about a video, or anything else, at the consulate prior to the attack. The CIA station chief in Libya had notified CIA deputy director Mike Morrell of this on September 15, prior to Ambassador Rice's claims. The Accountability Review Board tasked to investigate the attack also concluded, "There was no protest prior to the attacks."
- There was no mention of any Internet video sparking these attacks in any of the reporting from Libya or in the talking points prepared about the attack by the CIA.
- The initial talking points prepared by the CIA included the assertion that the U.S. government "knows that Is-

lamic extremists with ties to al Qaeda participated in the attacks."

As Stephen F. Hayes has reported, after an interagency meeting at the White House on September 15, 2012, the CIA removed all references to Islamic extremists, jihadists in Cairo, previous attacks on foreign interests in Benghazi, possible surveillance of the American facilities in Benghazi, and warnings about al Qaeda in Libya. In other words, they removed anything that suggested the involvement of al Qaeda affiliates in an attack on U.S. interests, and anything that suggested the State Department should have been aware of the danger. The new version of the talking points also softened the word "attacks" to "demonstrations."

There was an important video released on the Internet the day before the attacks. It was not, however, the one Secretary Clinton and President Obama attempted to blame for the attacks. It was a video released by Ayman al-Zawahiri, the leader of al Qaeda, on September 10, 2012. Zawahiri confirmed the death of his number two, Abu Yahya al-Libi, at the hands of the Americans. He urged his followers to puncture the "arrogance" of the "evil empire, America." Perhaps it was this video on which the president and secretary of state should have been focused.

One might ask why the administration worked so hard to ignore evidence and peddle a false narrative about what happened. The answer is the calendar. In the middle of an election campaign in which President Obama was claiming every day that al Qaeda had been defeated or was diminished, he could not admit to an al Qaeda attack on U.S. personnel and facilities on the anniversary of 9/11. His reelection was on the line. He had to find another story.

The outlines for the new story were in place by Friday, September 14, 2012, when Deputy National Security Advisor Ben Rhodes sent an email setting out goals for Ambassador Rice to achieve during her appearances on September 16 on five Sunday shows. She should, he wrote, "Underscore that these protests are rooted in an Internet video, and not a broader failure of policy." She should also, he emphasized, "Reinforce the President and Administration's strength and steadiness in dealing with difficult challenges." The Obama team's spin was clear.

They knew that a preplanned al Qaeda attack on American personnel and facilities would raise the question of whether senior officials had spent so much time claiming al Qaeda was defeated that they had failed to adequately guard against the possibility of an al Qaeda–linked attack. The facts, in this regard, are not helpful to either President Obama or Secretary Clinton. We know now:

- The attacks were preplanned, well organized, and carried out by the same al Qaeda affiliate that had launched previous attacks on U.S. and Western interests in Benghazi in the months immediately preceding September 11, 2012.
- There had been at least twenty attacks in Benghazi in 2012, in the midst of a rising wave of violence.
- The American facilities had been the target of al Qaeda–affiliated surveillance.
- Ambassador Chris Stevens had asked for additional security and been turned down. Secretary Clinton's State Department cut U.S. security staff in Libya prior to the attacks.
- The Libyan government had asked for additional security assistance just two months before the attacks, and the Obama administration had failed to provide anything meaningful.

- Al Qaeda's number two issued a video on September 10 calling on his followers to avenge the death of his number two, a Libyan operative, by attacking America.
- There were no demonstrations and no evidence that an anti-Muslim Internet video had anything to do with these attacks.

The steady drumbeat of evidence indicating that the president and the secretary had misled the American people came to a head when Secretary Clinton testified before the Senate Foreign Relations Committee in January 2013. As the senators tried to determine what Secretary Clinton knew and when she knew it, she responded angrily:

With all due respect, the fact is we had four dead Americans. Was it because of a protest or was it because of guys out for a walk one night who decided that they'd go kill some Americans? What difference at this point does it make?

This response was stunning because the alternative scenarios Secretary Clinton offered did not include what actually happened—the American facilities in Benghazi were the target of an al Qaeda–affiliated terrorist attack. Equally remarkable was her assertion (posed as a rhetorical question) that what caused the American deaths makes no difference—when, of course, it does. It is the difference between dismissing what happened as a one-off event and understanding it as part of an ongoing threat that we must guard against. Understanding what happened affects everything from how we assess what went wrong in the past to how we conduct ourselves to defeat the terrorists, to how we protect our people in the future.

At the most fundamental level, though, it is the difference between being honest about what happened in Benghazi on September 11, 2012, and adopting a false narrative because it serves political purposes. It is the difference between lying to the American people and dealing with them truthfully—which is what we deserve.

THE RISE OF ISIS

In March 2014, the authors of this book visited with a number of key leaders in the Middle East. One Arab head of state unfolded a map in front of us on his conference table and drew an arc with his finger from Raqqa in Syria to Anbar Province in Iraq. "The terrorists will control this entire territory if America doesn't act," he said. "Why won't your president act?" We could not answer the question. Not only was President Obama doing nothing consequential to stop the spread of ISIS across the Middle East, the rise of this most dangerous terrorist group was a direct result of his policies in Iraq and Syria.

When President Obama withdrew from Iraq, al Qaeda in Iraq had largely been defeated. The Shi'a militias had also been routed. President Obama's decision not to leave any U.S. forces behind created the space and the conditions for the rebirth of al Qaeda in Iraq, as well as the Islamic State of Iraq and Syria, ISIS.

Even before the Obama withdrawal was complete, President Obama's administration made clear that they had as little interest in maintaining political ties with Iraq as they did in maintaining a military presence there. A delegation of Iraqi government officials who visited Washington in early 2009 met with Obama administration officials and attempted to thank them for all America had done to liberate their country. The Iraqis reported that it was as though they were thanking representatives of a government that had nothing to do with their liberation. The officials had no interest in their gratitude, nor, apparently, any interest in their country.

Ambassador Ryan Crocker, who has served as U.S. ambassador

to Lebanon, Kuwait, Syria, Pakistan, Iraq, and Afghanistan, describes the severing of the U.S. relationship with Iraq this way:

> *We disengaged not only militarily at the end of 2011, we disengaged politically. The war was over. We were out. Let the chips fall where they may. Well, I don't think we thought through exactly how many chips were going to fall and what the consequences of that were going to be.*
>
> *Senior level phone calls, senior level regular visits basically ceased. There was exactly one visit to Iraq since the end of 2011 until mid-2014 by a cabinet level official. Given that we were hard-wired into their political system, they wouldn't be able to function effectively with each other, among communities, without us. I think that disengagement brought them all back to zero sum thinking.*

The day after the last American troops left Iraq in December 2011, the Shi'ite prime minister, Nouri al-Maliki, issued an arrest warrant for his Sunni vice president, Tariq al-Hashemi. Maliki also began to purge Sunni officers from the military, and he targeted the Sons of Iraq, the Sunni fighters who had fought alongside the United States during the surge. Although they had been given promises that they would be absorbed into the Iraqi Army, Maliki initially stopped paying them and then a number of them were arrested and killed.

Throughout this period, violence was rising in Iraq. Abu Bakr al-Baghdadi had become the leader of the Islamic State in Iraq in May 2010. As America withdrew, he orchestrated waves of car bombs and suicide attacks across the country.

Soon Baghdadi turned his attention to Syria, where, in early 2011, protests began against the regime of Bashar al-Assad. Launched first in Da'ara, a town near the Jordanian border, the demonstrations quickly spread. Protesters chanted the familiar refrain heard in Tahrir Square in Cairo: "The people want the regime to go."

The Obama administration sent mixed messages. Secretary of State Clinton appeared on CBS's *Face the Nation* on March 27, 2011. Host Bob Schieffer asked her whether the United States would use force to defend the Syrian people from attacks by the regime, as we had done in Libya. Pointing to the reign of terror of the Assad family, Schieffer suggested it was at least as bad as the brutality of Libyan leader Muammar Qaddafi. In her answer, Secretary Clinton defended Syrian president Assad:

> *There is a different leader in Syria now. Many of the members of Congress of both parties who have gone to Syria in recent months have said they believe he is a reformer.*

At the same time, U.S. ambassador to Syria, Robert Ford, who was under no illusions about the nature of the Assad regime and its leader, was traveling to sites of the anti-regime protests to show solidarity with the demonstrators. He was also urging Washington to act to provide support for the uprisings, which were at this point largely composed of secular, peaceful groups.

As Assad began ordering violent crackdowns, killing protesters in an attempt to end the demonstrations, the Obama administration imposed sanctions on some Syrian officials. President Obama announced on May 19, 2011, that if Assad was unwilling to lead the movement for reform, an unlikely possibility given that his forces were slaughtering protesters, then it was time for him to go:

> *The Syrian people have shown their courage in demanding a transition to democracy. President Assad now has a choice: He can lead that transition, or get out of the way. The Syrian government*

must stop shooting demonstrators and allow peaceful protests. It must release political prisoners and stop unjust arrests. It must allow human rights monitors to have access to cities like Dara'a; and start a serious dialogue to advance a democratic transition.

Assad stepped up his attacks on the demonstrators, and at dawn on July 31, 2011, he sent tanks into Hama, the city that had been the site of a horrific massacre ordered by Assad's father in 1982. The Obama administration imposed more sanctions and the president issued another stern instruction for Assad to step down:

The future of Syria must be determined by its people, but President Bashar al-Assad is standing in their way. . . . We have consistently said that President Assad must lead a democratic transition or get out of the way. He has not led. For the sake of the Syrian people, the time has come for President Assad to step aside.

The president was still unwilling, however, to take any action. It should have been clear that stern words were not enough to force Assad from office. It should also have been clear that America's credibility was diminished when the president instructed Assad to leave and he didn't.

The question of just what behavior from Assad might spark the use of American military force came up in a press conference on August 20, 2012. President Obama drew his red line:

I have at this point not ordered military engagement in the situation. . . . We have been very clear to the Assad regime, but also to other players on the ground, that a red line for us is we start seeing a whole bunch of chemical weapons moving around or being utilized. That would change my calculus. That would change my equation.

On August 21, 2013, Assad launched a sarin gas attack on the suburbs of Damascus where rebel groups were operating. The death toll was over 1,400 civilians. President Obama had drawn a red line. Assad had crossed it. Obviously, the United States would have to act.

Military preparations began. But then, according to Leon Panetta, who was secretary of defense at the time, "President Obama vacillated, first indicating he was prepared to order some strikes, then retreating and agreeing to submit the matter to Congress. The latter was, as he well knew, an almost certain way to scotch any action."

President Obama had blinked. The consequences were devastating. First, as Panetta explained:

> When the president as commander in chief draws a red line, it is critical that he act if the line is crossed. The power of the United States rests on its word, and clear signals are important both to deter adventurism and to reassure allies that we can be counted on. Assad's action clearly defied President Obama's warning; by failing to respond, it sent the wrong message to the world.

Amr al-Azm, a member of the Syrian opposition, described it this way:

> I think it was a terrible, terrible error on the part of this administration. I mean, it's not just a red line. This is the president of the United States, this is the White House, and a tinpot dictator challenges that and gets away with it? Who's going to believe you next time?

Inside Syria, the president's failure to act was a propaganda victory for ISIS, one that they used to convince Syrians that they couldn't count on the United States. Oubai Shahbandar, a member of the Syrian opposition, described what happened:

Immediately after [Obama's failure to attack], extremists and what eventually came to be ISIS were sending the message to the locals that, "Look, you have been betrayed by the world. Do not trust those nationalist rebel forces," that at this point were receiving nominal support from the United States and its regional allies.

As President Obama vacillated about whether to take action, the Russians sensed an opening. Russian foreign minister Sergei Lavrov offered to get the Assad regime to turn over its chemical weapons and agree to have them moved out of Syria. The Obama administration has claimed this as a diplomatic success. On July 20, 2014, Secretary of State John Kerry said, "We struck a deal where we got one hundred percent of their chemical weapons out." This claim is undoubtedly somewhat surprising to the Syrian civilians who were the victims of the thirty-five chlorine gas attacks that occurred between March 16 and May 26, 2015.

While the president was making threats and delivering ultimatums, the situation in Syria and Iraq continued to deteriorate. Baghdadi's influence and effectiveness spread as ISIS forces conducted an increasing number of operations in both countries. In July 2013, ISIS forces attacked Iraqi prisons on the outskirts of Baghdad and freed at least five hundred prisoners. In August 2013, ISIS took control in Raqqa, Syria, and made the city its headquarters. In October 2013, the situation in Iraq had gotten so bad that Prime Minister Maliki visited Washington to seek assistance.

Maliki's warnings to the Obama administration—that ISIS posed an existential threat to Iraq and that Iraq did not have control of its own borders—were echoed by intelligence reports the administration was receiving. President Obama's response was to provide a minimal amount of assistance to the Iraqis. Obama officials fundamentally viewed what was happening inside Syria and Iraq as not their problem. The constant refrain was "This is up to the Iraqis to sort out," "This isn't our fight," "We can't do it for them." All of which ignored the direct, clear, and present danger of ISIS to the security of the United States.

In 2014, after establishing a base of operations in Syria, and gathering strength and followers, ISIS spread full force back into Iraq. They bulldozed border crossings and began taking Iraqi cities. In January 2014, they took Fallujah. The Obama administration still failed to recognize the magnitude of the threat. In an interview published the same month ISIS took Fallujah, President Obama explained his view of the terrorist group: "The analogy we use around here sometimes, and I think it is accurate, is if a jayvee team puts on Lakers uniforms that doesn't make them Kobe Bryant." The terrorists President Obama described as the "jayvee team" would soon control more resources and territory than any other terrorist group in history.

In June, ISIS took Mosul. Baghdadi declared the establishment of a caliphate and, as caliph, preached a Ramadan sermon in Mosul's main mosque. The caliphate stretched across territory in Syria and Iraq, effectively erasing the former national boundaries, and securing a huge propaganda victory. It was a practical victory as well. The establishment of a caliphate imposes an obligation of allegiance upon those Muslims around the globe who share ISIS's apocalyptic, medieval interpretation of Islam. Since the declaration, tens if not hundreds of thousands of jihadists from around the globe have flooded into the caliphate.

ISIS's spread into territory that now reaches virtually from Baghdad to Damascus has continued despite American air strikes that began—in a limited fashion with onerous rules of engagement and no forward U.S. air controllers—in September 2014. In addition to the territory ISIS controls in Iraq and Syria, the group has established *wilayat*s or administrative districts in Yemen, the Sinai peninsula, Libya, Afghanistan, and Saudi Arabia.

During the period of ISIS's expansion, President Obama has minimized the threat, declared the war on terror over, proclaimed that it was U.S. policy to "degrade and ultimately defeat ISIS," declined to deploy the resources to accomplish this, and announced at least twice that we had no strategy to do so. His actions have served to accelerate progress by our enemies rather than safeguarding our interests. He has pointed to examples of his own success, only to see those policies deteriorate under the weight of the advance of militant Islam. Announcing his plans to combat ISIS in September 2014, for example, President Obama said the United States would adopt a plan similar to the counterterrorism strategy "that we have successfully pursued in Yemen . . . for years." Six months later, in the face of advancing Iranian-backed rebels, the United States was forced to close its embassy and pull out of the country. America had also been forced to close its embassies in Syria and Libya due to the violence and chaos unleashed by the rise of America's adversaries across the region.

Allowing this rise to continue nearly unabated, the president has pointed to one instance in which he would deploy U.S. ground forces: "If we discover that ISIL had gotten possession of a nuclear weapon and we had to run an operation to get it out of their hands, then yes, you can anticipate that not only would Chairman [of the Joint Chiefs of Staff Martin] Dempsey recommend me sending U.S. ground troops to get that weapon out of their hands, but I would order it." Is the president of the United States really willing to let ISIS get a nuclear weapon before he acts? Surely even this president and this national security team recognize that would be too late. Isn't there at least one person inside the Obama White House who could tell the president that his job is to prevent the terrorists from getting nuclear weapons, not to wait and act after the fact?

It is abundantly clear as we write this that the Obama strategy to defeat or even degrade ISIS is failing. General Jack Keane testified in front of the Senate Armed Services Committee on May 21, 2015:

> *Looking at this strategy today we know now that the conceptual plan is fundamentally flawed. The resources provided to support Iraq are far from adequate. The timing and urgency to provide arms, equipment, and training is insufficient. And as such, we are not only failing, we are in fact losing this war. Moreover, I can say with certainty, this strategy will not defeat ISIS.*

The president is undeterred. ISIS is Iraq's problem, not ours. Having lived through the attacks of 9/11, the president cannot claim ignorance about the threat to America posed by terrorists who have the territory, desire, resources, and commitment to attack America, and with the spread of ISIS, the threat America faces is grave and growing. No combination of armies, absent American leadership, will defeat them. Ambassador Ryan Crocker has described the situation this way:

> *It is hard to overstate the threat that this organization poses. I call it al Qaeda Version 6.0. The Islamic State is far better organized, equipped, and funded than the original. They are more experienced and more numerous. Several thousand carry Western passports, including American ones. All the terrorists have to do is get on a plane and head west. But perhaps the most important asset they possess is territory. For the first time since 9/11, a determined*

*and capable enemy has the space and security to plan complex,
longer-range operations. If we don't think we are on that list, we
are deluding ourselves.*

In his time left in office, President Obama would do well to remember the words of one of his Democratic predecessors. In 1948,
President Harry Truman spoke to Congress about the growing Soviet
threat to Western Europe. Urging Congress to act immediately to pass
the Marshall Plan and maintain America's military strength, Truman
said, "There are times in world history when it is far wiser to act than
to hesitate. There is some risk involved in action—there always is. But
there is far more risk in failure to act." President Truman continued,
"We must be prepared to pay the price for peace, or assuredly we shall
pay the price of war."

In years to come, President Obama will have to explain to his
fellow citizens why he chose inaction as the threat grew, spread, and
gathered strength? Why was he unwilling to stop those bent on America's destruction?

When history asks, how will he answer?

———— ◆ ————

FIVE

Appeasing Adversaries

*If history teaches anything, it teaches that simple-minded appease-
ment or wishful thinking about our adversaries is folly. It means the
betrayal of our past, the squandering of our freedom.*
—PRESIDENT RONALD REAGAN, MARCH 8, 1983

In his first inaugural address, on January 20, 2009, President Obama
had a message for dictators around the globe. "To those who cling
to power through corruption and deceit and the silencing of dissent,"
he said, "know that you are on the wrong side of history, but that we
will extend a hand if you are willing to unclench your fist." Leaders
in Tehran and Moscow had yet to take the measure of America's new
president, but over the next six years, as they were placated and even
appeased, they learned that the president's extended hand was full of
prizes for them and did not require—contrary to what he had said—
that they unclench their fists.

IRAN

Dubai, United Arab Emirates, 1987. The Iranian delegation arrived
with a check, in Swiss francs, for approximately $3 million. Represen-

tatives from A. Q. Khan's nuclear network, including S. M. Farouq and B.S.A. Tahir, met them in the hotel room carrying a briefcase containing designs for centrifuges used to enrich uranium. Once Farouq confirmed the Iranians' check would clear, Khan's team handed over the briefcase. Technical drawings for a centrifuge were just the beginning. Khan's sales to the Iranians would eventually include a starter kit for a centrifuge plant, centrifuge components, and instructions for enriching uranium to weapons-grade levels. The Iranians were Khan's first customers in what would become the most dangerous nuclear proliferation network in history.

MORE THAN TWENTY YEARS earlier, the Iranians had established a peaceful nuclear energy program. In 1967, the Tehran Research Reactor went online. In 1970, the Iranian parliament ratified the Nuclear Non-Proliferation Treaty (NPT), which aimed to halt the spread of nuclear weapons technology by creating a two-tiered structure for membership. The five countries that tested nuclear weapons before 1968—the United States, the Soviet Union, China, Great Britain, and France—joined the NPT as nuclear weapons states. Other states that signed the treaty, the non-nuclear-weapons states, promised not to develop nuclear weapons. In exchange, the NPT recognized the absolute right of all signatories to nuclear programs "for peaceful purposes," and the nuclear weapons states agreed to provide technical assistance and equipment for the development of peaceful programs. Nearly every country in the world has now signed the NPT.

In 1974, Iran entered into a safeguards agreement with the International Atomic Energy Agency (IAEA), giving the IAEA the right to inspect Iran's nuclear sites and verify that it was not developing nuclear weapons. Iran continued to work with the West, including the United States, throughout the 1970s to acquire technology and equipment necessary for its peaceful nuclear program.

Everything changed in 1979 when Iran's shah, Reza Pahlavi, was overthrown. Ayatollah Ruhollah Khomeini, who had been exiled by the shah, returned to Tehran, proclaimed the establishment of the new Islamic Republic of Iran, and became its first supreme leader. On November 2, 1979, militant Islamic students stormed the U.S. embassy in Tehran. The Iranians would ultimately hold fifty-two Americans hostage for 444 days.

Under Khomeini, Iran became the world's leading state sponsor of terror, targeting the United States, our allies, and our interests around the world. Iran's Islamic Revolutionary Guard Corps, the IRGC, oversees the suppression of opposition inside Iran and its support for terror externally, providing financing and training to groups like Hezbollah and Hamas. The IRGC also controls Iran's nuclear program and a large and growing share of the Iranian economy. Therefore, lifting sanctions on Iran's financial, oil, and transport sectors, and releasing frozen assets to the government in Tehran directly benefits the IRGC.

President Obama has also taken the previously unimaginable step of agreeing to lift sanctions on the IRGC itself, including on its military arm, the Quds Force. The Obama nuclear deal also provides for lifting sanctions on Quds Force commander Qassim Suleimani. Suleimani reports directly to Iran's supreme leader, Ayatollah Ali Khamenei. The Quds Force is responsible for the deaths of members of the U.S. armed forces in Iraq and Afghanistan. In Iraq, they trained, supplied, and funded Shi'ite militias to fight against our forces. Hezbollah, the Lebanese terrorist group sponsored by Iran, assisted the Quds Force in this effort. In Afghanistan, Iran has provided weapons and training to the Taliban and other insurgent groups. In both countries, improvised explosive devices with distinctive markings indicating that they were manufactured in Iran have accounted for significant numbers of American casualties. According to a Pentagon report published in October 2014, Iran was providing support for the killing of American soldiers in Afghanistan as Iranian representatives sat across the negotiating table from Secretary of State John Kerry in the nuclear talks.

Today, the Quds Force is active on battlefields across the Middle East. According to former director of the Defense Intelligence Agency General Michael Flynn, the Iranian regime significantly increased its destabilizing activities during negotiations over Iran's nuclear program. As of this writing, Iran or its proxies control at least four Arab capitals: Baghdad, Damascus, Sana'a, and Beirut, with a power and influence that is spreading.

ON WEDNESDAY, AUGUST 14, 2002, an Iranian opposition group held a press conference in Washington to announce that Iran was operating two secret nuclear facilities. They had evidence of a uranium enrichment facility near Natanz and a heavy-water reactor at Arak. As a signatory to the Non-Proliferation Treaty, Iran is required to report any new nuclear construction to the IAEA. These secret sites had not been disclosed.

Iran continued to claim that its program was peaceful in nature, but countries that are pursuing peaceful nuclear energy programs don't hide their nuclear facilities underground. They don't build heavy-water reactors. They don't insist on enriching their own uranium. They don't build intercontinental ballistic missiles.

The disclosure of these secret sites brought immediate requests by the IAEA for international inspectors to visit, which they did in February 2003. The inspectors identified two facilities at Natanz: an aboveground plant that could hold 1,000 centrifuges and underground facilities with room for 50,000. France, Germany, and Britain, known as the EU-3, began negotiations with Iran to halt work at these sites.

In March 2003, the United States and coalition forces invaded

Iraq. In the fall of 2003, the Iranians agreed to stop construction at the Natanz site and signed an additional agreement with the IAEA that would provide greater inspection access to any suspicious site inside the country. Iran had fought the Iraqi Army for a decade without being able to defeat it, and watching the Americans prevail in a matter of weeks likely focused the thinking of Iranian leaders. They halted portions of their nuclear program—temporarily it turned out—almost surely to keep America from targeting them next.

In a dance that would be repeated many times over the years, the Iranians played for time. They would agree to cooperate with inspections and then obstruct and delay. They would agree to suspend activities and then restart them. They would pretend to negotiate in good faith while they marched ahead aggressively with their nuclear program.

Iran's current president, Hassan Rouhani, led his country's nuclear negotiations during this period. Although the Obama administration has portrayed him as a "moderate" and a "reformer," he oversaw Iran's nuclear duplicity. He described it himself in his 2011 book: "While we were talking to the Europeans in Tehran, we were installing equipment in Isfahan."

From 2003 to 2005, the EU-3 offered the Iranians many opportunities and incentives to maintain a peaceful program while ending the activities that were clearly aimed at producing a weapon. Iran was offered, for example, light-water reactors and the feedstock needed to fuel them. The Iranians weren't interested. There simply was no benefit or "carrot" the international community could propose that was more valuable to Tehran than a nuclear weapon.

On August 3, 2005, Mahmoud Ahmadinejad assumed office as Iran's new president. On August 10, Iran broke the IAEA seals on their uranium enrichment facility at Isfahan. In January 2006, they broke the seals on three more facilities and restarted uranium enrichment at Natanz. The IAEA reported Iran's ongoing violations to the United Nations Security Council, which adopted UN Security Council resolution 1696 demanding that Iran halt all enrichment activity or face sanctions.

The EU-3 negotiations broke down and attention turned to imposing costs on Iran for continuing to pursue a nuclear weapons program. It was not immediately evident what additional steps America could take. Beginning with the 1979 seizure of the U.S. embassy in Tehran, America had imposed a series of ever-expanding sanctions on the Iranian regime. By 2005, the conventional wisdom was that Iran was "sanctioned out." That turned out not to be true. The brilliant work of a few dedicated public servants in the United States Treasury Department made it clear that there were additional and painful costs that could be imposed on the Iranian regime.

Stuart Levey, undersecretary of the Treasury for terrorism and financial intelligence, is probably the most important player you've never heard of in the effort to stop Iran's nuclear program. In the aftermath of 9/11, the Treasury Department used new authorities, granted through statute and executive order, to track and stop terrorist financing. Treasury could use the same approach, Levey deduced, to target and block the illicit activities of rogue regimes like North Korea, Iran, and Libya. The real innovation was to engage the private sector in the effort, actively and aggressively.

In the past, the United States had focused on convincing foreign governments to cut off potentially lucrative commercial activity with a sanctioned country, but the private sector frequently resisted and put pressure on their governments not to support the American efforts. Levey, Secretary of the Treasury Hank Paulson, and a team that included Assistant Secretary of the Treasury Juan Zarate and other experts realized they could turn this approach on its head.

America's global financial power is such that any bank operating in international markets is likely to need access to the American financial system. Any transaction denominated in dollars, for example, must at some point pass through a dollar-clearing account, most often in New York. Banks that are cut off from America's networks find it hard to survive.

Section 311 of the Patriot Act gives the United States Treasury the power to isolate banks that traffic in illicit activities by designating them as "primary money laundering concerns." "No number strikes fear into bankers' hearts," the *Economist* reported in June 2015, "like 311. . . . For firms badly behaved or unlucky enough to be targeted, a 311 designation is more often than not a death sentence."

Iran's vulnerability was due in part to the fact that the regime regularly mixes illicit with legitimate financial activity in order to hide the illicit activity. The IRGC has so thoroughly infiltrated Iran's economic and financial systems that it is nearly impossible to be sure any transaction involving Iranian businesses is free of taint.

In 2006, after attempts at diplomacy had failed and the Iranians had relaunched their uranium enrichment efforts, President Bush undertook a multitrack approach to stop their nuclear program. On one track, Secretary of State Condoleezza Rice announced that the United States would join direct negotiations between the Europeans and the Iranians, if the Iranians suspended their enrichment and reprocessing activities. When the Iranians rejected the offer, action moved to the United Nations Security Council, where the United States would secure four resolutions over the next two years, including three that were unanimous, demanding that Iran halt its uranium enrichment and plutonium reprocessing efforts and imposing sanctions when Iran failed to comply.

The second track was Treasury's. Levey began traveling the world meeting directly with the CEOs and compliance officers of financial institutions and warning them about Iran's illicit financial activities.

Levey's weapon in these meetings was information. He would begin his briefings with an overall view of Iran's economic structure and financial system, explaining, among other things, the infiltration of the IRGC across Iran's economy and its use of front companies to hide illegal transactions. These transactions might involve financing for terrorism or the acquisition of goods necessary for Iran's military or nuclear program. Levey would conclude his briefings by providing specific information to the bank CEO about such mattters as illicit Iranian activity in accounts held in that very bank.

Former assistant secretary Juan Zarate explained, "These meetings were not intended to be an accusation of complicity . . . but a wake up call to lift the veil of Iranian financial activity and raise suspicions." The Treasury Department was "exposing Iranian behavior" and, in Zarate's words, signaling "that it would not be ignored, especially if Iranian money was flowing through the banking system."

No other nation in the world has the financial power to do what Levey and the U.S. Department of the Treasury did. Their message to foreign governments and financial institutions was not political. It was about safeguarding the American and, by extension, the international financial sector by blocking tainted transactions. Following these meetings, banks often closed questionable accounts and began limiting their exposure to Iranian businesses.

The Treasury Department also used its authorities to directly target Iranian banks and cut them off from the international financial system. In September 2006, Bank Saderat, which was used by the Iranian government to funnel funds to Hezbollah, Hamas, and other terrorist organizations, was designated as a terrorist-financing institution. In January 2007, Bank Sepah was designated for its role in funding proliferation activities. In October 2007, Bank Mellat was designated for providing financial services for Iran's efforts to acquire nuclear materials. In December 2008, Bank Melli and its affiliates were similarly designated.

Other governments followed America's lead. In June 2008, the European Union targeted Bank Melli and froze its assets. In September 2008, Australia imposed sanctions on Bank Melli and Bank Saderat. Banks across the Arab world also cut back their dealings with Iran, as did the Chinese.

At the same time, Iranian businesses most closely tied to terror financing or nuclear proliferation activities were targeted. These included Iranian shipping and insurance concerns. In October 2007, the United States designated the IRGC and Iran's Ministry of Defense, cutting them off from the international financial system for their role in attempting to acquire nuclear capabilities and supporting terror.

By the time Barack Obama took office in January 2009, the Bush administration had put in place an unprecedented series of sanctions targeting Iran. The Treasury Department had magnified the impact of the formal designations through Undersecretary Levey's work with private financial institutions and businesses around the globe. President Obama wisely asked Undersecretary Levey to continue to serve at the Treasury Department in the new administration. Then he told him to put his work isolating Iran on hold.

President Obama was going to try a different approach. He had campaigned on a policy of engagement, and continuing to squeeze the Iranians financially was inconsistent with an outstretched American hand. The problem with our Iran policy, as the Obama administration saw it, was not the Iranians. "When we took office, let me remind you," Vice President Biden explained, ". . . we were the problem." The theory seemed to be that an American lack of willingness to engage was causing the Iranians to pursue a nuclear weapons program.

Engagement, of course, had been tried. In October 1979, after the Islamic Revolution but before the Iranians stormed our embassy and took our diplomats hostage, President Carter's national security advisor, Zbigniew Brzezinski, met with a delegation of Iranian officials in Algiers. Brzezinski told the delegation that America would recognize the new regime and could form an alliance with them. We shared a common enemy in the Soviet Union, he explained, and we were prepared to sell the new Iranian regime the weapons we had planned to sell the shah. The Iranians rejected all Brzezinski's offers. Three days later the American embassy in Tehran was overrun.

Twenty-one years later, on March 17, 2000, the Clinton administration made its own public effort at reconciliation. The Iranian regime had long demanded an apology from the United States for the CIA's alleged role in the 1953 coup that overthrew Iranian prime minister Mohammad Mosaddeq. Calculating that fulfilling this request would open the door to a new era of cooperation, Secretary of State Madeleine Albright apologized. Calling the coup "a setback for Iran's political development," Albright said, "it is easy to see now why many Iranians continue to resent this intervention by America in their internal affairs." She also indicated we had been wrong to support the shah and invoked President Clinton in asserting that "the United States must bear its fair share of responsibility for the problems that have arisen in U.S.-Iranian relations." It was a remarkable statement, suggesting America's conduct had been on a par with that of a nation that had held our citizens hostage and carried out terrorist attacks against us.

A few days later Ayatollah Khamenei delivered the Iranian response. He mockingly noted that the Americans had finally admitted to their terrible sins, but why should he be impressed? "An admission years after the crime was committed," he said, "while they might be committing similar crimes now, will not do the Iranian nation any good."

On Friday, March 20, 2009, President Obama launched his own outreach effort. In a video greeting on the occasion of the Persian holiday of Nowruz, the president offered a reinterpretation of thirty years of U.S.-Iranian relations. Gone were America's objections to the storming of our embassy, the holding hostage of our diplomats, the killing of our soldiers, the Iranian-sponsored terrorist attacks on our people and interests. In their place, according to Obama, we just had "serious differences." In this view, there wasn't any moral distinction between the way America and Iran had operated on the world stage, there were just matters on which we seriously didn't agree. Addressing his remarks directly to the regime in Tehran, the president said:

> *So, in this season of new beginnings, I would like to speak clearly to Iran's leaders. We have serious differences that have grown over time. My administration is now committed to diplomacy that addresses the full range of issues before us, and to pursuing constructive ties among the United States, Iran, and the international community. This process will not be advanced by threats. We seek instead engagement that is honest and grounded in mutual respect.*
>
> *You, too, have a choice. The United States wants the Islamic Republic of Iran to take its rightful place in the community of nations. You have that right—but it comes with real responsibilities, and that place cannot be reached through terror or arms, but rather through peaceful actions that demonstrate the true greatness of the Iranian people and civilization.*

The next day, Iran's supreme leader, Ayatollah Khamenei, responded. He told a crowd chanting "Death to America!" that the United States was hated around the world for its arrogance.

The president continued to pursue engagement, keeping the Treasury Department financial sanctions program on hold and providing valuable time for the Iranians to pursue their nuclear program. Building and maintaining the international pressure brought to bear through private banks cutting off business relationships with Iran required constant tending. The longer the program was on hold, the less effective it would be and the harder to reinvigorate.

In April 2009, Secretary of State Clinton announced the United States was prepared to join Britain, France, Russia, and China in directly negotiating with Iran. There were no preconditions. In May 2009, President Obama sent a letter to Iran's supreme leader. According to press accounts, the president's letter stressed that America sought "cooperation in regional and bilateral issues" and a resolution of disagreements about Iran's nuclear program.

Two months later, Iran held a presidential election. On Saturday, June 14, massive protests erupted in the streets of Tehran when the Interior Ministry announced that President Ahmadinejad had been reelected with 62.6 percent of the vote. Supporters of former prime minister Mir Hossein Mousavi charged that the election had been rigged and took to the streets. The mullahs, faced with the most significant challenge to their legitimacy in the thirty-year history of their rule, responded with violence to crush the protests. President Obama's initial response was silence, followed by tepid criticism of the mullahs' actions. Any support he expressed for the protesters could put his efforts to court the regime in jeopardy.

In September 2009, French president Nicolas Sarkozy, British prime minister Gordon Brown, and President Obama announced the discovery of a secret Iranian uranium enrichment facility on an Iranian military base outside Qom. The Iranians claimed the facility was for peaceful purposes, and Ahmadinejad declared, "I don't think Mr. Obama is a nuclear expert."

In a pattern that would be repeated many times over the course of the next six years, Iranian cheating was met with the offer of a deal. The Obama administration proposed a swap: if the Iranians agreed to ship 80 percent of their enriched uranium to Russia, they would receive the fuel they needed for the Tehran Research Reactor. The Iranians went along for a while, buying time while they continued to enrich, but then the supreme leader publicly criticized the offer, ending the round of negotiations.

Back in Washington, Stuart Levey provided a briefing for the National Security Council on restarting the effort to isolate Iran financially. UN ambassador Susan Rice objected. She argued that the United States should seek a new UN Security Council resolution before restarting Treasury's program. President Obama agreed with Rice, and Levey's program remained on hold.

Congress began work on a new round of legislatively imposed sanctions. Although President Obama claims credit for implementing an historically tough and extensive set of sanctions on Iran, a review of the record demonstrates that his administration, and Secretary Clinton's State Department, in particular, opposed and attempted to water down every congressional effort to impose tighter sanctions on Iran.

Secretary Clinton's deputy James Steinberg sent a letter to Senate Foreign Relations Committee chairman John Kerry in December 2009 explaining that the State Department had "serious substantive concerns" about the "unintended foreign policy consequences" that could be caused by the sanctions legislation under consideration. Steinberg wrote that the administration was worried about the bill's "inflexibility," in particular. Secretary Clinton's team did not succeed in killing the legislation, but they were able to weaken the sanctions provisions and delay the final bill, the Comprehensive Iran Sanctions, Accountability, and Divestment Act (CISADA), providing yet more time for Iranian uranium enrichment activities. President Obama ultimately signed CISADA into law in July 2010.

As it became clear CISADA was not having a sufficient impact on the Iranian nuclear program, a bipartisan group of ninety-two senators wrote to President Obama urging that he "impose crippling sanctions on Iran's financial system by cutting off the [Central Bank of Iran]." In November, a bipartisan group of senators introduced amendments to the 2012 defense authorization bill to target Iran's oil industry and central bank. Secretary Clinton and President Obama opposed the sanctions. Despite aggressive efforts by the Obama NSC, Treasury Department, and State Department, detailed in a piece in the *Weekly Standard* by Joel Winton, titled "Rewriting History: The Real Hillary Record on Iran Sanctions," the amendment passed unanimously, 100–0.

To his credit, President Obama had given the green light to Treasury to relaunch its efforts in the summer of 2010 after a new UN Security Council resolution was passed imposing additional sanctions on Iran. The combined effect of the new multilateral sanctions, additional U.S. sanctions, and Treasury's financial isolation campaign started to have a profound impact on Iran's economy. Getting the sanctions lifted became a top Iranian priority.

It should be noted, however, that there is no evidence that even these sanctions, tougher than any implemented before, had an impact on the Iranian nuclear program. The reason for their apparent ineffectiveness may well be that the Obama administration began looking for ways to relieve the pressure on Iran almost as soon as the new sanctions regime was in place. Six months after UNSC resolution 1929 was passed, Secretary Clinton started working with the Sultan of Oman to open a secret back channel for direct negotiations between the United States and Iran. A senior official in one of the governments in the Middle East described what happened next this way: "Just when the sanctions started working and Iran was feeling real economic pressure, Obama threw them a lifeline."

The Associated Press has reported that the secret meetings launched by Secretary Clinton began in mid-2011. According to Clinton the first US-Iran meeting took place in Oman in July 2012. In either case, it was in these meetings, according to senior Obama administration officials, that the outline of the nuclear framework agreement signed between Iran and the United States in November 2013 began to emerge. Two items in particular were of the utmost importance to Iran: They wanted the Americans to agree to drop the long-standing demand of the international community that Iran halt its uranium enrichment programs; and they wanted immediate sanctions relief. Iran also managed to secure a commitment that the United States would provide nearly $12 billion in cash payments, from frozen Iranian assets, over the course of the negotiations. The Iranians are reputed to be excellent negotiators, but getting the United States to cave on two fundamental points *prior* to the beginning of the actual negotiating, while also securing a commitment that the Iranians would be paid to stay at the negotiating table, must have surpassed Tehran's highest hopes. It also set a pattern for concession after concession that followed during the framework negotiations—none made by the Iranians.

The most damaging of the original American concessions, by far, was the Obama team's willingness to allow Iran to continue to enrich. This position immediately gutted all six UN Security Council resolutions passed over the previous decade demanding a halt to Iran's enrichment activities. It also seriously threatened the entire nuclear nonproliferation structure, codified in the NPT, which has been in place since 1968. The NPT guarantees every nation the right to peaceful nuclear programs. The Iranians extend this, asserting that they have a right to "peaceful nuclear programs, *including the right to enrich.*" These five words open the possibility of many other nations demanding this nonexistent right and moving forward with their own enrichment programs.

We now know that a number of President Obama's key policy decisions, including his decision in 2013 not to enforce the red line he had drawn concerning Syria's chemical weapons use, were made while these secret talks were ongoing. As we discussed in chapter 4, failing to act against the Syrian regime, after it blatantly violated the red line Obama had drawn, damaged America's credibility and handed a propaganda victory to ISIS. President Obama's decision not to strike Bashar al-Assad was likely an effort to avoid offending the Iranians, Assad's patrons.

In an October 2014 letter to Ayatollah Khamenei, the president emphasized that America's military operation against ISIS in Iraq and Syria would not target Assad or his forces. Since then, the lack of any coherent American strategy to defeat ISIS has opened the way for Iran to step in, increasing its regional role, presence, and responsibility at the expense of America's allies and interests in the region, not to mention the people of Iraq and Syria.

ON JULY 14, 2015, President Obama announced a new nuclear agreement had been reached with Iran. An early indication of how unfavorable the deal was for the United States—and how favorable to Iran—was the president's speech about it from the red-carpeted Cross Hall of the White House. Had the deal been a fair one, he would have spoken frankly about it. Instead, within the first two minutes of the Cross Hall speech, the president told three falsehoods about the agreement.

The first falsehood was his claim that the deal "will prevent [Iran] from obtaining a nuclear weapon." The truth is the opposite: This agreement will guarantee an Iranian nuclear arsenal. It allows the Iranians to maintain every element of their nuclear infrastructure and removes restrictions from their nuclear program within a decade. Even if one assumes for the sake of argument that the Iranians comply with the deal for the next ten years, at that point, they will have the ability, as the president has himself admitted, to achieve almost immediate nuclear breakout. The ten-year "sunset" provision is most accurately understood as the sun rising on an Iran armed with nuclear weapons. The president's assertion that the Iranians have "pledged to the international community that they will not develop a nuclear weapon" is of little comfort, given that the Iranians have cheated on every nuclear agreement into which they have ever entered.

The president's second falsehood was that the deal "stopped the spread of nuclear weapons in this region." In fact, the agreement guarantees and even accelerates it by legitimizing for the first time ever an Iranian uranium enrichment program, something previously held by the United Nations and the International Atomic Energy Agency to be illegal. Combine this with the removal of other key restraints, such as those on Iran's ballistic missile program (about which more below), on its ability to ship conventional weapons to terrorists, and on the IRGC, which oversees Iran's support for terror and is fomenting chaos and violence as Iran attempts to dominate the region, and there is more than enough reason for Iran's neighbors to decide they must pursue their own nuclear weapons programs. Having watched President Obama retreat from the Middle East, and realizing that he capitulated on nearly every key issue in the negotiations with Iran, is it any wonder our allies have concluded they can't count on us to defend them? Is it surprising they would question our ability to use our nuclear umbrella to protect them as they watch President Obama cut the size of our nuclear arsenal? The Obama deal will not stop nuclear proliferation. It will unleash it.

The president's third falsehood was that "the international community will be able to verify that the Islamic Republic of Iran will not develop a nuclear weapon." The claim is deceitful in two ways, first by misstating again what the agreement will accomplish. It will not keep the Iranians from developing a nuclear weapon. It legitimizes a pathway for them to do so. Secondly, it presents the verification provisions as though they were foolproof, which they are far from being. They are also a world away from what the administration publicly said they would be. Energy Secretary Ernest Moniz said in April that "we expect to have anywhere-anytime access." The same month President Obama's deputy national security advisor Ben Rhodes said the deal would include "go anywhere-anytime, twenty-four/seven access as it relates to the nuclear facilities that Iran has." Despite these reassurances, the Obama Iran deal gives the Iranians months to delay any request from international inspectors for access to suspicious sites, more than enough time for Iran to remove evidence of illicit activity. Instead of ensuring the international community's ability to verify, the Obama Iran deal seems structured to allow any deception that might go on to be unverifiable.

A truly verifiable deal would include not only go-anywhere-anytime inspections, but it would also require that Iran disclose all its nuclear activity, past and present, military and civilian. Such knowledge is essential for knowing the starting point from which future nuclear developments begin. Secretary of State John Kerry seemed to understand this when he was asked in April 2015 whether the United States would accept a deal in which the Iranians failed to disclose their past activity. "No," he replied, "They have to do it. It will be done. If there's going to be a deal, it will be done." Two months later, in June 2015, Kerry's position had evolved. "We're not fixated on Iran specifically accounting for what they did at one time or another," he said. "We know what they did. We have no doubt. We have absolute knowledge with respect to the certain military activities that they were engaged in." No responsible American official would make such a claim, and one wonders what changed between April and June. Likely it was the Iranians' making clear that they wouldn't accept such a provision.

According to the agreement reached in July, Iran is not required to provide a complete disclosure of its past or current activities. There is nothing in the agreement about the military facility at Parchin, for example, where Iran has engaged in suspicious nuclear-related activity and to which the IAEA has been denied access. There are secret annexes—or side deals—that reportedly govern verification at Parchin and other sensitive sites. The IAEA has refused to share these annexes with Congress. On July 22, 2015, Secretary of State Kerry admitted he hadn't seen them either. In other words, despite promising that he would never accept a deal based on trust, President Obama has agreed to a deal in which he has no idea what some of the most important verification provisions are.

On the day after the agreement with Iran was announced, the president held a press conference in which he made assertions similar to those in his July 14 speech—claims that deny facts and logic. Journalist and Middle East analyst Omri Ceren astutely noted, "As always, you're left asking, 'Does the president really believe this? And would it be better or worse if he did?' "

In so many ways the Obama Iran agreement is worse than those concerned about it could possibly have imagined before the negotiations concluded. On June 10, 2015, former undersecretary of state for arms control and disarmament Robert Joseph testified about the danger of an agreement that did not address Iran's ballistic missile program. That failure, combined with other flaws in the agreement, Joseph testified, would mean that "the threat to the U.S. homeland and to our NATO allies of an Iran armed with nuclear-tipped ballistic missiles will increase not decrease under the anticipated agreement." What the president had in mind, it turns out, was even more dangerous. Rather than stopping Iran's ballistic missile program, the Obama deal lifts restrictions that prohibit Iran from building these missiles.

One week before the deal was announced, Secretary of Defense Ash Carter and Chairman of the Joint Chiefs of Staff Martin Dempsey testified that American security depended upon "stopping Iran from having an ICBM program." Carter said this was important because "the 'I' in ICBM stands for 'intercontinental,' which means having the capability to fly from Iran to the United States, and we don't want that. That's why we oppose [Iran's] ICBMs." General Dempsey directly addressed the Obama-Iran agreement being finalized. "Under no circumstances," he said, "should we relieve pressure on Iran relative to ballistic missile capabilities and arms trafficking." The president agreed, nonetheless, to lift both restrictions, enabling Iran to build ICBMs after eight years and to traffic in conventional weapons after five.

In the run-up to the agreement with Iran, the president made promise after promise that he subsequently broke. He said that sanctions wouldn't be lifted until the Iranians fulfilled their obligations, but during the negotiating process itself he lifted sanctions in a wide array of areas, including some sanctions that were imposed for non-nuclear purposes. In addition, over the course of the negotiations, the United States provided nearly $12 billion in cash from frozen Iranian assets to the regime in Tehran—and according to the agreement announced in July, they will have access to over $150 billion more. Iran will also have a financial windfall as it begins selling its oil on world markets and accessing international financial and commercial markets. This money will undoubtedly be used by Iran to fund its military and terror-sponsoring activities around the globe. President Obama's claims that Iranian President Rouhani will be constrained by his campaign promises to use the money to improve the lives of everyday Iranians were absurd.

The president promised international sanctions would "snap back" into place if Iran cheats. Instead, the agreement actually commits the European Union and the UN Security Council to *refrain* from re-imposing or re-introducing sanctions lifted under this agreement. It also prohibits the UN Security Council and the European Union from imposing any new nuclear-related sanctions. The United States similarly commits "to refrain from re-introducing or re-imposing" sanctions that are lifted under this agreement. If those commitments aren't sufficient to prevent any attempt to impose "snapback" sanctions, the agreement says "Iran . . . will treat such re-introduction or re-imposition of sanctions . . . or such an imposition of new nuclear-related sanctions, as grounds to cease performing its commitments" under the agreement. If Iran cheats, and we learn about it despite the absence of a go-anywhere-anytime verification regime, the protracted international debate about whether the cheating happened and how significant it was will take place under the shadow of the Iranian threat—codified in the agreement—to abandon all their commitments. If history is any guide, President Obama will argue that the trade-off isn't worth it. After all, one can almost hear him saying, we wouldn't want to risk Iran abandoning the deal.

President Obama assures us that his "commitment to Israel's security is, and always will be, unshakeable." Although no nation is under greater threat from a nuclear-armed Iran than the state of Israel, President Obama has consistently demonstrated more determination to constraining Israeli action than Iranian action. The impact on Israel's security of Obama's attempted détente with Iran has already become evident. On January 18, 2015, Israel struck a convoy traveling in the Golan Heights. The convoy was carrying senior Hezbollah and Iranian officers, including a general in the IRGC. "By treating Syria as an Iranian sphere of influence," former national security council senior director Michael Doran noted, "Obama is allowing the shock troops of Iran to dig in on the border of Israel—not to mention the border of Jordan."

President Obama has said consistently that all options remain on the table to prevent Iran from attaining a nuclear weapon, including the military option. That was until May 31, 2015, anyway. In an interview on Israeli TV that day, the president took the military option off the table. His deal was really the only option, he said, because military strikes wouldn't be effective. "A military solution won't fix it," he continued, "even if the U.S. participates." The Iranians had already noted the change. "There are very few people in today's world who take these military threats seriously," Ayatollah Khamenei said in a speech in July 2014.

The president has also agreed as part of this deal to remove restrictions on those who facilitated, over the last thirty-five years, Iran's efforts to gain a nuclear weapon. In particular, he has agreed to remove sanctions on individuals who were at the heart of the worst nuclear proliferation network in history, the A. Q. Khan network. In a little-noticed action on April 3, 2015, the day after the outlines of the framework agreement were announced, the U.S. Treasury Department lifted sanctions on B.S.A. Tahir, the man who met the Iranians in the Dubai hotel with the briefcase full of centrifuge designs in 1987. Tahir was the point man, providing technology and centrifuge parts as the Iranians built their illicit nuclear program. He was the CEO, CFO, COO, chief money-launderer, and right-hand man for A. Q. Khan and his global proliferation network. In the deal announced on July 14, 2015, sanctions were also lifted on Gerhard Wisser, another of the key suppliers for Iran in A. Q. Khan's network. Why would President Obama, who claims to want to halt proliferation, lift sanctions on two of the world's worst offenders? Obviously, it was an Iranian demand as part of the deal, and there seems to be no limit to President Obama's appetite for concessions.

The president has said repeatedly that he is committed to stopping Iran's support for terror and its destabilizing activities across the Middle East. Instead, he now seems intent on ushering in an era of Iran as a political, economic, and military power. Not only has he been unwilling to take action against Iran's interests in the Middle East, he seems to have convinced himself that it is in America's interest for Iran to play a dominant role in the region. And the concessions he has granted in this agreement enhance their ability to do so.

One principle the president has lived up to is something he announced in his June 2009 Cairo speech. "No single nation," he said, "should pick and choose which nations hold nuclear weapons." It is as though President Obama sees no moral difference between an Iranian nuclear weapon and an American one. The agreement he approved in July 2015 cedes our right to keep the world's greatest state sponsor of terror from obtaining the world's worst weapons.

President Obama told us no deal is better than a bad deal. Now he tells us this deal, which is so bad it *guarantees* the very things he said he was trying to prevent, is the only option. There was another option: America could have negotiated from a position of strength. The president could have left the sanctions in place instead of releasing the pressure just as Iran was beginning to feel the impact. He could have left the military option on the table instead of announcing in May 2015 that there was no workable military solution. He could have recognized that the credible threat of war makes war less, not more, likely. He could have learned from the example of Ronald Reagan's negotiations with the Soviets at Reykjavik that no deal really is better than a bad deal, and some things cannot be conceded. He could have stood firm for the principle that Iran must not have a nuclear weapon.

He could have secured a deal that enhanced America's security. Instead, he agreed to one that puts us at risk.

The Obama nuclear agreement with Iran is tragically reminiscent of Prime Minister Chamberlain's Munich agreement. Both were negotiated from a position of weakness and conceded nearly everything to appease an ideological dictator. Hitler got Czechoslovakia. The mullahs in Tehran get billions of dollars and a pathway to a nuclear arsenal.

The July 14, 2015, agreement jettisons forty years of an international arms control regime, guts the United Nations Security Council's ability to restrict Iran's nuclear weapons program, ends prohibitions on Tehran's ability to build ballistic missiles to carry their nuclear warheads, lifts the embargo on the import of conventional weapons Iran uses and supplies to terrorists around the globe, and removes sanctions that have limited the ability of the IRGC to proliferate nuclear technology, support terror, and kill Americans. Munich led to World War II. The Obama agreement will lead to a nuclear-armed Iran, a nuclear arms race in the Middle East, and more than likely, the first use of a nuclear weapon since Hiroshima and Nagasaki.

RUSSIA

ON APRIL 25, 2005, Vladimir Putin delivered the Russian equivalent of a State of the Union address—his annual speech to the Federal Assembly of the Russian Federation. Speaking of the challenges facing Russia, he said it was necessary to consider Russia's recent history. "Above all, we should acknowledge that the collapse of the Soviet Union was a major geopolitical disaster of the century." Where most saw the triumph of freedom over tyranny, Putin saw geopolitical disaster. He has spent his years in office trying to restore what he believes Russia lost.

With bullying, extortion, blackmail, covert operations, the threat of nuclear strikes, and outright military invasion, Putin is desperately trying to reestablish Russia as a global power and reimpose Russian dominance over large swaths of Europe. The sovereignty of his neighbors is of little concern to him. Under the pretext of coming to the aid of Russian-speaking populations, Putin is using force to redraw the map of Europe. In the early years of the Obama administration, President Obama and Secretary Clinton were either unable or unwilling to recognize Putin's true intentions. When those intentions turned into actions, President Obama consistently failed to take any meaningful steps to stop him.

President Obama's approach to Russia began where his approach to Iran did—with the assumption that America was to blame for the tensions in the relationship. The problem was not Vladimir Putin's behavior but rather George Bush's. To drive this point home, and signal a time of new beginnings, Secretary of State Clinton presented Russian foreign minister Lavrov with the now-infamous "reset" button in front of the world's press in Geneva in March 2009. The button was a grand gesture, presented in a box tied up with a bow. After he opened the box, Lavrov looked down on the button as the cameras rolled. "You got it wrong," he said. The label on the button said "overcharge," not "reset." Later, Secretary Clinton's staff chased down the Russian delegation pleading with them to allow the Americans to fix the label.

The translation mistake could have happened to anyone. Secretary Clinton has explained that it was really the thought that counted, the policy behind the "reset" button. Unfortunately, the policy was as flawed as the translation on the label.

President Obama visited Moscow in July 2009. In a speech at the New Economic School, he described the world of the Cold War:

At that time, the American and Soviet armies were still massed in Europe, trained and ready to fight. The ideological trenches of the last century were roughly in place. Competition in everything from astrophysics to athletics was treated as a zero-sum game. If one person won, then the other had to lose.

It's the perfect picture of a world divided between two morally equivalent powers dug in to their individual "ideological trenches," conveniently leaving out that only one side oppressed, terrorized, built walls, and killed to keep its people within its borders. The Cold War, as Obama told it in Moscow that day, wasn't won or lost. It "reached a conclusion."

Twenty years later, Obama continued, America now rejected the idea of powerful nations leading a global world order. "As I said in Cairo, given our interdependence any world order that elevates one nation or one group of people over another will inevitably fail. The pursuit of power is no longer a zero-sum game—progress must be shared." In this new world, governed by an idealized "international system," Obama explained, "rules must be binding, violations must be punished, and words must mean something."

Obama's vision was simultaneously prescriptive and passive— these things all "must" happen, yet there is no mention of who will make them happen. "Progress must be shared"; states that attempt to dominate others "will inevitably fail." There was no recognition, and worse, no apparent understanding, that the triumph of freedom was the result of the *actions* of free nations—especially the United States. The Cold War simply "reached a conclusion," like a lecture does, or a particularly boring book. The president's failure to understand this fundamental truth—that freedom must be defended and America must lead that defense—has been the fatal flaw in his policies. It was on full display that day at the New Economic School in Moscow.

After serving two terms as Russia's president from 2000 to 2008, Vladimir Putin was prevented by the Russian constitution from serving a third. When Obama visited Moscow in the summer of 2009, Putin had stepped aside as president, although he was still running the country, and he hosted Obama at his country house outside Moscow.

The meeting opened with a lecture from Putin on America's misconduct and lies. Then he moved on to Russia's role in Europe. Putin had launched his efforts to regain lost Soviet territory with the 2008 invasion of Georgia, and now he demanded that the United States recognize Russia's sphere of influence over all the former Soviet republics. U.S. ambassador to Russia Michael McFaul called Putin's lecture "grossly inaccurate," adding, "but that's his theory of the world."

President Obama was nevertheless anxious to further the "reset" of the relationship. This meant eliminating irritants. The missile defense system planned for Poland and the Czech Republic was at the top of this list. In his speech at the New Economic School, the president acknowledged Russia's concerns and announced that the United States would be undertaking a review of the plans.

America's new Russia policy was causing grave concern in Central and Eastern Europe. As President Obama's trip to Moscow came to an end, twenty-two former heads of state, cabinet ministers, ambassadors, and scholars from Central and Eastern Europe published an open letter to the American president. They urged that America not walk away from Europe or give in to Russian bullying. "Our nations are deeply indebted to the United States," it began:

> Many of us know firsthand how important your support for our freedom and independence was during the Cold War years. U.S. engagement and support was essential for the success of our democratic transitions after the Iron Curtain fell twenty years ago. Without Washington's vision and leadership, it is doubtful that we would be in NATO and even the EU today.

It was critically important, they continued, that America "reaffirm its vocation as a European power and make clear that it plans to stay fully engaged on the continent." The free nations of Europe faced many challenges. Russia was at the top of the list. They were under no illusions as to Russia's plans. America shouldn't be, either. The leaders explained:

> *Our hopes that relations with Russia would improve and that Moscow would finally fully accept our complete sovereignty and independence after joining NATO and the EU have not been fulfilled. Instead Russia is back as a revisionist power pursuing a 19th century agenda with 21st century tactics. . . . It challenges our claims to our own historical experiences. It asserts a privileged position in determining our security choices. It uses overt and covert means of economic warfare, ranging from energy blockades and politically motivated investments to bribery and media manipulation in order to advance its interests and challenge the transatlantic orientation of Central and Eastern Europe.*

They stressed the critical importance of the planned missile defense installations in Poland and the Czech Republic. The system had become "a symbol of America's credibility and commitment to the region." Despite Russia's objections to the system, they wrote:

> *The small number of missiles involved cannot be a threat to Russia's strategic capabilities, and the Kremlin knows this. We should decide the future of the program as allies and based on the strategic plusses and minuses of the different technical and political configurations. The Alliance should not allow the issue to be determined by unfounded Russian opposition. Abandoning the program entirely or involving Russia too deeply in it without consulting Po-*

land or the Czech Republic can undermine the credibility of the United States across the whole region.

President Obama sided with the Russians. On September 17, 2009, he announced he was canceling the installations in Poland and the Czech Republic.

Both the Poles and the Czechs had expended significant political capital to secure parliamentary approval for the systems. They had been assured the project would proceed. "We heard first from the media," said Witold Waszczykowski, deputy in Poland's national security bureau. Poland's prime minister was so angry about the cancellation that he refused to take President Obama's call, which came at midnight Poland time. Foreign Minister Radek Sikorski spoke for many when he was overheard saying, "The Polish-American alliance is worthless, even harmful, as it gives Poland a false sense of security."

The president has been willing to gamble not just the security of our allies, but of the United States as well, by appeasing the Russians with regard to missile defense. On Monday, March 26, 2012, President Obama was caught on an open microphone making what he thought were private comments to Russian president Medvedev: "On all these issues, but particularly missile defense, this can be solved, but it's important for [Putin] to give me space." Putin had just been elected to return to the Russian presidency. "This is my last election," Obama continued. "After my election I have more flexibility." Medvedev replied, "I understand. I will transmit this information to Vladimir." In this case, Obama was good for his word. The following year, six weeks after President Obama was sworn in for his second term, the United States announced it was canceling the final stage of the European missile defense program the Russians had so strenuously opposed.

Three months later, Russian president Vladimir Putin welcomed Edward Snowden to Moscow, granting asylum to the traitor responsible for one of the greatest thefts of American intelligence in history. Whether Snowden was a Russian operative at the time he stole the U.S. secrets is the subject of debate, although it is hard to conceive of his landing in Moscow as a coincidence. What is clear is that he is fully Putin's tool now. On April 18, 2014, Snowden participated in one of Putin's government-controlled television shows. He "called in" to ask Putin, "Does Russia engage in mass surveillance of its population?" Of course not, Putin answered. Those who herald Snowden as a hero fighting for freedom ought to consider the propaganda services he is now providing for a man who, among other things, routinely has journalists and political opponents murdered.

A CENTERPIECE OF PRESIDENT Obama's reset with the Russians and of his efforts to reduce America's strategic nuclear arsenal was the New START Treaty he signed with Russian president Medvedev in Prague in April 2010. The original START Treaty, signed in 1991 by President George H. W. Bush and Soviet premier Gorbachev, had expired in 2009. The Obama administration heralded New START as a "serious step" toward achieving the president's announced goal of ridding the world of nuclear weapons.

Secretary Hillary Clinton described all the treaty would accomplish in a speech at the U.S. Institute of Peace in October 2009. In those early days of the administration, when promises were made and performance remained to be judged, she laid out lofty goals for this treaty. By reducing our nuclear arsenal, it would "bolster our national security." By setting "the stage for even deeper cuts," New START would make us even safer in the future. We had more nuclear weapons than we needed anyway, she said—"nuclear weapons in excess of our security needs," as she put it. Staying at those numbers would only "give other countries the motivation or excuse to pursue their own nuclear weapons." Reducing them would help us "build trust and avoid surprises."

It is not clear on what basis Secretary Clinton determined that cutting our arsenal would make us safer or that our nuclear forces were "in excess of our security needs." There had been no strategic review supporting this conclusion. A few months later, in testimony before the Senate Foreign Relations Committee, General Kevin Chilton, commander of the U.S. Strategic Command, addressed the size of our arsenal:

> *I do not agree that [the number of nuclear weapons in the U.S. arsenal] is more than is needed. I think the arsenal we have is exactly what is needed today to provide the deterrent. And I say this in light of—when we talk about the non-deployed portion of the arsenal—it is sized to be able to allow us to hedge against both technical failures in the current deployed arsenal and any geopolitical concerns that might . . . cause us to need more weapons deployed.*

The assertion about America's "excess" nuclear weapons was crafted to support President Obama's goal of getting to nuclear zero. Cutting America's arsenal through reductions adopted in New START was the easiest place to begin.

The Obama administration claimed that Russian nuclear forces would be reduced by a third as a result of the treaty. Instead, the Russians have used the years since the treaty was signed to increase spending on and modernization of their nuclear forces. As a result of the treaty, Russia now has more strategic warheads deployed than the United States does. Contrary to Secretary Clinton's promise of verifiable reductions that would build mutual trust, inspections have been tightly managed by the Russians and are far from go-anywhere-anytime.

While the United States has been reducing its nuclear arsenal, the Russians have also been violating the Intermediate-Range Nuclear Forces Treaty (INF Treaty), signed by President Reagan and Soviet premier Gorbachev in 1987, by testing missiles prohibited by the treaty. Secretary Kerry was reportedly briefed on the cheating in November 2012 when he was chairman of the Senate Foreign Relations Committee. The United States at first attempted to ignore the violations, then deal with them privately. The Russians, predictably, have denied the cheating and resisted all entreaties, including from President Obama, to stop cheating and comply with their treaty obligations.

ON FEBRUARY 28, 2014, as Russian troops crossed the Ukrainian border, Russian foreign minister Lavrov was on the phone with Secretary of State John Kerry. Lavrov failed to mention the troops on the march. Kerry briefed the press after the phone call, seemingly still unaware of events on the ground in Ukraine. Lavrov, Kerry reported, told him the Russians "do not intend to violate the sovereignty of Ukraine." Furthermore, they "are prepared to be engaged and involved in helping to deal with the economic transition that needs to take place."

A few hours later, when it became clear what was happening, President Obama issued a statement warning that "there will be costs" for any Russian invasion of Ukraine. After watching him fail to enforce the infamous red line in Syria, is it any wonder the Russians ignored this warning?

Since then, Putin has formally annexed Crimea and sent troops farther into Ukraine. In May 2015, Ukrainian president Petro Poroshenko warned that Russia had 50,000 troops deployed on Ukraine's border and more than 40,000 "separatist" proxy troops inside the country. Between the signing of the second cease-fire agreement in Minsk in February, and May 2015, the Ukrainian government reported it had lost twenty-eight towns to the Putin-backed "separatist fighters."

The United States and the European Union have imposed several rounds of sanctions but otherwise allowed the invasion to stand. Ukrainian requests for the United States to provide military support were met with blankets and meals ready to eat (MREs). Early in the crisis, President Obama took the military option off the table, explaining in March 2014, "We are not going to be getting into a military excursion in Ukraine."

Putin likely already knew that or else he wouldn't have risked the invasion in the first place. He is now turning his sights toward other countries in Europe with significant Russian-speaking populations, including the Baltic states, which are members of NATO. Putin's objective is threefold: 1) to return territory to Russia in an effort to reclaim its historic power and standing; 2) to diminish American power and influence in Europe; and 3) to destroy the NATO alliance.

Putin's invasion of Ukraine and annexation of Crimea have also done lasting damage to the international nuclear nonproliferation structure. In 1994, the United States, the United Kingdom, and Russia signed the Budapest Memorandum on Security Assurances, as Ukraine signed the NPT as a non-nuclear weapons state. In exchange for Kiev's agreement to send its nuclear materials and weapons to Russia, the U.S., U.K., and Russia agreed "to respect the independence and sovereignty and existing borders of Ukraine" and to "refrain from the threat or use of force against the territorial integrity or political independence of Ukraine." Russia is clearly in violation of its obligation under this agreement. Ambassador Eric S. Edelman, undersecretary of defense for policy under President George W. Bush, has pointed out that Russia's invasion of Ukraine, "left standing . . . will establish that security assurances offered by nuclear weapons states to states that willingly give up their weapons or weapons programs mean precisely nothing."

As the credibility of U.S. security guarantees comes into question, Moscow continues to escalate its nuclear rhetoric and threats. In March 2015, the Russian ambassador to Denmark warned that Russia would aim nuclear missiles at Danish ships if Denmark, a NATO member, joined NATO's missile-defense system. The Russians have deployed nuclear-capable missiles to Kaliningrad, which borders NATO members Poland and Lithuania, threatened to deploy nuclear weapons in Crimea, and simulated a nuclear attack on Warsaw during annual military exercises.

Cheating on the INF Treaty, building up and modernizing their strategic nuclear forces, undertaking increasingly hostile military exercises, threatening the use of nuclear force against countries that ally themselves with the West, invading and occupying Crimea, invading Ukraine—these are Russian policies in the aftermath of the reset. Not only did the reset clearly not improve U.S.-Russia relations, it did real damage to America's global strategic interests and standing.

Six years into the Obama administration, the Iranian nuclear weapons program is advancing rapidly, and Iran's power and influence have spread across the Middle East. The threat to America and our allies is grave and growing. Nuclear proliferation, which President Obama promised to halt, will instead be guaranteed as a result of the Obama nuclear deal allowing Iran to enrich uranium. Russia has invaded Ukraine, threatens the Baltic states and other European nations, is cheating on its obligations under the INF Treaty, is expanding its nuclear capabilities, and is providing advanced antiaircraft missiles to the Iranians. Meanwhile, President Obama reduces our nuclear arsenal, dismantles key elements of our missile defense, and imposes significant cuts on our conventional forces as he ushers Vladimir Putin back into the Middle East as a global power.

The "outstretched hand" to Iran and the "reset" with Russia have failed. Regimes like the ones in Tehran and Moscow don't "unclench their fists" when America "extends" a hand. They don't feel constrained by the "international system" or the "new world order" in which President Obama puts so much faith.

They arm themselves, mass their forces, capture territory, and seize their chance to dominate as much of the globe as possible with their tyrannical rule.

———◆———

SIX

Disarming America

We maintain our strength in order to deter and defend against aggression—to preserve freedom and peace.
—PRESIDENT RONALD REAGAN, MARCH 23, 1983

Our successful defense of freedom was not due to the words we used, but to the strength we stood ready to use on behalf of the principles we stand ready to defend.
—PRESIDENT JOHN F. KENNEDY, REMARKS
PREPARED FOR DELIVERY NOVEMBER, 22, 1963

For seventy years, the foundation of America's security has been the unmatched might of our armed forces. Our military superiority and our willingness to use our forces when necessary have guaranteed freedom and peace for millions around the world. We have been, in the words of President John F. Kennedy, "by destiny rather than by choice, the watchmen on the walls of world freedom."

It's a duty no other nation can fulfill. America does it at a tremendous cost but the price of inaction would be far higher. The 2014 bipartisan National Defense Panel explained it this way:

There is clearly a cost to this kind of leadership, but nowhere near what America paid in the first half of the 20th century when conflict was allowed to fester and grow until it rose to the level of general war. Indeed, our policy of active global engagement has been so beneficial and is so ingrained that those who would retreat from it have a heavy burden of proof to present an alternative that would better serve the security interests and well-being of the United States of America.

Today, this burden of proof rests with Barack Obama. He has overseen a reduction in U.S. military resources and readiness and a corresponding decline in the capacity of the United States to influence events in key parts of the world.

Dedicated to a vision of an idealized community of nations where none lead, none follow, and all progress is shared, President Obama apparently sees no danger in abandoning our leadership role in the world and diminishing our power. Convinced, it seems, of his own powers of persuasion, he sees little need for conventional or nuclear deterrence. Certain that "the arc of history bends toward justice," he appears unconcerned with the need to ensure America can defeat her enemies. In fact, in August 2014 and again in May 2015, he told the world we have no strategy to do so with respect to ISIS. Committed to a progressive agenda of immense increases in domestic spending, he strips the military of the resources it needs to defend the nation.

In President Obama's first year in office, his then defense secretary, Robert Gates, recognized the Pentagon would be facing increased pressure for cuts. He undertook what he described as a preemptive effort to prevent other policy makers and legislators from seeing "the defense budget as the place to solve the nation's deficit problems." Gates tasked each service to come up with savings from wasteful or underperforming programs. He promised the service chiefs—based on assurances from the president—that the exercise would not result in overall cuts in the defense budget. The services, Gates said, would be able to keep the funds they saved to invest "in programs of higher value."

After identifying approximately $78 billion in savings, Gates announced the cuts he planned to make at a press conference at the Pentagon on January 6, 2011. Even though the reductions he announced were deep and included cuts in the overall size of the Army and Marine Corps, Gates's effort to protect military spending from further cuts failed. He couldn't protect the defense budget from President Obama. On April 20, 2011, President Obama announced he would seek an additional $400 billion in cuts in military spending on top of what Gates had already proposed. Gates later described his sense of betrayal:

> I felt [President Obama] had breached faith with me both on the budget numbers for FY2012–2016 that [Obama budget director Peter] Orszag, [White House chief of staff] Rahm Emanuel, and I had agreed on—with Obama's approval—in the fall of 2009, and on the promise that Defense could keep all the efficiencies savings for reinvestment in military capabilities. . . . I felt that agreements with the Obama White House were good for only as long as they were politically convenient.

The situation grew even worse in August 2011, when Congress passed the Budget Control Act with a sequestration provision that would compound the damage already being done by President Obama's cuts. Part of an agreement to authorize lifting of the debt ceiling, the act provided for $1.2 trillion in spending cuts and, if a joint House and Senate committee failed to agree on a plan to cut another $1.2 trillion, then sequestration would go into effect. This would require across-the-board arbitrary cuts, 50 percent from domestic discretionary spending and 50 percent from the defense budget, even though military spending accounts for only roughly 17 percent of government spending.

Sequestration was intended to be an alternative so drastic that Congress would be compelled to find a way to avoid triggering it. They failed. Sequestration required roughly a $500 billion cut in the defense budget. This was additional to cut reductions the president had already ordered, resulting in more than $1 trillion being slashed from the nation's military budget over the next ten years.

Not only are the cuts far too deep, but the system of mandatory across-the-board reductions prevents the Department of Defense from having any input into the budget process. The funding cuts are arbitrary, rather than being the product of strategic assessments about what is necessary to defend the nation. There has not been a defense budget based on a serious analysis of the threats facing the nation and an assessment of the military capacity necessary to defend against those threats since the Gates 2012 budget.

It should also be noted that defense spending is not the main driver of our deficits. These cuts that are so devastating to our national security contribute little to the effort to get federal spending under control.

In January 2015, Army Chief of Staff General Ray Odierno told the Senate Armed Services Committee that because of the budget cuts, the U.S. Army is as unready as it has been at any other point in its 239-year history. At the same hearing, Air Force Chief of Staff General Mark Welsh said America's current aircraft fleet is "now the smallest and oldest in the history of our service." Added Welsh, "It is also the least ready—less than half of our combat coded units are fully combat capable." The Air Force, Welsh explained, "simply cannot get smaller and still meet the demand of current and projected operations."

In testimony in March 2015 before the Senate Appropriations

Committee, Chief of Naval Operations Admiral Jonathan Greenert warned that "Navy readiness is at its lowest point in many years." Marine Corps Commandant General Joseph Dunford told members of the House Appropriations Committee in February 2015, "Approximately half of our non-deployed units—and those are the ones that provide the bench to respond to unforeseen contingencies—are suffering personnel, equipment and training shortfalls." This will, he said, delay response times and put American lives at risk unnecessarily.

In July 2015 the Army announced it would be necessary to reduce the size of the force by 40,000 due to the budget reductions, leaving the Army smaller than it has been since before World War II. Budgetary constraints may also force the Navy to pull the USS *Theodore Roosevelt* out of the Persian Gulf in the fall of 2015 before another carrier is ready to take its place. The U.S. would then be left with no carrier presence in the Middle East in the midst of the growing threats from ISIS, al Qaeda, and Iranian-backed terror groups.

The difference between the amount the Pentagon projected it would need in the Gates 2012 budget and the amount it has received gives some idea of the critical nature of the situation. According to the National Defense Panel:

> *Including the 2015 budget request, the Defense Department has already lost $291 billion compared to the funding plan Secretary Gates recommended for fiscal year 2012, with $646 billion of still more reductions ahead unless current law is changed—bringing the projected total cuts to $937 billion.*

The situation is likely far worse than even the nearly $1 trillion shortfall the National Defense Panel warned about. The 2012 Gates budget was developed prior to the rise of ISIS, the establishment of the caliphate across a large swath of Iraq and Syria, the collapse of the Iraqi security forces, the aggressive spread of Iranian influence throughout the Middle East, the Russian invasion of Ukraine and annexation of Crimea, the loss of U.S. embassies in Libya, Yemen, and Damascus, and increasing aggression by China in the South China Sea and East China Sea. While Washington has been drastically cutting America's defense budgets, the threats to our nation have been growing. On January 28, 2015, General Odierno testified.

> *In my thirty-eight years of service, I have never seen a more dynamic and rapidly changing security environment than the one we face now. We no longer live in a world where we have the luxury of time and distance to respond to threats facing our nation. Instead, we face a diverse range of threats operating across domains and along seams—threats that are rapidly changing and adapting in response to our posture.*

Former secretary of state Henry Kissinger agreed. "The United States," he told the Senate Armed Services Committee, "has not faced a more diverse and complex array of crises since the end of the Second World War."

Given the increasingly dangerous threat environment, the United States should be increasing, not decreasing, its military capabilities. As Michèle Flournoy, who served as undersecretary of defense in the Obama administration, explained:

> *The international security environment is more complex and volatile, and as we have seen, I would emphasize it is only going to get more challenging. . . . U.S. leadership could not be at more of a premium right now. It's also a time that requires investment to ensure that we retain a strong and agile military to shape the*

international environment, to deter and defeat aggression when
we must, to reassure allies and partners, and to ensure that this
president and future presidents have the options that they need for
an increasingly dangerous world.

Rather than ensuring that America's military has the resources it needs to confront growing threats, President Obama and sequestration have set us on a path that will make it difficult, if not impossible, to provide for the nation's security in the decades ahead.

The president has adopted strategies that contribute to America's vulnerabilities. Since the Cold War, one of the fundamental tenets of our force structure has been the requirement that the United States maintain the ability to defeat two adversaries simultaneously in two different geographic theaters. The Defense Department's 1997 Quadrennial Defense Review explained the importance of this concept:

Maintaining this core capability is central to credibly deterring
opportunism—that is, to avoiding a situation in which an aggres-
sor in one region might be tempted to take advantage when U.S.
forces are heavily committed elsewhere—and to ensuring that the
United States has sufficient military capabilities to deter or defeat
aggression by an adversary that is larger or under circumstances
that are more difficult than expected. . . . Such a capability is the
sine qua non of a superpower and is essential to the credibility of
our overall national security strategy.

In 2012 President Obama abandoned this concept. Rather than sizing our force to be able to defeat enemies simultaneously in two theaters, President Obama's strategic guidance required only that "when U.S. forces are committed to a large scale operation in one region, they will be capable of denying the objectives of—or imposing unacceptable costs on—an opportunistic aggressor in a second region."

President Obama's troop reductions and budget cuts, compounded by sequestration, raise the question of whether the United States could carry out even this new limited objective. For example, although the strategy guidance envisions that the United States will be engaged in counterinsurgency and stability operations, it includes this caveat: "U.S. forces will no longer be sized to conduct large-scale, prolonged stability operations." In other words, regardless of what America's enemies have in mind, America will have sufficient forces to fight only small, short wars.

In his cover letter transmitting the new strategy, President Obama asserted that the United States was able to make changes to our national security strategy "as we end today's wars." His assumption is that withdrawal of American forces from Iraq and Afghanistan will make large-scale conflict a relic of the past. The president offered no facts to support such a notion, but one can see why he would want to believe it. A world without large wars provides a rationale for draconian cuts to the military.

At about the time the president issued his new defense strategic guidance, a senior Obama political appointee in the Pentagon called one of the authors of this book. It was likely that he was making courtesy calls to all the former secretaries of defense to preview the new strategic guidance. The official explained elements of the new strategy, especially what would become known as the "pivot to Asia." The idea seemed to be that because President Obama was ending the wars in Iraq and Afghanistan and we had killed Osama bin Laden, America could now turn its attention away from the Middle East and focus on Asia.

Asia is critically important, as we will discuss shortly, but America is a superpower, and our security depends upon an ability to focus on more than one geopolitical region at a time. A decision to "pivot" away from the Middle East entails significant risk, and one would assume such a major shift must have some strategic analysis behind it. When pressed for the strategic underpinning for the "pivot," the Pentagon official finally said, "Mr. Vice President, it's all about budgets." President Obama was pretending the war on terror was over so that he wouldn't have to continue to allocate significant military resources to the Middle East. He was pretending the world had become safer and more stable so that he wouldn't have to fund a force sized to fight and win two wars simultaneously.

The president's new strategic guidance was inadequate. It neither contemplated nor provided for the number or nature of the threats we face. Its purpose, as the Obama political appointee made clear, was to justify budget cuts.

Those cuts are not only causing a serious deficit in readiness and force structure, they are also resulting in the potential loss of preeminence for the United States military in key areas. "The nation faces unprecedented technology challenges," Representative Mac Thornberry, chairman of the House Armed Services Committee, has said, "with enemies and potential competitors working every day to exploit vulnerabilities in our capabilities." They are focused, he said, on developing technologies that will offset America's military strength. While much of the information about efforts under way in this area is classified, Chairman Thornberry quoted a senior Defense Department official describing the magnitude of the threat:

> We are at risk, and the situation is getting worse. . . . We came out
> of the Cold War with a very dominant military . . . [and] people
> have had quite a bit of time to . . . do things about how to defeat
> that force. And what I am seeing in foreign modernizations . . .
> is a suite of capabilities that are intended clearly . . . to defeat
> the American way of doing power projection, American way of

warfare . . . and, without saying too much about this, the Chinese, in particular—and, again, to a lesser extent, the Russians—are going beyond what we have done. They are making advances beyond what we currently have fielded.

For the last seventy years, the United States has had no peers in terms of the power of our military. The advent of cyberwarfare and the technological advances being made by our adversaries threaten to change that. In an appearance on *Fox News Sunday* on January 11, 2015, Chairman of the Joint Chief of Staff Martin Dempsey described the shift. "In every domain, we generally enjoy a significant military advantage," Dempsey said, "but we have peer competitors in cyber. . . . We don't have an advantage. It's a level playing field. And that makes this chairman very uncomfortable."

The United States also risks losing the preeminence of its nuclear arsenal. "Since the start of the atomic age," according to former undersecretary of state for arms control and international security Robert Joseph, "from Harry Truman to George W. Bush, the United States has sought to maintain, in the words of John F. Kennedy, a nuclear-weapons capability 'second to none.' " As Joseph went on to say, they have all understood "that it was vital for the United States not to concede nuclear pre-eminence to any country." During the Cold War, this meant ensuring that America's arsenal was of sufficient size and capability to deter the Soviet nuclear threat. Today, as the United States faces the reality of multiple adversaries armed with nuclear weapons, maintaining America's nuclear superiority is more important than ever, but President Obama has abandoned this goal.

In his first months in office President Obama proclaimed his commitment to eliminating all nuclear weapons. The first step, he explained, was to cut America's own arsenal. In pursuit of this goal,

President Obama signed the New START Treaty with the Russians. As former undersecretary of defense ambassador Eric Edelman noted in testimony before the Senate Foreign Relations Committee, New START has imposed significant limits on American capabilities while requiring no drawdowns in Russia's nuclear force structure. President Obama agreed, for example, to limit the number of deployed missile launchers to 700 for each side, despite the fact that the Department of Defense and Department of Energy found that a force of 900 launchers was necessary to maintain America's deterrence capability. In addition, Russia was already below 700 prior to the treaty, so this limitation would require cuts only from the United States.

New START also limits our missile defense capabilities. In particular, Article V prohibits converting existing intercontinental (ICBM) or submarine-based (SLBM) launchers for the placement of missile defense interceptors. In what is an all-too-familiar pattern, the Obama administration first claimed the treaty would include no such limitations. Undersecretary of State for Arms Control and International Security Ellen Tauscher was asked in a briefing on March 29, 2010, about Russian claims that the treaty included missile defense limitations. "There is no limit or constraint on what the United States can do with its missile defense systems," Tauscher replied, "no way, no how." When the language in the treaty became public, and the missile defense limitations could not be denied, the administration changed its rhetoric. As former undersecretary of state Bob Joseph pointed out, "No way, no how" became "no meaningful limitations" and "no constraints on current and planned" programs. Limiting America's ability to defend itself from nuclear attack in a world in which we face threats not just from Russia, but also from a nuclear-armed North Korea, a nuclear-armed China, and potentially a nuclear-armed Iran, is reckless. Such a concession was so sure to increase opposition to the treaty that the administration had no desire to be candid about it with the American people.

The same week that President Obama signed the New START Treaty, his administration also issued a new nuclear policy for the nation. The 2010 "Nuclear Posture Review" imposes additional restraints on America's ability to maintain and modernize its nuclear forces. Despite the fact that China and Russia are aggressively pursuing expanded arsenals and improved technology, President Obama has prohibited the United States from developing any new nuclear warheads or any new components for existing warheads. He has also banned efforts that would lead to "new military missions or provide new military capabilities" for our nuclear arsenal. Our adversaries want to deny us nuclear superiority. President Obama's policies are making their task easier.

The president has continued to seek even further nuclear arms reductions. Speaking at the Brandenburg Gate in June 2013, he explained that New START was just the beginning. America could cut its deployed nuclear arsenal by one-third, he announced. "And, I intend," he said, "to seek negotiated cuts with Russia to move beyond Cold War nuclear postures." At the time that the president made this announcement, his administration had confirmed Russia was violating its existing arms reduction obligations under the INF Treaty. Putting America's nuclear arsenal at the mercy of another arms control treaty with the Russians when they weren't living up to existing obligations is counterintuitive, to say the least.

The INF Treaty, signed in 1987 by President Reagan and Soviet premier Gorbachev, prohibits, among other things, testing missiles with a range between 500 and 5,000 kilometers. The Russians have been doing precisely that. As a result, because the United States is abiding by its obligations under the treaty, we are the only nation in the world today prohibited from testing intermediate-range missiles.

Efforts to broaden membership in the treaty, including during the Bush administration, were unsuccessful. Other countries did not see it to be in their interest to limit their capabilities.

The president's ongoing efforts to reduce our nuclear arsenal indicate that he views it as a relic of the Cold War. He seems not to recognize that in today's world, its deterrent effect is more crucial than ever. If our arsenal is degraded, outdated, or unreliable, our ability to prevent the hostile actions of others is significantly diminished.

One example of the impact of our nuclear deterrence occurred during the 1991 Gulf War. Though the Iraqis had large stocks of chemical and biological weapons, they did not use them. All of the Scud missiles they fired at Israel and Saudi Arabia were armed with conventional warheads. A number of high-ranking U.S. officials, including President George H. W. Bush, had warned Saddam Hussein in strong terms against launching a chemical or biological attack. "You and your country will pay a terrible price if you order unconscionable acts of this sort," President Bush wrote in a letter to Saddam. After the war, the Iraqis explained that, although they had armed a number of missiles and bombs with their WMD, they didn't launch them because they feared a nuclear response from America, based largely on warnings like the one issued by President Bush.

America's nuclear weapons are also important for the assurances they enable us to provide other nations. For decades the United States has extended the protection of its "nuclear umbrella" to allies. These assurances have contributed significantly to preventing the proliferation of nuclear weapons. Countries need not develop their own nuclear arsenals if they can rely on ours. Cutting the size of America's arsenal and preventing its modernization significantly reduce the value and credibility of the American nuclear umbrella. This will undoubtedly lead more nations to pursue their own nuclear weapons programs.

We live in a world in which America's most significant adversaries are expanding the size and capabilities of their nuclear arsenals, in which terrorist groups are gathering strength, territory, resources, and seeking nuclear weapons, in which the Iranians are poised to become a nuclear weapons state, and in which the North Koreans are increasing their arsenal and capabilities. We cannot afford to let wishful thinking blind us to the reality that now more than ever, America must maintain its nuclear preeminence.

Time and again throughout our history, we have cut our military too deeply in the aftermath of wars, only to have to rearm when enemies threaten. Barack Obama is the only president in American history—perhaps the only world leader in all of history—to slash defense spending in the midst of a war.

CHINA

THE ARRAY OF THREATS facing America today is vast, from the rise of ISIS to the potential of a nuclear-armed Iran to Russian aggression against Ukraine and threats against the Baltics. None, however, is greater than the challenge posed by China. Embarked upon a decades-long effort to defeat the United States militarily and economically, China is pursuing this objective with determination and strategic commitment. Aiming to surpass the United States economically and militarily, the Chinese are moving along multiple fronts simultaneously, building up their conventional, nuclear, and technological weapons capabilities.

During a 2011 trip through the Pacific, President Obama delivered a speech to the Australian parliament in which he announced a broad shift in American policy, a "pivot to Asia," as it became known. He emphasized America's strength and determination to defend its interests and allies in Asia, and said that he had directed his national security team "to make our presence and mission in the Asia Pacific a top priority." He did not directly say so, but he was widely understood to signal America's intention to maintain its preeminent status against the Chinese challenge.

Particularly on the military front, however, there was a decided lack of follow-through. On March 4, 2014, the assistant secretary of defense for acquisition, Katrina McFarland, spoke the blunt truth. Cuts in the defense budget meant the pivot wouldn't happen. "Right now," she said, "the pivot is being looked at again, because candidly, it can't happen." A few hours later, she issued a typical Washington "clarification," explaining that what she meant was "The rebalance to Asia can and will continue." Having announced that we would increase our presence significantly and provide protection for our allies in the region while discouraging China's aggressive moves, the United States failed to deliver. It was a policy outcome that can only have emboldened China.

While we've been undertaking massive cuts, China has been building the military forces necessary to become a global power. Their defense spending increased more than 12 percent between 2013 and 2014, and with the exception of 2010, has increased every year since 1989 by double digits. These are only the publicly known figures. Beijing routinely omits major defense-related expenditures from its announced numbers, so the expansion has likely been significantly greater. Chinese military capacity is advancing in every sector as a result of these expenditures.

In its annual report to Congress for 2014, the U.S.-China Economic and Security Review Commission described some of China's accomplishments in the missile sector, an area of obvious concern for U.S. security:

> *China maintains the largest and most lethal short-range ballistic missile force in the world; fielded the world's first anti-ship*

ballistic missile in 2010; deployed its military's first long-range, air-launched land-attack cruise missile in 2012; and will widely deploy its military's first indigenous advanced long-range submarine-launched anti-ship missile in the next few years, if it has not already. In 2014, China conducted its first test of a new hypersonic missile vehicle, which can conduct kinetic strikes any-where in the world within minutes to hours, and performed its second flight test of a new road-mobile intercontinental missile that will be able to strike the entire continental United States and could carry up to ten independently maneuverable warheads.

Since the report was submitted, China has conducted three more tests of its hypersonic missile. According to the U.S. Office of Naval Intelligence, China has also deployed its new YJ-18 supersonic antiship cruise missile on warships and submarines, posing "a major threat to U.S. and allied vessels."

While investing in a vastly expanded missile capability, China is also building a navy capable of projecting Chinese power regionally and globally. In January 2014, the first Chinese aircraft carrier was deployed on a long-term training mission, and the Chinese navy conducted its first combat deployment in the Indian Ocean. If current trends continue, according to the U.S.-China Economic and Security Review Commission, by 2020 the Chinese could have more than 350 submarines and missile-equipped surface ships in the Asia-Pacific. By contrast, the U.S. Navy projects that it will have 67 submarines and surface ships "stationed in or forward deployed to" the Asia-Pacific by 2020.

Ignoring international law, the Chinese have claimed sovereignty over most of the South China Sea and are embarked upon a massive land reclamation and construction program to bolster these claims. They have built nearly two thousand acres of artificial islands on top of submerged reef, and they have attempted to restrict U.S. military flights over the islands. Satellite imagery confirms they are building airstrips and other military facilities on the reclaimed land.

China is also making strides in its ability to conduct warfare in space and disable American satellites. The Chinese are building their own drone force, jamming communications in U.S. drone flights, and developing a range of weapons systems aimed at eliminating America's military advantage. These include rocket-propelled sea mines and tactical high-energy laser weapons.

Their efforts in many of these areas are a result of a decades-long commitment to the development of technologies that exploit particular areas of American weakness. Some of these projects sound like the stuff of science fiction, but many of them are part of a larger effort known as *shashoujian*, or "Assassin's Mace," a term derived from an ancient Chinese folktale. In the story, a weaker hero triumphs over a mighty adversary with a macelike weapon hidden in his sleeve. Michael Pillsbury, director of the Center for Chinese Strategy at the Hudson Institute, explains the term in the military context: "Assassin's Mace refers to a set of asymmetric weapons that allows an inferior enemy to defeat a seemingly superior adversary by striking at an enemy's weakest point." China has been embarked upon an effort to develop Assassin's Mace weapons for use against the United States for the better part of twenty years.

One central element of this effort is China's cyberwar against the United States. This has included massive targeting of both U.S. government and industry. In May 2013, the *Washington Post* reported that the Chinese had obtained designs for a number of America's most advanced weapons systems, and were undertaking aggressive efforts to steal intellectual property from the U.S. private sector. In May 2015, the U.S. Office of Personnel Management announced that someone had hacked into their systems stealing personnel and security clearance information on U.S. government employees. Twenty-two million people may have been affected. The Chinese government, it is widely thought, is to blame. According to former director of the CIA and NSA General Michael Hayden, "The Chinese have pretty much had a freehand in American databases for the better part of a decade and the attacks fit their policy, their needs, their tactics and their tools."

In addition to cyberespionage, the Chinese have focused on developing electromagnetic pulse (EMP) weapons that could take down our power grid, destroy communications networks, and render military command-and-control centers inoperable. Until relatively recently, launching an EMP attack would require exploding a nuclear device several hundred miles above the wide area to be affected. The method the Chinese are focusing on achieves the same end but with none of the complications of a nuclear explosion—and it can be targeted. In his book, *The Hundred-Year Marathon*, Pillsbury points out that the Chinese see America's ever-increasing dependence on electronic technology as putting us particularly at risk. According to an official newspaper of the People's Liberation Army, "The United States is more vulnerable to attacks than any other country in the world."

China is matching its technological advances, military buildup, and cyberespionage programs with policies aimed at countering American influence globally. They have proliferated missile technology to rogue states like Iran, Libya, and Syria. They are expanding trade ties, weapons sales, and military cooperation with Russia, building a relationship based on challenging America's preeminence. "They see [America's] grip on the rest of the world rapidly loosening," writes Dmitri Trenin, director of the Carnegie Moscow Center:

Both Moscow and Beijing see the world going through an epochal change away from U.S. domination and toward a freer global

order that would give China more prominence and Russia more
freedom of action.

Neither China nor Russia, it is safe to say, plans to use these anticipated gains in prominence to further the cause of global freedom, security, or peace. Nor do they seem to agree with President Obama's assertion that the days when global power "was a zero-sum game" are over.

IN THE SEVENTY YEARS since World War II, no American president has done more damage to our nation's defenses than Barack Obama. His determination to cut defense spending and reduce the size of the U.S. military has served two of his fundamental objectives. He came to office determined to increase domestic spending, and cutting defense spending was a way of getting the resources to do it.

He also came into office determined to reduce America's role in the world. Bret Stephens of the *Wall Street Journal* described Obama's philosophy this way:

> *Above all, progressivism believes that the United States is a coun-*
> *try that, in nearly every respect, treads too heavily on the Earth:*
> *environmentally, ideologically, militarily, and geopolitically. The*
> *goal, therefore, is to reduce America's footprint; to "retrench," as*
> *the administration would like to think of it, or to retreat, as it*
> *might more accurately be called.*

Slashing the size, readiness, and equipment of our forces is a way of guaranteeing America will be unable to play a larger role in the world.

In what may turn out to be one of the tragedies of American history, President Obama has been aided in his misguided efforts by partisan gridlock in the U.S. Congress. Unable to reach agreement on cuts in the federal budget, Congress has allowed sequestration to further devastate our defense capabilities.

The misguided cuts being made now will have long-lasting negative effects on the nation. Weapons systems take years—and dedicated assembly lines—to produce. Cuts of the magnitude we are seeing now gut our industrial capacity as well as our current war-fighting capability. A strong military force requires a consistent and long-term investment. Officers must be developed over multiyear careers. Adequate training requires time and money. Cutting the size of the force, reducing training budgets, and denying our men and women the equipment they need guarantee we will have a less capable, less ready force years down the line. We are also likely to be reminded that it is far costlier to rebuild a military than it is to maintain it.

If not reversed in the very near term, current defense budget cuts will significantly limit the ability of future presidents to defend the nation. Even today, twenty-seven years after Ronald Reagan left office, we are still benefiting from his defense buildup. Many of the most important weapons systems on which we rely were designed, procured, and built during the Reagan era. As former undersecretary of defense for policy Eric Edelman has said, we have been "eating the seed corn" that was laid down then. President Obama's legacy will be far different. It is hard to imagine anyone who succeeds him in the Oval Office looking back in gratitude for what he has done to our capacity to defend ourselves.

One can't help but wonder what some of President Obama's Democratic predecessors would have thought of his neglect of the nation's military power. In June 1941, when London was standing virtually alone against the Nazis, President Roosevelt sent a letter to a special convocation of Oxford University. He told the story of America's ambassador to England visiting the House of Commons and Westminster Abbey after they'd been bombed, and seeing the statue of

Abraham Lincoln, our Great Emancipator, still standing as a symbol and sentinel "in this great battle for freedom." Roosevelt knew this was America's cause:

> *We, too, born to freedom, and believing in freedom, are willing to fight to maintain freedom. We, and all others who believe as deeply as we do, would rather die on our feet than live on our knees.*

President John F. Kennedy knew this, too. For our own sake, and for the sake of global peace and freedom, he believed America must always maintain "a national security position which is first, not 'first, but'; not 'first, if'; not 'first, when'; but first." America must, he warned, maintain a military power that is "second to none." Everything else—*everything*—depends on this.

PART THREE

What Must Be Done

·◆·

SEVEN

Restoring American Power

The free peoples of the world look to us for support in maintaining their freedoms. If we falter in our leadership, we may endanger the peace of the world. And we shall surely endanger the welfare of this nation.

—HARRY S. TRUMAN, MARCH 12, 1947

Let the word go forth from this time and place, to friend and foe alike, that the torch has been passed to a new generation of Americans— born in this century, tempered by war, disciplined by a hard and bit- ter peace, proud of our ancient heritage—and unwilling to witness or permit the slow undoing of those human rights to which this nation has always been committed, and to which we are committed today at home and around the world. Let every nation know, whether it wishes us well or ill, that we shall pay any price, bear any burden, meet any hardship, support any friend, oppose any foe to assure the survival and success of liberty.

—JOHN F. KENNEDY, INAUGURAL ADDRESS,

JANUARY 20, 1961

Presidents Truman and Kennedy knew that neither America's freedom nor its security was self-sustaining. Each was guaran- teed by American power. Both men were shaped by World War II: President Kennedy by his heroic Navy service and President Truman by the duty he inherited and the leadership he provided in securing victory for the Allies. Neither man was naïve enough to think that America could be safe if we retreated behind our oceans. They had seen too much of the evil of our enemies and the powerful reach of their weapons to have been lulled by the false comfort of isolationism or appeasement.

Nor would either man have suggested that American unilateral disarmament would inspire the Soviets to follow suit. When Truman had to decide whether America should develop the hydrogen bomb, he asked one question: "Can the Soviets do it?" Told that they could, he ordered America's program to proceed. When Soviet premier Khrushchev built the Berlin Wall and threatened to cut off America's access to the western side of the city, Kennedy didn't offer American concessions. He instructed his deputy secretary of defense to announce publicly how far the American nuclear arsenal exceeded the Soviets' arsenal in size and capabilities. He wanted to be certain the Soviets were under no illusions about America's nuclear supremacy and the deadly costs of escalation. Both men had a clear understanding of the nature of America's adversaries, the magnitude of the threats we faced, the importance of our military power, and the indispensable role we played in the world.

Although they were Democrats, it is unlikely they would find much that is prudent—or even explicable—in the national security policies of the Democrat who inhabits the Oval Office today. It will be up to America's next president to look to the examples of men like Truman and Kennedy, Eisenhower and Reagan as he or she works to undo the significant damage that's been done.

The next president's top priority must be rebuilding America's military to ensure it has the personnel, resources, and equipment necessary to defend the nation in an environment of escalating and multiplying dangers. Not since before World War II have we faced a situation of such disparity between the threats we face and our capability to defend against them. There will be no more important or urgent task for our next commander in chief than repairing the damage done by the Obama-era defense budget cuts.

Even before our next president is inaugurated:

- **Congress should move immediately to repeal the Budget Control Act and end the sequestration cuts.** If Congress fails to act, two more rounds of sequestration cuts will go into effect before January 20, 2017, when the next president is inaugurated. Former general Jim Mattis described the damage these cuts are doing to our nation's defenses: "No foe in the field can wreak such havoc on our security [as] mindless sequestration is achieving today." They should be repealed immediately.

In addition, the next commander in chief should:

- **Use the Gates fiscal 2012 budget as a minimum baseline on which to build in setting funding levels for the Department of Defense.** The Gates FY 2012 budget was the last defense budget prepared using the normal defense planning process, assessing the threats to the nation and the resources necessary to meet those threats. That budget requested $661 billion for national defense for FY 2016. This FY 2012 budget was developed prior to the rise of ISIS, the collapse of the government in Iraq, the civil war in Syria, the fall of Libya to militant Islamists, the fall of Yemen to Iranian-backed rebels, Russia's invasion of Ukraine, China's most recent aggressive actions in the South China Sea, and the cyberattack on the U.S. government personnel systems for which the Chinese were apparently responsible. The FY 2012 budget should be supplemented to ensure sufficient resources in light of this increased threat environment.

- **Direct the Department of Defense to prepare a list of immediate readiness requirements to remedy shortfalls.** The president should work with Congress to seek an emergency supplemental providing the funding necessary to restore these shortfalls. Allowing readiness to continue to decline will, as noted in the National Defense Panel QDR Review for 2014, lead to the possibility of a hollow force "that loses its best people, underfunds procurement, and shortchanges innovation."

- **Instruct the Department of Defense to adopt an updated force-sizing construct.** In 2012, President Obama abandoned the "two-war" strategy, which provided for a force sized to defeat two enemies in two geographically separate theaters simultaneously. By abandoning this requirement, the president was able to abandon the need for a force sized to accomplish it. In light of the growing complexity of the international situation and the rising threats we face, even a return to a force sized to meet the "two-war" construct is likely insufficient. The United States must have a force today that is structured to defeat adversaries in multiple geographically separate theaters simultaneously, while maintaining the ability to defend the homeland and engage in other critical missions.

- **Reverse cuts to the size of the Army, Navy, Air Force, and Marine Corps.** The current Obama budgets, combined with sequestration, have put us on a path to having a Navy smaller than at any time since 1915, an Army smaller than it has been since 1940, and an Air Force operating the smallest and oldest force of combat aircraft in its history. Those levels would be inadequate in a time of peace and stability. They are inexcusable in the face of today's threats. The recommendations of the bipartisan 2014 National Defense Panel are a responsible place to start in reversing these cuts. In particular, the panel recommends that Congress should task the Defense Department with conducting a thorough review, "without undue emphasis on budgetary constraints," to determine how it would construct a force to meet the current threat environment.

- **Ensure the Pentagon budget includes a robust program to invest in the technologies necessary to maintain our military superiority.** Important areas identified for particular focus in the NDP include: armed intelligence surveillance and reconnaissance systems, space capabilities, cyberspace, joint and coalition command and control, air superiority, long-range and precision strike capability, undersea and surface naval warfare, and electric and directed-energy weapons.

- **Upgrade America's offensive and defensive cyber-capabilities.** The successful cyberattack on the U.S. government's personnel and security clearance databases makes clear that we do not have adequate cyberdefenses. Former NSA and CIA director General Michael Hayden has said that the United States must bear much of the blame for this attack because we have left ourselves vulnerable. He also noted that many of the same members of Congress who voted to limit the authorities of the NSA, "America's most powerful cyberforce," were demanding, forty-eight hours later, "to know how the personal records of millions of Americans could have been violated by a foreign power."

Our next president must lead the nation in recognizing that limiting our own intelligence abilities aids our adversaries.

• **Develop and build a robust, modern, and effective missile defense system.** Cuts made to missile defense programs must be restored, and we should invest in upgraded programs that enable us to defend against new capabilities, such as China's hypersonic weapons. In a world in which America's adversaries have nuclear weapons and the missiles to deliver them, we cannot leave ourselves unprotected.

• **Harden American targets that are most vulnerable to EMP attack.** One of our greatest vulnerabilities is the threat posed by electromagnetic pulse attacks to our military and civilian infrastructure. Congress established the Commission to Assess the Threat to the United States from Electromagnetic Pulse Attack. The next president should sign the executive order prepared by the EMP commission and ignored by President Obama, to protect essential infrastructure targets. He or she should also ensure America's missile defense system is structured to provide protection against an EMP attack. Congress should take immediate action to pass legislation proposed by the commission to enable the hardening of targets, including the nation's electric grid. The next president should use the commission's recommendations as a basis to build on to ensure we are taking all necessary steps to defend against this threat.

• **Modernize and upgrade our aging nuclear arsenal.** We must recognize the continued importance of maintaining nuclear superiority with a strategic arsenal that is "second to none." Our nuclear arsenal should not be viewed as a relic of a long-ago time. It is a crucial element in the security of the nation, particularly in a world in which the spread of nuclear weapons has become reality. Failing to upgrade, modernize, and maintain our nuclear force, in a world in which our adversaries are improving and modernizing their arsenals, puts our security at risk. The Defense Department should help restore the loss of human capital in all areas related to nuclear capabilities, including investing in programs that will help fund the education of the next generation of nuclear specialists.

- **Reverse Obama-era environmental policies that may harm our national security.** Environmental Protection Agency policies, such as those aimed at reducing emissions from coal-fired power plants, can lead to reductions in the reliability of our power grid and interfere with efforts we should be undertaking to decrease Europe's dependence on Russian energy by exporting some of our growing surplus of natural gas to European markets. The current EPA "Clean Power Plan" requires taking one-third of coal-fired power plants off the grid by 2020. This is inconsistent with ensuring the reliability of our grid and will have no demonstrable positive impact on our environment, particularly so long as countries such as China and India continue to produce far greater quantities of pollutants.

In the difficult budget environment in which we find ourselves, it has been tempting for some to think we can cut funds from our nation's defenses as a way to fund domestic programs or to reduce the overall size of the deficit. In reality, cutting defense only harms our capacity to secure the nation and does not solve our fiscal problems. The defense budget is not driving our deficits—entitlement spending is. We must reform entitlements as part of a larger effort to guarantee the long-term health of the U.S. economy, which will also be beneficial to our national security.

Maintaining America's global supremacy is necessary for our freedom and security. As author Mark Helprin recently noted, "Upon our will to provide for defense, all else rests."

AS WE REBUILD AMERICA'S armed forces, we must also take steps to win the war against militant Islam. Our adversaries in this war include ISIS, al Qaeda and its affiliates, and Iran and the terror groups it sponsors.

The urgent task facing us today is the defeat of ISIS and the denial of the territory on which it has established its caliphate. We must:

- **Recognize that America's current strategy, to the extent there is one, is failing.** The limited military operations authorized by President Obama are insufficient to defeat ISIS. The $500 million program to train Syrian rebels is a national embarrassment, having produced, according to Secretary of Defense Ash Carter, sixty vetted candidates. America and its allies are not winning.
- **Dedicate the American forces necessary to prevail.** Former vice chief of staff of the Army General Jack Keane has detailed these near-term requirements: We should deploy U.S. and coalition military advisors to accompany indigenous frontline forces fighting ISIS. Thousands of advisors, not hundreds, are required, and they need the ability to call in air strikes. We also need direct-action special operations forces, both ground and air, targeting ISIS leaders. American and coalition combat brigades should be designated for deployment and moved to Kuwait to be ready if needed.

- **Reverse President Obama's policy of retreat and rebuild our alliances with key Arab states, including Saudi Arabia, the United Arab Emirates, Egypt, and Jordan.** Provide them the support they need to win against ISIS, al Qaeda, and other insurgent groups, especially those backed by Iran. Recognize that alliances must be based on trust and on reliability. Countries in the Middle East must know that America will not abandon them and that our word means something. We must never issue empty threats.

- **Rebuild our alliance with Israel.** Recognize that America has no stronger ally or partner, including in the war against militant Islam, than the state of Israel. The deterioration of the relationship over the last six years must be halted and reversed.

- **Provide military assistance directly to the Kurdish Peshmerga forces.** The Peshmerga are a capable fighting force aggressively challenging ISIS. They need and will make effective use of U.S. military support.

- **Develop an effective air campaign to deny ISIS sanctuary in Syria, as well as Iraq.** We should increase the pace of our air campaign, establish a no-fly zone to deny Assad's use of airpower and create a buffer zone to protect refugees. We must target and destroy ISIS's lines of communication, staging areas, and bases inside Syria.

- **Recognize that the longer we allow ISIS to survive and expand, the more powerful they become.** Every month, they are recruiting thousands of fighters to their cause. They cannot be contained, and since America's security requires their defeat, we must take decisive action to bring that about.

We must take additional steps to defeat al Qaeda and its affiliates, and to prevent further attacks on the United States. Contrary to President Obama's claims, al Qaeda is not on the road to defeat. His withdrawal from the field of battle has resulted in gains for our enemies. We must:

- **Halt the withdrawal of American forces from Afghanistan and tailor America's ongoing presence there based on conditions on the ground, not American political timetables.** America's complete withdrawal from Iraq and the vacuum it left for ISIS and Iran to fill should be a clear warning about the dangers we face if we follow the same course of action in Afghanistan. Though we have seen progress there, President Obama's decision to deploy 25 percent fewer surge forces than his commanders requested, coupled with his decision to withdraw them early to meet a U.S. political timetable, means that there are still safe havens in Afghanistan that will be exploited by America's enemies if we walk away. We must maintain our presence there and our support for the Afghan National Security Forces until they are truly able to secure their nation and prevent terrorists from establishing safe havens on their sovereign territory.

- **Restore authority to the NSA to effectively track and monitor terrorist communications.** We now know that the 9/11 hijackers were in the United States prior to the attacks, communicating with known terrorists overseas. Had the terrorist surveillance program been in place then, according to former NSA director General Mike Hayden, we may well have been able to prevent those attacks. We are at war with the same enemy, under at least as serious a threat as we were then. Restrictions that were imposed on NSA, including in the USA Freedom Act should be lifted, and the next president should ensure that NSA has all of the authorities necessary to effectively track America's adversaries.

- **Reinstitute the enhanced interrogation program and stop releasing terrorists from Guantánamo.** We should continue the aggressive use of drones to kill terrorists, and we should supplement that program with equally aggressive efforts to capture and interrogate them. We need intelligence to win this war and that requires effective interrogation. There may be instances where intelligence necessary to prevent attacks cannot be obtained using only Army Field Manual techniques. In addition, we need to keep enemy combatants off the field of battle, and that requires detaining them. Detainees who have been released from Guantánamo have returned to the field of battle, including the former detainee who is currently the lead recruiter for ISIS in Afghanistan and Pakistan.

- **Recognize the Muslim Brotherhood shares the goals and objectives of militant Islamist terrorist groups.** They provide the ideological foundation for these groups and are allied with them. The United States should not be providing support to the Muslim Brotherhood or any of its affiliated groups or individuals.

- **Recognize that Iran is America's enemy and that its objectives are inconsistent with peace, stability, and security in the Middle East.** President Obama has reversed decades of U.S. policy with respect to Iran. By withdrawing from the Middle East, lifting sanctions on an array of Iranian entities, including the IRGC, removing obstacles to Iran's ballistic missile program, and ending the embargo on conventional weapons transfers, he has facilitated their efforts to dominate the Middle East and threaten the United

States and our allies. He has also created the impression he is attempting to align American policy with Iran's interests, by refusing, for example, to enforce his declared redline against Iran's client, Bashar al-Assad and proclaiming that America believes Iran should be "a very successful regional power." His reasoning is incomprehensible. America's security demands that we deny, not promote, Iran's dreams of regional domination. America's next president must reverse course in order to prevent Iran from threatening our allies and interests in the region.

IN 1992, AFTER THE Cold War came to an end and the United States emerged as the world's sole superpower, the Department of Defense produced planning guidance laying out actions necessary to ensure the continued security of the nation. The guidance contained this objective:

> *To preclude any hostile power from dominating a region critical to our interests and also thereby to strengthen the barriers against the reemergence of a global threat to the interests of the United States and our allies. These regions include Europe, East Asia, the Middle East/Persian Gulf, and Latin America. Consolidated nondemocratic control of the resources of such a critical region could generate a significant threat to our security.*

President Obama's policies have enabled the rise of such a threat in three critical regions simultaneously: Iran in the Middle East, China in Asia, and Russia in Europe. Efforts to rebuild America's military will have a positive impact in each of these regions as a warning to potential adversaries that the United States no longer intends to retreat from the world. A revitalized American military will also serve as assurance to our allies that we have the forces necessary to defend our interests. In addition, the next president should take specific steps, detailed below, in each region to preserve and protect the interests of the United States.

THE NEXT PRESIDENT MUST ensure Iran does not obtain a nuclear weapon. This task has been made exponentially more difficult by the concessions President Obama granted the Iranians in the nuclear agreement announced in July 2015. The agreement allows Iran to preserve every element of its nuclear infrastructure, including thousands of centrifuges and its uranium enrichment program. It lifts sanctions on an array of terrorist-supporting entities, including the IRGC, IRGC-Quds Force, and IRGC Air Force. The agreement provides billions in cash payments to Iran, lifts restrictions on the Iranian ballistic missile program, commits to ending the conventional weapons arms embargo, and includes a wholly inadequate verification regime. It is the most dangerous arms control agreement ever entered into by an American president.

President Obama has argued that his agreement is the only alternative to war, when in fact the Obama nuclear deal makes war more—not less—likely. Neither Congress nor America's next president should accept President Obama's false choice. To undo the tremendous damage of this agreement and prevent Iran from obtaining nuclear weapons, the U.S. Congress should:

- **Reject the agreement entered into by the Obama administration and recognize that, contrary to President Obama's claims, there is a better deal possible.** We know that sanctions and the credible threat of force have worked effectively in the past to affect Iran's behavior. The sanctions regime the president opposed, and now claims credit for, was working. Rather than maintain the sanctions, President Obama eased them just as they began to have an impact. Instead of maintaining a credible threat of force, the president took force off the table. Instead of negotiating from a position of strength, and, in the words of the *Wall Street Journal*, "showing determination so an adversary under pressure concludes that it must make more concessions," the president showed desperation for a deal and conceded nearly every key point. The Iranians got the better of him.

America's next president should:

- **Affirm that the following non-negotiable elements must be part of any agreement with Iran concerning its nuclear program:**
  1. Iran must halt all enrichment and reprocessing activities.
  2. Iran must halt all ballistic missile activities.
  3. Iran must provide a full and complete accounting of all its nuclear activities, past and present, military and civilian. Without such an accounting, verification of any agreement is impossible.
  4. Iran must provide complete go-anywhere-anytime access to international inspectors, including at its military sites.
  5. The U.S. should not support any effort to repeal sanctions until such time as Iran has fulfilled these obligations.
- **Immediately re-impose all U.S. sanctions, with a particular focus on the IRGC, IRGC Quds Force, and IRGC Air Force.** The IRGC has American blood on its hands, provides direct support for terrorist groups around the world

and is working for the destruction of Israel. The next president should make it a top priority to once again impose serious restrictions on their ability to operate.

- **Withdraw American support for lifting restrictions on Iran's ballistic missile program and for ending the conventional weapons embargo on Iran.** Iran's ballistic missiles, which have no purpose other than to transport nuclear warheads, can reach the United States, as well as our friends and allies in Europe and the Middle East. Without the conventional arms embargo in place, Iran will be able to import deadly weapons from Russia and China, and further destabilize the Middle East by supplying weapons to terrorists bent on the destruction of Israel and the United States.

- **Stop all cash payments under way or planned to Iran. Instruct the Treasury Department to issue new designations, if necessary, to freeze Iranian assets and prevent the transfer of further cash from the United States to the regime in Tehran.** Transferring cash to Tehran, while the regime kills American soldiers in Afghanistan, sponsors terror across the region, and seeks the destruction of Israel is indefensible.

- **Reinvigorate the Treasury Department program to work directly with private entities around the world to block Iran's use of the international financial system for illicit purposes.** This program, begun in earnest in 2006 by undersecretary of Treasury Stuart Levey, successfully limited Iran's access to international financial and commercial markets and increased the impact of the multilateral sanctions regime. The next president should direct the Treasury Department to re-launch this effort.

- **Develop a strategy in consultation with our allies in the Middle East to address Iran's state sponsorship of terror and use of the IRGC to undermine other governments in the region.** Iran or its proxies now largely control capitals in four Arab countries: Yemen, Syria, Lebanon, and Iraq. Iranian domination of the Middle East and unfettered IRGC terror are clearly inconsistent with American interests and security. America must work with its allies to develop a strategy to deny Iran's objectives and roll back the regional gains it has made under President Obama.

- **Ensure that our allies and the Iranians recognize that all options are on the table if Iran refuses to halt its nuclear program through a diplomatic process.** The president should instruct the U.S. military to prepare plans for military strikes on Iran's nuclear facilities and other key military and economic targets. The United States should undertake visible exercises and publicized tests of specific capabilities, such as the precision-guided Massive Ordnance Penetrator, which could be used in a strike on Iran's facilities.

OUR POLICY TOWARD CHINA must reflect the fact that they are simultaneously a significant strategic threat and a major economic partner. America's next president must counter China's increasingly hostile actions, impose costs for their cyberattacks on the United States, deny their ambitions for conquest, and ensure America builds the technology and capabilities necessary to prevent China from overtaking our most important defensive capabilities. At the same time, America must recognize that China will be an enduring power for many years to come and that the complexity of the relationship between the United States and China requires consistent, serious diplomatic engagement at the highest levels. The next American president should:

- **Aggressively counter Chinese cyberattacks on U.S. government and industrial systems.** We must harden our own targets and ensure we have the capability to counter their attacks. We must impose significant costs on China for engaging in cyberespionage and other forms of cyberattack. The sophistication of the Chinese attacks and the sensitive content they have stolen from the United States for military and industrial purposes represent a very real threat to our security. In addition, their potential ability to access systems that control America's infrastructure, such as the power grid, communications networks, and military command-and-control systems, is a clear and present danger that we must strengthen our defenses against.

- **Expand our military presence in Asia to counter China's efforts at regional domination.** We should engage in increased military exercises, reinvigorate security dialogues, and provide military assistance and arms sales to our key allies in the region. These efforts will aid our allies in building their own capacity to counter the Chinese threat and send the clear signal that China's increasingly provocative and threatening actions will not go unanswered.

- **Increase investments in military technologies and capabilities necessary to counter advances the Chinese are making in areas such as hypersonic weapons and anti-ship missiles.** Ensure that our investments in technology and weapons systems are sufficient to guarantee we do not cede superiority in any sector to the Chinese.

- **Recognize that China is upgrading, modernizing, and expanding its nuclear arsenal.** Our next president should ensure that we are making investments in our own nuclear arsenal sufficient to maintain superiority and provide a credible deterrent against any contemplated nuclear use by the Chinese. We must build up missile defense systems capable of defending against the Chinese missile threat. In addition to conventional anti-ballistic-missile defenses, the United States should be investing in directed-energy weapons that can defend against China's new hypersonic weapons.

- **Task the Department of Defense with developing a new regional defense strategy for Asia.** We must ensure that the United States is taking all actions necessary to protect our interests and our allies, to prevent China from fulfilling its hegemonic ambitions, and to ensure that we maintain supremacy in military capability.

- **Reassess economic cooperation policies.** Economic cooperation continues to be an important area in the U.S.-China relationship. However, the assumption that increasing China's economic opportunities and openness would lead to similar progress in the area of political reform has not proven accurate. The United States should assess the benefit and effectiveness of existing economic cooperation programs, particularly in light of aggressive Chinese theft of American intellectual property from U.S. businesses.

- **Impose tighter restrictions on China's access to American technology.** The Chinese are exploiting technology cooperation exercises. They have, for example, illegally converted civilian nuclear technology for military use. The United States should work with its allies to impose tighter restric-

tions on Chinese access to Western technology, including
dual-use technology.

- **Continue to raise publicly and in meetings with Chinese
leadership China's human rights violations and repres-
sions of freedom.**

- **While undertaking necessary efforts to defend ourselves
and our allies, the United States must also engage in
expanded, serious, consistent diplomatic engagement
with the Chinese government.** Recognizing that Chinese
power will be a long-term feature of events in the Pacific
and recognizing also that America is a Pacific power, it
is crucial that our two nations participate in the kind of
high-level engagement across the range of issues that com-
prise our relationship. The false promises of the Obama
administration's "pivot to Asia" should be replaced with a
genuine effort to deepen the dialogue between our two nations.

THE NEXT AMERICAN PRESIDENT should take steps to defend America's interests in Europe and the sovereignty of our NATO
allies against the regional ambitions of Vladimir Putin. Putin has
called the collapse of the Soviet Union "one of the greatest geopolitical catastrophes of the twentieth century." He is attempting to recover
some of what was lost when the Cold War ended. He clearly wants to
undermine NATO and demonstrate its ineffectiveness. He would like
to force states in Eastern Europe and the Baltics to withdraw from
NATO. The next American president should:

- **Restore and reinvigorate the NATO alliance.** NATO has
been the most successful military alliance in history, but it
has suffered in recent years from reduced defense expen-

ditures and weak American leadership. The next president
must make clear that America's commitment to the trans-
atlantic security alliance is unwavering and is backed by our
leadership and military might.

- **Ensure that NATO sends a clear signal to Moscow that
Article 5 applies to all members of NATO.** Russia should
have no doubt that any military action against a NATO
member, including the Baltics and those states that were
once members of the Warsaw Pact, will be considered a
move against all, triggering Article 5.

- **Signal American determination to stand by our NATO
allies through periodic deployment of forces to the territory of NATO members bordering Russia.**

- **Task NATO with reviewing its existing strategies, commitments, and obligations in light of the aggressive policies of Vladimir Putin. Call for NATO members to meet
their financial obligations to the alliance.** Recognize that
the 2014 Quadrennial Defense Review (QDR) failed to
take into account the reality of the threat posed by Putin's
Russia, identifying Europe as a "net producer of security."
Direct the Department of Defense to undertake a special
review of the QDR and recommend necessary adjustments
in this area.

- **Restore the missile defense systems President Obama
canceled in Poland and the Czech Republic.** Provide expanded coverage across Europe for shorter-range missiles
with a system similar to Israel's Iron Dome.

- **Recommit the United States to abiding by its obligations
under the Budapest Memorandum of 1994,** in which the
United States, the United Kingdom, and Russia committed

to upholding Ukraine's territorial integrity in exchange for Ukraine's agreement to send its nuclear arsenal to Moscow. Recognize that failure to uphold this agreement diminishes the value of guarantees the United States gives in the future to encourage nuclear weapons states to give up their weapons.

- **Provide additional military assistance to Ukraine.**
- **Impose additional sanctions on Russia if they don't halt their military action in Ukraine.**
- **Lift current U.S. restrictions on energy exports and begin providing oil and natural gas to Europe to diminish Russia's ability to use energy as a weapon.** Build a liquefied natural gas export terminal on the East Coast of the United States to facilitate these shipments. Former national security advisor Steve Hadley and former secretary of defense Leon Panetta have advocated this approach, noting that as the United States has long been "the arsenal of democracy," we should now also become "the great arsenal of energy."
- **Recognize that the New START Treaty does not further America's security interests and allow it to expire in 2021.** The treaty restricts our missile defense capabilities and limits our deployed launchers to 700, below the number that the Department of Defense and the Department of Energy determined was necessary for purposes of deterrence. The treaty should be allowed to expire when it ends in 2021.
- **In light of Russian cheating on the Intermediate-Range Nuclear Forces (INF) Treaty, the United States should allocate funds for research and development for the Pershing III intermediate-range ballistic missile.** The president should also instruct the Department of Defense to

conduct a review of America's likely long-term requirements for missiles, both conventional and nuclear, in the intermediate range. Neither of these actions violates the treaty, and they are prudent in light of Russian deception.

THE NEXT PRESIDENT SHOULD take steps to limit the potential spread of nuclear weapons and minimize the threat that expanded proliferation poses to the United States. The risk from the proliferation of nuclear weapons is increasing, as the Iranians pursue a nuclear weapons program, the North Koreans and Pakistanis expand their arsenals, the Russians and Chinese improve, modernize, and enlarge theirs, and terrorist organizations seek access to nuclear weapons. The next president must:

- **Reestablish the primacy of America's nuclear arsenal.** Discard the Obama-era fallacy that cutting America's arsenal will encourage rogue nations to abandon their nuclear programs or ambitions. President Obama's policies, which have cut our arsenal and limited our ability to modernize what remains, have increased, not decreased, the risk of war. Recognize that America's security requires that we maintain a nuclear arsenal that is, in the words of John F. Kennedy, "second to none." Restore the credibility and deterrence effect of America's nuclear umbrella by maintaining, modernizing, and extending our nuclear arsenal.
- **Develop and build an effective missile defense system to defend ourselves and our allies.** According to former undersecretary of defense Eric Edelman and former undersecretary of state Robert Joseph, "President Obama has canceled or reduced every program to protect the United States

from ballistic-missile attack." In the current threat environment this must be reversed.

- **Recommit the United States to enforcing the international arms control regime.** Despite the fact that President Obama claims nuclear nonproliferation is his top national security priority, his actions have significantly weakened the international nonproliferation regime. Allowing Iran to continue to enrich uranium, ignoring their ongoing IAEA violations, giving up key verification provisions in New START, and seeking further arms treaties with Moscow without insisting Russia stop cheating on the INF Treaty are among the most damaging steps he has taken. The next president should make it a priority to restore the strength of the international arms controls system.

- **Work with our allies to update and improve the international regime.** The Nuclear Non-Proliferation Treaty, which nearly all the world's nations have signed, has been perhaps the most effective arms control treaty in history. It has likely prevented a much larger expansion in the numbers of nuclear weapons states. However, if Iran obtains a nuclear weapon and others in the Middle East follow, that may be a tipping point that renders the NPT increasingly ineffective. The United States should develop, on an urgent basis, a strategy to update and improve the existing regime, in light of the increasingly likely possibility of a nuclear-armed Iran.

- **Use Ronald Reagan's playbook in effective arms control negotiations.** Reagan knew what he was willing to concede and what he wasn't. He was prepared to walk away from the table or have the Russians walk away rather than compromise America's security. While negotiating, he also built up America's conventional forces, undertook a massive program to modernize our nuclear forces, and launched the Strategic Defense Initiative to protect us from attack. It would not have occurred to Reagan to negotiate from a position of weakness.

- **Invest in America's intelligence capabilities with respect to the detection of nuclear weapons programs.** Our history is not impressive in this regard. The United States has been surprised by the development of many of the world's nuclear weapons programs. We need to improve our collection and analysis capability in this area.

- **Recognize that the realistic and credible threat of military force gives substance and meaning to our diplomacy.** Rogue nations and state sponsors of terror attempting to acquire nuclear weapons must believe that the United States is serious when it says "all options are on the table." History has shown the effectiveness of military action in deterring or stopping nuclear programs. In Iraq, Saddam Hussein's nuclear program was destroyed in 1981 when the Israelis bombed the reactor at Osirak. He reconstituted his program and it was destroyed again in 1991 during the Persian Gulf War. In 2003, when the United States and our coalition partners invaded Iraq, the Iranians temporarily halted at least a portion of their program. Five days after we captured Saddam Hussein in December 2003, Libyan leader Muammar Qaddafi announced he was surrendering his nuclear materials, including weapons design, centrifuges, and uranium feedstock. In the aftermath of Qaddafi giving up his program, the United States was able to dismantle the nuclear black market operation of A. Q. Khan. Khan, father of the Pakistani bomb, was selling centrifuge technology and feedstock to nations in the Middle East and Asia. Military action was also effective in 2007 when the Israelis took action to destroy a North Korean–built nuclear reactor in the Syrian Desert. In light of this history, if rogue nations recognize that the cost of pursuing nuclear weapons programs may be significant and may include the use of military force, they may be less likely to choose that path.

THE CHALLENGES FACING OUR next president will be significant and complex. We have discussed only a handful here, intentionally focusing on those that represent the most significant threats and will require the most urgent action.

In some instances, the U.S. Congress should act immediately. Delay in repealing the Budget Control Act, improving America's offensive and defensive cyber-capabilities, or hardening American targets against the potential of an EMP attack, would leave America more vulnerable and would be highly irresponsible. Congress bears a solemn obligation to improve, not diminish, America's defense and intelligence capabilities. We would note that a Congress that fails to repeal the Budget Control Act or pass cybersecurity legislation while devoting hundreds of hours to *limiting* America's cyber-capabilities— through the USA Freedom Act—needs to reassess its priorities.

One common thread running through all we must do to meet these threats is the importance of leadership—American leadership and presidential leadership.

Our next president must be committed to restoring America's power and strength.

Our security and the survival of freedom depend upon it.

The Last, Best Hope of Earth

On December 1, 1862, facing the gravest threat to the survival of the Republic in our history, Abraham Lincoln delivered his annual written message to the U.S. Congress. This "state of the union" message, required by the U.S. Constitution, opened with detailed reports, including information about the nation's accounts, our relations with foreign powers, the operation of the post office, the conditions of the public lands, and the status of the Indian tribes. Then Lincoln turned to the war and spoke to the American people of the responsibility that was theirs, of the burden they carried, the precious burden of preserving this nation, which was, he said, "the last, best hope of earth."

The responsibility remains with us today to sustain and perpetuate America as a model for all those who aspire to live in freedom, but we are also now something more. Since World War II, we have been "the last, best hope of earth" because we are freedom's defender, not just for ourselves, but also for millions around the world. We do this because it is right, because it is necessary, because our security depends upon it, and because there is no other who can.

This duty comes with a tremendous cost, but we must never forget that the cost of inaction is higher. Imagine a world where the rules are set not by America and the allies of freedom, but by Iran or Russia or China. Imagine a world where militant Islam, unchallenged, spreads its venomous ideology and control over ever-expanding swaths of the globe. What if America continues its retreat from the Middle East, leaving Iran, al Qaeda, and ISIS to fill the void? How long until Iran gets a nuclear weapon? How long until others do? How long after that until one is used? What if China is allowed to dominate Asia, developing military capability targeted specifically at the United States? Imagine Europe controlled by Putin, free nations enslaved, and NATO in tatters. These are the costs of inaction.

Some choose to ignore the threats or to blame America. We are the problem, they say, and if we would just retreat, the threats would diminish. Such an assertion requires a willful disregard of the truth. Ignoring dangers did not bring us through World War II or the Cold War. Confronting them did.

Conceived in liberty, we were founded by men of uncommon courage, willing to risk all for the cause of freedom. Through the fire of a great civil war, we were sustained by Abraham Lincoln, who knew that, "The nation is worth fighting for, to secure such an inestimable jewel." Threatened by the depraved tyranny of fascism, we were roused by Franklin Roosevelt to become "the arsenal of democracy," our forces mobilized and commanded by George C. Marshall, who secured the greatest military victory in history—in defense of freedom. Confronted with the soul-killing evil of communism, America's might was marshaled once again by men like Harry Truman, Dwight Eisenhower, and John F. Kennedy, who knew we had to be "the watchmen on the walls of freedom," and by Ronald Reagan, who understood that "war comes not when the forces of freedom are strong, it is when they are weak that tyrants are tempted."

This is one of the themes of America's great story, but many, President Obama prominent among them, want us to take a different view, want us to see the United States as having had and continuing to have a malign role in the world. This fashionable ideology, which would have us retreat and deliberately diminish our power, plays a part not only in our politics, but in the larger culture—and increasingly in education. In the books they are assigned, in the tests they take, and in the instruction they receive, our children and grandchildren are too often being told that the legacy they have inherited is a shameful one.

Neither we nor our children and grandchildren should be uncritical of our country. Despite the self-evident truth that "all men are created equal," slavery continued after we declared our independence. The Constitution, signed in 1787, failed to end the system of slavery, nor did it address the oppression of women. Among the wonders of this country, however, is that that document, our constitution, was the instrument for remedying our failures, for abolishing slavery, granting women the right to vote, and working to ensure equality of opportunity for all. That we are a resilient country, able to correct wrongs, is among the lessons we should embrace and our children should learn. We have worked to make ourselves better—and we have succeeded. No nation has ever been freer or more prosperous. No nation has ever worked so successfully to extend freedom to others. No nation, in the history of mankind, has ever been such a force for good.

As we have written this book, we have sometimes been dispirited. The damage that Barack Obama has done to our ability to defend ourselves is appalling. It is without historical precedent. He has set us on a path of decline so steep that reversing direction will not be easy. But then we call to mind America's resilience and the historical fact that great leaders have rallied us before and surely will again.

Great leaders have called us together to perform hard and noble tasks in large measure by reminding us that we are, as Lincoln said, "the last, best hope of earth." We are not just one more nation, one more indistinguishable entity on the world stage. We have been essential to the preservation and progress of freedom, and those who lead us in the years ahead must remind us, as Roosevelt, Kennedy, and Reagan did, of the special role we play. Neither they nor we should ever forget that we are, in fact, exceptional.

ACKNOWLEDGMENTS

The authors would like to thank Lynne Cheney, whose contributions to this book and to our lives are beyond measure, as is our love for her. This book could not have happened without her. Her involvement touched every aspect of its production, including substance, style, editing, writing, and punctuation. We are deeply grateful—and any misplaced commas are entirely the responsibility of the authors. We would also like to thank our friend Kara Ahern, whose input to this project—ranging from substantive advice, to research, to PR and marketing, to hauling horses—has been incomparable. This is the third Cheney book that Jim Steen, a dear friend and colleague for more than forty years, has worked on with us. He has spent hours reading, editing, and fact-checking the manuscript, making key suggestions about content, and catching our mistakes. Any that remain are ours, not Jim's.

We are indebted to Ambassador Eric Edelman, General Jack Keane, Michael Doran, Robert Karem, John Hannah, Scooter Libby, David Addington, Juan Zarate, and Marc Thiessen for their suggestions and input on key portions of the manuscript. We have traveled many miles over the years with our friend Gamal Helal. His advice and analysis of U.S. policy, and of events across the Middle East, continue to be invaluable.

We consulted hundreds of articles, books, newspapers, and websites in the preparation of this book and are particularly grateful for the extraordinary analysis, research, scholarship, and reporting of Steve Hayes, Tom Joscelyn, Bill Kristol, Max Boot, Robert Joseph, Bret Stephens, Reuel Gerecht, Andrew McCarthy, Jennifer Rubin, Catherine Herridge, Lee Smith, Mark Dubowitz, Emanuele Ottolenghi, Omri Ceren, Bill Gertz, and, the incomparable Charles Krauthammer. Elizabeth Perry, our daughter and granddaughter, was a first-rate intern and research assistant.

Terry O'Donnell skillfully represented us and provided outstanding advice and guidance throughout this process. We would also like to thank the wonderful team at Simon & Schuster, beginning with CEO Carolyn Reidy and Threshold Editions publisher Louise Burke. They were a joy to work with once again, as was our terrific editor, Mitchell Ivers. Mitchell provided crucial perspective and editorial comment through many drafts and changing world events. We are grateful to the entire Simon & Schuster team: Natasha Simons, Jean Anne Rose, Jennifer Long, Felice Javit, Al Madocs, Susan Rella, Lisa Litwack, Tom Pitoniak, Jaime Putorti, and Liz Psaltis. The production of the audio book was made possible by the skill and patience of Tara Thomas and George Morris.

We are grateful to Kris Koch, Gus Anies, Sarah Eaton, Debbie Heiden, Juana Gonzales, Jodi and Brian Edwards, and Abbey and Rob Hardeman for their support, assistance, friendship, and good humor as we wrote this book.

Liz Cheney would like to express her deepest gratitude and love to her husband, Phil Perry, and their children, Kate, Elizabeth, Grace, Philip, and Richard. They were supportive throughout this project, tolerant of the long hours she spent buried in research and writing, and finally learned to quit asking "Isn't that book done yet?"

NOTES

———◆•◆———

PROLOGUE: YES, WE ARE EXCEPTIONAL

1 *"great drama of human affairs"*: Daniel Webster, Oration at the Dedication of the Bunker Hill Monument, June 17, 1825, https://www.dartmouth.edu/~dwebster/speeches/bunker-hill.html.

2 *"must be: all three"*: Andrew Roberts, *A History of the English-Speaking Peoples Since 1900* (New York: HarperCollins, 2007), p. 13.

2 *"the one essential country"*: Walter Berns, *Making Patriots* (Chicago: University of Chicago Press, 2001), p. x. Berns's full quote is worth noting here: "Our lot is to be the one essential country, 'the last, best hope of earth,' and this ought to be acknowledged, beginning in our schools and universities, for it is only then that we can come to accept the responsibilities attending it."

3 *"another will succeed"*: President Barack Obama, Remarks to the United Nations General Assembly, September 23, 2009, https://www.whitehouse.gov/the-press-office/remarks-president-united-nations-general-assembly.

3 *"to defend itself"*: Jean-François Revel, quoted by Ambassador Jeane Kirkpatrick, Speech to the 1984 Republican National Convention, August 20, 1984, http://www.cnn.com/ALLPOLITICS/1996/conventions/san.diego/facts/GOP.speeches.past/84.kirkpatrick.shtml.

4 *"bends toward justice"*: Remarks by President Obama, Press Briefing, June 23, 2009, http://www.nytimes.com/2009/06/23/us/politics/23text-obama.html?pagewanted=all.

4 *"the 20th, FDR"*: Charles Krauthammer, "Martin Luther King in Word and Stone," *Washington Post*, August 25, 2011, quoted in *Things That Matter: Three Decades of Passions, Pastimes, and Politics* (New York: Crown Forum, 2013), p. 250.

6 *"always be free":* President Ronald Reagan, Remarks Commemorating the 40th Anniversary of D-Day, Omaha Beach Memorial, Normandy, France, June 6, 1984, http://www.wsj.com/articles/reagan-at-normandy-1401968701.

CHAPTER 1: FOR THE GOOD OF ALL MANKIND

9 *"good of all mankind":* George C. Marshall to Dwight D. Eisenhower, May 7, 1945, Marshall Library Files, W-78438, cited in Forest C. Pogue, *George C. Marshall: Organizer of Victory, 1943–1945* (New York: Viking Press, 1973), p. 583.

9 *pack of Camels:* This and other details about the audience and atmosphere are from "The President Speaks," *Time,* January 6, 1941.

9 *"talk on national security":* Franklin D. Roosevelt, Fireside Chat 16: On the "Arsenal of Democracy," December 29, 1940, http://millercenter.org/president/fd roosevelt/speeches/speech-3319.

11 *justice Harlan Stone:* Ed Cray, *General of the Army: George C. Marshall, Soldier and Statesman* (New York: Rowman & Littlefield, 1990), p. 143.

11 *called to the telephone:* Lincoln Barnett, "General Marshall: Commander and Creator of America's Greatest Army," *Life,* January 3, 1944, p. 54.

11 *Constitution Avenue:* Ibid.

12 *"God bless us all":* Franklin D. Roosevelt, Day-by-Day, A Project of the Pare Lorenz Center at the FDR Presidential Library, September 1, 1939, http://www .fdrlibrary.marist.edu/daybyday/event/september-1939/.

12 *"by radio at once":* FDR's handwritten bedside note re: the German invasion of Poland, September 1, 1939, Franklin D. Roosevelt, Day-by-Day, A Project of the Pare Lorenz Center at the FDR Presidential Library, http://www.fdrlibrary .marist.edu/daybyday/resource/september-1939/.

12 *sixty divisions:* Andrew Roberts, *The Storm of War: A New History of the Second World War* (New York: HarperCollins, 2011), p. 6.

12 *columns of fleeing refugees:* Ibid., p. 7.

12 *defeated on October 6:* Thomas E. Greiss, ed., *The Second World War in Europe and the Mediterranean,* Department of History, U.S. Military Academy, West Point (Wayne, NJ: Avery, 1989), p. 20.

12 *was significantly larger:* Dwight D. Eisenhower, *Crusade in Europe* (New York: Doubleday, 1948) p. 2.

12 *smaller than Romania's:* Rick Atkinson, *An Army at Dawn* (New York: Henry Holt, 2002), p. 8.

12 *174,000 enlisted men:* George C. Marshall, *Biennial Reports of the Chief of Staff of the United States Army to the Secretary of War,* July 1, 1939 to June 30, 1941, p. 2, http://www.ibiblio.org/hyperwar/USA/COS-Biennial/COS-Biennial-1 .html.

13 *no armored divisions:* Eisenhower, *Crusade in Europe,* p. 2.

13 *1,175 planes:* Ibid.

13 *wooden machine guns:* Ibid., p. 7.

13 *"for immediate action":* Remarks by George C. Marshall, "National Organization for War," American Historical Association Meeting, Mayflower Hotel, Washington, D.C., December 28, 1939, http://marshallfoundation.org/library /digital-archive/speech-to-the-american-historical-association/.

13 *"for quick delivery":* L. C. Speers, "Our New Army Chief," *New York Times,* May 14, 1939.

13 *one-off fashion:* Cray, *General of the Army,* loc. 3194.

14 *"if we don't get it":* Forrest C. Pogue, *George C. Marshall: Ordeal and Hope, 1939–1942* (New York: Viking Press, 1966), p. 29.

14 *the president's schedule:* Transcript of phone call to Edwin "Pa" Watson from Henry Morgenthau Jr., May 11, 1940, Diaries of Henry Morgenthau Jr., April 27, 1933–July 27, 1945, vol. 261, May 10–11, 1940, Franklin D. Roosevelt Presidential Library and Museum, http://www.fdrlibrary.marist.edu/_resources /images/morg/md0349.pdf.

14 *"You've filed your protest":* John Morton Blum, *Years of Urgency, 1938–1941 (From the Morgenthau Diaries)* (New York: Houghton Mifflin, 1965), p. 140.

14 *"hearing him at all":* Forrest C. Pogue, *George C. Marshall: Interviews and Reminiscences* (Lexington, VA: George C. Marshall Foundation, 1986), Tape 11, Recorded November 15, 1956, p. 329.

14 *"he didn't grasp":* Ibid.

15 *"Of course":* Ibid., p. 330.

15 *"than of flying":* Ibid.

15 *dedicate only 15,000 men:* Cray, *General of the Army,* p. 155.

15 *everything was needed:* Ibid.

15 *"to this country":* Pogue, *George C. Marshall: Interviews and Reminiscences,* p. 330.

15 *appropriation he needed:* Cray, *General of the Army,* p. 155.

16 *for the Army:* Franklin D. Roosevelt, "Message to Congress on Appropriations for National Defense," May 16, 1940, American Presidency Project, http:// www.presidency.ucsb.edu/ws/?pid=15954.

16 *"not won by evacuations"*: Winston Churchill, Speech to Parliament, June 4, 1940, http://www.winstonchurchill.org/resources/speeches/1940-the-finest -hour/we-shall-fight-on-the-beaches.

17 *"liberation of the old"*: Ibid.

17 *deemed already beaten:* Winston Churchill, *Their Finest Hour: The Second World War,* vol. 2 (New York: Houghton Mifflin, 1949), p. 123.

17 *"incandescent with courage"*: Ronald Reagan, Address to Members of the British Parliament, June 8, 1982, http://www.reagan.utexas.edu/archives/speeches /1982/60882a.htm.

17 *Churchill later said:* Jean Edward Smith, *FDR* (New York: Random House, 2007), p. 485.

18 *"not be forthcoming"*: Churchill, *Their Finest Hour,* p. 495.

18 *"meet this need"*: Ibid., p. 498.

18 *"artillery, and tanks"*: Ibid., p. 500.

18 *"other supplies"*: Ibid.

19 *"fire is over"*: Franklin D. Roosevelt, Press Conference, December 17, 1940, http://docs.fdrlibrary.marist.edu.od11pc2.html.

19 *"of any nation"*: Churchill, *Their Finest Hour,* p. 503.

20 *"never experienced before"*: Charles A. Lindbergh, "We Are Not Prepared for War: Our Dangers Are Here at Home," Testimony before the Senate Foreign Relations Committee, February 6, 1941, http://www.ibiblio.org/pha/policy /1941/1941-02-06a.html.

20 *"by either side"*: Ibid.

20 *the opening article: Life,* June 3, 1940.

20 *"Threatens the World"*: Ibid.

20 *"have conquered"*: Ibid.

21 *"to fight alone"*: Edna St. Vincent Millay, "There Are No Islands, Any More: Lines Written in Passion and in Deep Concern for England, France, and My Own Country," *New York Times,* June 14, 1940, http://www.nytimes.com /1940/06/14/books/millay-islands.html.

22 *sail for America:* Max Hastings, *Winston's War: Churchill, 1940–1945* (New York: Knopf, 2010), p. 184.

22 *party of eighty:* Ibid.

22 *flew to Washington:* Ibid., p. 186.

22 *"My heart filled"*: Doris Kearns Goodwin, *No Ordinary Time: Franklin & Eleanor Roosevelt: The Home Front in World War II* (New York: Simon & Schuster, 1994), p. 301.

22 *twelve times:* Hastings, *Churchill's War,* p. 186.

22 *single commander:* Andrew Roberts, *Masters and Commanders: How Four Titans Won the War in the West, 1941–1945* (New York: HarperCollins, 2009), p. 67.

22 *"of the twentieth century"*: Roberts, *A History of the English-Speaking Peoples Since 1900,* p. 299.

23 *outside the Capitol:* "U.S. at War: The Presidency—Great Decisions," *Time,* January 5, 1942, p. 12.

23 *"in every land"*: Winston S. Churchill, Address to the U.S. Congress, December 26, 1941, http://www.senate.gov/artandhistory/history/minute/Churchill_Addresses_Congress.htm.

23 *"trusting in the Lord"*: Ibid.

23 *"cast away the scabbard"*: Ibid.

23 *"of all time"*: *Time,* January 5, 1942.

23 *"forces of the U.S."*: Ibid.

24 *"general line of action"*: Eisenhower, *Crusade in Europe,* p. 22.

24 *"of money required"*: Ibid., p. 495.

24 *"to save them"*: Ibid.

24 *"as soon as possible"*: Stephen E. Ambrose, *The Supreme Commander: The War Years of Dwight D. Eisenhower* (New York: Doubleday, 1970), p. 16.

25 *"to fight on"*: Rick Atkinson, *An Army at Dawn: The War in North Africa, 1942–1943* (New York: Henry Holt, 2002), p. 537.

25 *experience of command:* Ibid., p. 533.

26 Enterprise, Hornet, *and* Yorktown: Roberts, *A History of the English-Speaking Peoples Since 1900,* p. 317.

26 *three of Japan's four carriers:* Martin Gilbert, *The Second World War: A Complete History* (New York: Holt Paperbacks, 2004), loc. 7340.

26 *sunk the next day:* Ibid.

26 *in twenty-four hours:* Eisenhower, *Crusade in Europe,* p. 249.

26 *"justified great risk"*: Ibid.

27 *"poised and ready"*: *Time,* June 19, 1944, p. 26.

27 *had been unfortified:* Stephen E. Ambrose, *D-Day: June 6, 1944, The Battle for the Normandy Beaches* (New York: Simon & Schuster, 1994), p. 39.

27 *weighed 300 pounds: Time,* June 19, 1944, pp. 26–27.

27 *"her armed forces":* Combined Chiefs of Staff Directive to General Eisenhower, February 12, 1944, reprinted in "Report by the Supreme Commander to the Combined Chiefs of Staff on the Operations in Europe of the Allied Expeditionary Force, 6 June 1944–8 May, 1945," Center for Military History, United States Army, 1994, http://www.history.army.mil/html/books/070/70-58/CMH _Pub_70-58.pdf.

27 *"going to prevail":* Stephen Ambrose, interview, C-SPAN, *Book TV,* May 25, 1994, http://www.c-span.org/video/?57267-1/book-discussion-dday-june-6 -1944.

28 *"in your life":* John Reville, oral history, Eisenhower Center, University of New Orleans, quoted in Ambrose, *D-Day,* p. 581.

28 *"every church people prayed": Time,* June 12, 1944, p. 21.

29 *"went to pray":* Ibid.

29 *"in their faith":* Franklin Roosevelt, Prayer on D-Day, June 6, 1944, http:// docs.fdrlibrary.marist.edu/odddayp.html.

29 *"invasion has begun":* Anne Frank, *The Diary of a Young Girl: The Definitive Edition* (New York: Doubleday, 1995), pp. 306–7.

30 *"there is life":* Ibid.

30 *on April 12:* Ibid., p. 334.

30 *wounded and dying soldiers: Time,* December 4, 1944, p. 27.

30 *"awesome to behold":* Ibid.

30 *through her tent:* Ibid.

30 *School of Nursing:* Bob Welch: *The Story of Frances Slanger, Forgotten Heroine of Normandy* (New York: Atria, 2004), loc. 1302.

31 *"became America":* Ibid., loc. 324.

31 *"not to doubt":* Ronald Reagan, Remarks at a Ceremony Commemorating the 40th Anniversary of the Normandy Invasion, D-Day, June 6, 1984, http:// www.reagan.utexas.edu/archives/speeches/1984/60684a.htm.

31 *are buried:* American Battle Monuments Commission, Normandy American Cemetery, http://www.abmc.gov/cemeteries-memorials/europe/normandy -american-cemetery#.VYdGYevZr9E.

32 *"our fellow countrymen":* Ibid.

32 *Warm Springs, Georgia:* Senate Historical Office, "Harry S. Truman, 34th Vice President, 1945," http://www.senate.gov/artandhistory/history/common /generic/VP_Harry_Truman.htm.

32 *"Board of Education":* Ibid.

32 *of the United States:* Harry S. Truman, *Memoirs: 1945: Year of Decisions* (New York: Doubleday, 1955), p. 8.

32 *congressional leadership:* Franklin Roosevelt, Day by Day, A Project of the Pare Lorenz Center at the FDR Presidential Library, Diary Logs for January 20, 1945, March 8, 1945, and March 19, 1945, http://www.fdrlibrary.marist.edu /daybyday/search/?str=Truman&start_date=1945-01-01&end_date=1945-04 -20&type=daylog&search_submit=&submitted=t.

32 *Senate Office Building:* David McCullough, *Truman* (New York: Simon & Schuster, 1992), loc. 6491.

32 *"as a senator":* Truman, *1945: Year of Decisions,* loc. 3940.

32 *"to defy description":* Ibid., p. 7.

33 *"accepted in our land":* Ibid.

33 *Europe despaired:* McCullough, *Truman,* p. 350.

33 *by the Americans:* Ibid.

33 *"merely to propaganda":* Letter from General Eisenhower to General Marshall, United States Holocaust Memorial Museum, http://www.ushmm.org /information/exhibitions/online-features/special-focus/buchenwald-concentration -camp.

34 *"Wed. 25. HST":* Henry Stimson to Harry S. Truman, April 24, 1945, Confidential File, Truman Papers, http://www.trumanlibrary.org/whistlestop/study _collections/bomb/large/documents/index.php?documentdate=1945-04-24 &documentid=9-14&pagenumber=1.

34 *"a whole city":* Henry L. Stimson, "The Decision to Use the Atomic Bomb," *Harper's,* February 1947, p. 97.

34 *in the future:* Ibid.

34 *nature of the weapon:* Ibid., p. 100.

35 *"situation was hopeless":* McCullough, *Truman,* p. 438.

35 *had ever surrendered:* Ibid.

36 *12,000 American service members killed:* SSgt Rudy R. Frame, "Okinawa: The Final Great Battle of World War II," *Marine Corps Gazette,* November 2012, https:// www.mca-marines.org/gazette/2012/11/okinawa-final-great-battle-world-war-ii.

36 *more than 100,000:* Ibid.

36 *on Kyushu alone:* Roberts, *A History of the English-Speaking Peoples since 1900,* p. 374.

36 *"on his home grounds":* Truman, *1945: Year of Decisions,* p. 417.

36 *"like a beautiful flower?":* McCullough, *Truman,* p. 459.

36 *council was adjourned:* Ibid.

36 *"teletyped to Washington":* *Time,* August 20, 1945, p. 20.

37 *dispatch from the War Department:* Ibid.

37 *remained on his throne:* Ibid., p. 21.

37 *"Declaration are achieved":* Ibid.

37 *"surrender of Japan":* Harry S. Truman: "The President's News Conference," August 14, 1945, American Presidency Project, http://www.presidency.ucsb.edu/ws/?pid=12383.

37 *broke into cheers: Time,* August 20, 1945, p. 19.

38 *failed to use it:* McCullough, *Truman,* p. 439.

38 *"countrymen in the face":* Stimson, *Harper's,* p. 106.

38 *spotlight shone: Time,* December 4, 1944.

39 *"as its keystone":* Roberts, *History of the English-Speaking Peoples Since 1900,* p. 304.

40 *"the next millennium":* Atkinson, *An Army at Dawn,* p. 3.

40 *"Armies and Navies":* William Manchester, *The Glory and the Dream: A Narrative History of America, 1932–1972* (Boston: Little, Brown, 1973), p. 386.

40 *"of the Free World":* Roberts, *A History of the English-Speaking Peoples Since 1900,* 350.

40 *"fight like hell":* "Eisenhower Says We'll Fight Like Hell for Peace," *Evening Independent,* November 22, 1944, https://news.google.com/newspapers?nid=950&dat=19441121&id=8fRPAAAAIBAJ&sjid=HFUDAAAAIBAJ&pg=5032,5008271&hl=en.

40 *"to unparalleled might":* Eisenhower, *Crusade in Europe,* loc. 180.

41 *"to the Arctic Sea":* Lincoln Barnett, "General Marshall: Commander and Creator of America's Greatest Army," *Life,* January 3, 1944, p. 54.

CHAPTER 2: FREEDOM VICTORIOUS

43 *Shortly before 10 P.M.:* Nicolaus Mills, *Winning the Peace: The Marshall Plan & America's Coming of Age as a Superpower* (Hoboken, NJ: Wiley, 2008), loc. 1835.

43 *with a red pencil:* Ibid., loc. 1846.

44 *"the time after that":* Cray, *General of the Army,* p. 605.

44 *It was Soviet policy:* Ibid.

44 *"Communism thrived on":* Forrest C. Pogue, *George C. Marshall,* vol. 4, *States-man, 1945–1959* (New York: Viking, 1987), p. 196.

44 *"they could not be":* George C. Marshall, oral history interview with Forrest C. Pogue, November 14, 1956, cited in Pogue, *Statesman,* p. 196.

44 *"the Iron Curtain":* Robert Murphy, *Diplomat Among Warriors* (New York: Prae-ger, 1976), p. 342, cited in Pogue, *Statesman,* p. 196.

44 *"meaningless election on earth":* Time, February 18, 1946, p. 29.

45 *were on the ballot:* Ibid.

45 *vote in Moscow:* Ibid.

45 *capitalist system survived:* John Lewis Gaddis, *The United States and the Origins of the Cold War* (New York: Columbia University Press, 1972), p. 299.

45 *"since V-J Day":* Time, February 18, 1946, p. 29.

45 *read the speech with care:* Interview with Paul Nitze, CNN, *Cold War,* Episode 2, "Iron Curtain 1945–1947."

45 *"is to be secure":* Telegram, George Kennan to George Marshall ["Long Tele-gram"], February 22, 1946, Harry S. Truman Administration File, Elsey papers, Part Five, p. 14, https://www.trumanlibrary.org/whistlestop/study_collections /coldwar/documents/pdf/6-6.pdf.

45 *"peaceful and stable world":* George G. Kennan, "The Sources of Soviet Con-duct," *Foreign Affairs,* July 1947, https://www.foreignaffairs.com/articles/russian -federation/1947-07-01/sources-soviet-conduct.

46 *"messages were shockers":* Dean Acheson, *Present at the Creation: My Years at the State Department* (New York: Norton, 1969), p. 217.

46 *insurrection was under way:* Roberts, *A History of the English-Speaking Peoples Since 1900,* p. 410.

46 *against the Soviet threat:* Acheson, *Present at the Creation,* p. 217.

47 *"break up the play":* Ibid., p. 219.

47 *"not a free one":* Address of the President to Congress, Recommending Assistance to Greece and Turkey, March 12, 1947, Harry S. Truman Administration, Elsey Papers, https://www.trumanlibrary.org/whistlestop/study_collections/doctrine /large/documents/index.php?pagenumber=1&documentdate=1947-03-12 &documentid=5-9.

47 *"suppression of personal freedoms":* Ibid.

47 *"destinies in their own ways":* Ibid.

48 *"welfare of our own Nation":* Ibid.

48 *majorities in both houses:* Acheson, *Present at the Creation,* p. 225.

48 *assist the European recovery:* Mills, *Winning the Peace,* p. 108.

49 *"placed upon our country":* George C. Marshall Remarks at Harvard University, June 5, 1947, Transcription Version, http://marshallfoundation.org/marshall/the-marshall-plan/marshall-plan-speech/.

49 *his prepared remarks:* John T. Bethell, "The Ultimate Commencement Address," *Harvard Magazine,* May 1977, https://harvardmagazine.com/1997/05/marshall.html.

49 *twelve-minute speech:* Ibid.

49 *understood its significance:* Ibid.

49 *sixteen European countries:* "History of the Marshall Plan," George C. Marshall Foundation, http://marshallfoundation.org/marshall/the-marshall-plan/history-marshall-plan/.

49 *in 2015 dollars:* Bureau of Labor Statistics, CPI Inflation Calculator, http://www.bls.gov/data/inflation_calculator.htm/.

49 *to outline assistance needs:* Acheson, *Present at the Creation,* p. 234.

49 *conference in Paris:* Ibid., p. 235.

50 *ordered them not to attend:* CNN *Cold War,* Episode 3, "Marshall Plan, 1947–1952."

50 *"as Stalin's slave":* Interview with Antonin Sum, ibid.

50 *"nothing against the state":* Anne Applebaum, *Iron Curtain: The Crushing of Eastern Europe, 1944–1956* (New York: Doubleday, 2012), loc. 178.

50 *secret police forces:* Ibid., loc. 339.

50 *radio stations:* Ibid., loc. 348.

50 *ethnic cleansing:* Ibid., loc. 357.

50 *young people's organizations:* Ibid., loc. 348.

50 *"observation and restraint":* Ibid., loc. 358.

50 *"own the future":* Ibid., loc. 3447.

51 *trains loaded with coal:* Air Force Historical Support Division, "The Berlin Airlift," Fact Sheet, June 28, 2012, http://www.afhso.af.mil/topics/factsheets/factsheet.asp?id+17711.

51 *and other supplies:* Harry S. Truman Presidential Library, Berlin Airlift Fact Sheet, https://www.trumanlibrary.org/educ/presidentialyears/22-Berlin%20Air lift.doc.

51 *"plant of East Germany":* Roberts, *A History of the English-Speaking Peoples Since 1900,* p. 382.

51 *"could dispel these fears":* Harry S. Truman, *Memoirs: 1946–52, Years of Trial and Hope* (New York: Doubleday, 1956), loc. 6635.

52 *Treaty was signed:* Ibid., loc. 6671.

53 *"in France's cemeteries?":* Roberts, *A History of the English-Speaking Peoples Since 1900,* p. 469.

53 *state of Israel:* Martin Gilbert, *Israel: A History* (New York: Harper Perennial, 2008), p. 186.

53 *"idea of a Jewish state":* Truman, *1946–1952, Years of Trial and Hope,* loc. 4330.

53 *pulled out:* Gilbert, p. 191.

54 *not include South Korea:* Secretary of State Dean Acheson, Remarks at the National Press Club, January 12, 1950, https://web.viu.ca/davies/H102/Acheson .speech1950.htm.

54 *invade the South:* John Lewis Gaddis, *The Cold War: A New History* (New York: Penguin Press, 2005), p. 42.

54 *in Indochina:* Ibid.

54 *June 24, 1950:* Truman, *1946–1952, Years of Trial and Hope,* p. 332.

54 *withdraw its forces immediately:* Ibid., p. 336.

54 *to the South Korean army:* Ibid.

55 *"back away from it":,* Ibid., p. 334.

55 *worldwide dimensions:* Ibid., p. 337.

55 *amphibious assault:* McCullough, *Truman,* loc. 15575.

56 *imprisonment, and starvation:* Stephane Courtois et al. and Mark Kramer, *The Black Book of Communism* (Cambridge, MA: Harvard University Press, 1999), pp. 463–64, cited in Lee Edwards, PhD, "The Legacy of Mao Zedong Is Mass Murder," Heritage Foundation, February 2, 2010, http://www.heritage.org /research/commentary/2010/02/the-legacy-of-mao-zedong-is-mass-murder.

56 *died in combat:* Department of Veterans Affairs, "America's Wars Fact Sheet," May 2015, http://www.va.gov/opa/publications/factsheets/fs_americas_wars .pdf.

56 *"intentions of the West":* President Ronald Reagan, Address to Members of the British Parliament, June 8, 1982, http://www.heritage.org/research/reports /2002/06/reagans-westminster-speech.

56 *thermonuclear bomb:* McCullough, *Truman,* loc. 14752.

57 *"working on an H-bomb":* Paul H. Nitze, *From Hiroshima to Glasnost: At the Center of Decision* (New York: Grove Weidenfeld, 1989), p. 90.

57 *directly to the president:* Acheson, *Present at the Creation,* p. 349.

57 *cut the presentation short:* Nitze, *From Hiroshima to Glasnost,* p. 91.

58 *"of the individual":* "NSC 68: United States Objectives and Programs for National Security, A Report to the President Pursuant to the President's Directive of January 31, 1950," April 14, 1950, Part II, http://fas.org/irp/offdocs/nsc-hst /nsc-68.htm.

58 *"to their authority":* Ibid., Part III.

58 *"its fundamental design":* Ibid., Part V.

59 *of the free world:* Ibid., Part IX, D.

59 *"military position weakened":* Acheson, *Present at the Creation,* p. 376.

59 *"to their enemies":* NSC 68, Part VIII.

59 *"We will bury you":* "Raging Soviet Boss Shouts at the West: We Will Bury You," *Sarasota Journal,* November 19, 1956, p. 1.

60 *"compared to rockets":* Time, November 25, 1957, p. 27.

60 *"just as vulnerable":* Ibid.

60 *merits of communism versus capitalism:* see Transcript, "The Kitchen Debate," July 24, 1959, Vice President Richard Nixon and Soviet Premier Nikita Khrushchev, U.S. Embassy, Moscow, Soviet Union, http://www.foia.cia.gov /sites/default/files/document_conversions/16/1959-07-24.pdf; Harrison E. Salisbury, "Nixon and Khrushchev Argue in Public as U.S. Exhibit Opens; Accuse Each Other of Threats," *New York Times,* July 24, 1959; "1959: Khrushchev and Nixon Have War of Words," BBC, On This Day, http://news .bbc.co.uk/onthisday/hi/dates/stories/july24/newsid_2779000/2779551.stm.

61 *"our military establishment":* President Dwight Eisenhower, Farewell Address, January 17, 1961, http://www.eisenhower.archives.gov/research/online_documents /farewell_address/Reading_Copy.pdf.

63 *followed events closely:* William Manchester, *The Glory and the Dream,* p. 1112.

63 *refugees from the East:* Aleksandr Fursenko and Timothy Naftali, *Khrushchev's Cold War: The Inside Story of an American Adversary* (New York: Norton, 2006), p. 355.

63 *would respond militarily:* Ibid., p. 364.

64 *"Roughest thing in my life":* Manchester, *The Glory and the Dream,* p. 1115.

64 *"intimidated and blackmailed":* Ibid.

64 *days of August alone: Time,* August 25, 1961, p. 20.

64 *"steel on cobblestones":* Ibid.

64 *"As the troops arrived at scores of border points":* Ibid.

65 *"bullets, bayonets, and barricades":* Ibid.

66 *"self-destruction on his part":* Address by Roswell L. Gilpatric, Deputy Secretary of Defense, Before the Business Council at the Homestead, Hot Springs, Virginia, Saturday, October 21, 1961, http://nsarchive.gwu.edu/NSAEBB/NSAEBB56 /BerlinC6.pdf.

66 *"intend to be defeated":* Ibid.

67 *"answer was missiles":* Nikita Khrushchev, *Khrushchev Remembers,* translated and edited by Strobe Talbott (New York: Bantam, 1971), p. 546.

67 *"leads to war":* President John F. Kennedy, Address to the Nation, Cuban Missile Crisis, October 22, 1962, http://www.americanrhetoric.com/speeches /PDFFiles/John%20F.%20Kennedy%20-%20Cuban%20Missile%20Crisis .pdf.

67 *"upon the Soviet Union":* Ibid.

67 *they turned around:* Manchester, *The Glory and the Dream,* loc. 21067.

68 *within six months:* Roberts, *A History of the English-Speaking Peoples Since 1900,* p. 454.

68 *remove the missiles:* Manchester, *The Glory and the Dream,* p. 1189.

68 *advisors in Vietnam:* John F. Kennedy President Library and Museum, "Historical Briefings: JFK, The Cold War and Vietnam," http://www.jfklibrary.org/~/media /assets/Education%20and%20Public%20Programs/Education/Lesson%20 Plans/Vietnam%20Lesson%20Plan.pdf.

69 *"unable to win":* General William Westmoreland, *A Soldier Reports* (New York: Plenum, 1976), p. 142.

69 *"of the American public":* Henry A. Kissinger, *Years of Renewal* (New York: Simon & Schuster, 1999), loc. 1640.

70 *"Communist conqueror":* Ibid., loc. 7868.

70 *"finished as far as America is concerned":* Remarks by Gerald R. Ford, Tulane University, April 23, 1975, http://www.fordlibrarymuseum.gov/library/speeches /750208.asp.

71 *"in the Middle East"*: Kissinger, *Years of Renewal,* loc. 1727.

71 *"Don't do stupid stuff"*: See, for example, Mark Landler, "Obama Warns U.S. Faces Diffuse Terrorism Threats," *New York Times,* May 28, 2014.

71 *"we'd made history"*: Interview with Henry Kissinger, CNN *Cold War,* Episode 15, "China."

72 *"of the United States"*: Associated Press wire story, August 8, 1974.

74 *"to see Solzhenitsyn"*: Memorandum from Dick Cheney to President Ford, July 8, 1975, cited in Stephen F. Hayes, *Cheney: The Untold Story of America's Most Powerful and Controversial Vice President* (New York: HarperCollins, 2007), pp. 92–93.

74 *"manner as possible"*: Kissinger, *Years of Renewal,* loc. 11092.

74 *"unrecognized by contemporaries"*: Ibid., loc. 10788.

74 *"Declaration of Human Rights"*: Conference on Security and Cooperation in Europe, "Final Act," Helsinki, August 1, 1975, http://www.osce.org/docs/English /1990-1999/summits/helfa75e.htm.

75 *"Who can force us?"*: Interview with Anatoly Dobrynin, CNN *Cold War,* Episode 16, "Détente."

75 *"The Soviet Union and the Warsaw Pact"*: Interview with President Gerald Ford, CNN *Cold War,* Episode 16, "Détente."

75 *"of an official document"*: Gaddis, *The Cold War,* p. 190.

75 *"of the Soviet leadership"*: Ibid.

76 *"Charter 77" manifesto*: Ibid., 191.

76 *"under a Ford administration"*: Gerald R. Ford, "Presidential Campaign Debate," October 6, 1976, American Presidency Project, http://www.presidency.ucsb .edu/ws/?pid=6414.

76 *"communist zone?"*: Ibid.

76 *national security team*: Rowland Evans and Robert Novak, "Nuclear Blockbuster," *Washington Post,* January 27, 1977, p. A23.

77 *flatly rejected it*: Interview with Anatoly Dobrynin, CNN *Cold War,* Episode 19, "Freeze."

77 *"deep stab wound"*: Interview with Les Gelb, CNN *Cold War,* Episode 19, "Freeze."

77 *"because we are free"*: President Jimmy Carter, Commencement Address at University of Notre Dame, May 22, 1977, American Presidency Project, http:// www.presidency.ucsb.edu/ws/?pid=7552.

77 *from the Soviets:* Roberts, *A History of the English-Speaking Peoples Since 1900,* p. 519.

78 *"on a very clear course":* "The Neutron Bomb Furor," *Time,* April 17, 1978.

78 *"foul-up":* "Costly U.N. 'Mistake': Carter Angers Both Sides in the Arab-Israeli Contest," *Evening Independent,* March 6, 1980, https://news.google.com/news papers?nid=950&dat=19800306&id=p2FQAAAAIBAJ&sjid=sVgDAAAAIB AJ&pg=6657,1414362&hl=en.

78 *fifty-two Americans:* "The Iran Hostage Crisis, 31 Years Later—Pictures," *National Journal,* January 19, 2012, http://www.nationaljournal.com/pictures -video/the-iran-hostage-crisis-31-years-later-pictures-20120119.

79 *"to do anything":* Address by Governor Ronald Reagan Accepting the Republican Nomination for the Presidency, July 17, 1980, http://www.presidency.ucsb .edu/ws/?pid=25970.

79 *"country as pope":* Gaddis, *The Cold War,* p. 192.

80 *"speaks with my voice":* John O'Sullivan, *The President, the Pope, and the Prime Minister: Three Who Changed the World* (Washington, DC: Regnery, 2006), p. 93.

80 *"before your own conscience":* George Weigel, *Witness to Hope: The Biography of Pope John Paul II* (New York: HarperCollins, 1999), pp. 307–9.

80 *"thousand-year-right of citizenship":* Ibid., p. 306.

80 *"history of Poland":* Peggy Noonan, "We Want God: When John Paul II Went to Poland, Communism Didn't Have a Prayer," *Wall Street Journal,* April 7, 2005.

80 *"We want God":* Ibid.

80 *"people want the Pope":* Hella Pick, "Party for the People but People for the Pope," *Manchester Guardian Weekly,* June 17, 1979.

80 *the archbishop's residence:* Weigel, *Witness to Hope,* p. 313.

81 *"Sto lat!":* Ibid.

81 *the pope sang:* Ibid.

81 *Kraków Commons:* Ibid., p. 318.

81 *"the Holy Spirit":* Noonan, "We Want God."

81 *"spiritual freedom":* Weigel, *Witness to Hope,* p. 319.

82 *Thirteen million Poles:* Ibid., p. 320.

82 *In an interview:* Peggy Noonan, "Make Him a Saint: How Pope John Paul II Worked a Political Miracle," *Wall Street Journal,* April 28, 2011.

82 *pen bearing John Paul II's picture:* Gaddis, *The Cold War,* p. 218.

82 *"coffin of Communism"*: Ibid., p. 222.

83 *"ash-heap of history"*: President Ronald Reagan, Address to Members of the British Parliament, June 8, 1982, http://www.reagan.utexas.edu/archives/speeches /1982/60882a.htm.

83 *"squandering of our freedom"*: President Ronald Reagan, Remarks at the Annual Convention of the National Association of Evangelicals in Orlando, Florida, March 8, 1983, http://www.reagan.utexas.edu/archives/speeches/1983 /30883b.htm.

84 *"day by day"*: President Ronald Reagan Address to the Nation on Defense and National Security, March 23, 1983, http://www.reagan.utexas.edu/archives /speeches/1983/32383d.htm.

85 *share the technology:* Ronald Reagan, Speech on the Geneva Summit, November 21, 1985, http://www.millercenter.org/president/speeches/speech-3924.

85 *toward significant arms reductions:* Ibid.

85 *were on the table:* Lou Cannon, "Reagan-Gorbachev Summit Talks Collapse as Deadlock on SDI Wipes Out Other Gains," *Washington Post*, October 13, 1986, http://www.washingtonpost.com/wp-srv/inatt/longterm/summit/archive/oct86 .htm.

85 *laboratory testing:* Ibid.

85 *Reagan would not agree:* Ronald Reagan, Address to the Nation on the Meetings with Soviet General Secretary Gorbachev in Iceland, October 13, 1986, http:// www/reagan.uteyas.edu/archives/speeches/1986/101386a.htm.

86 *"tear down this wall"*: President Ronald Reagan Remarks on East-West Relations at the Brandenburg Gate, West Berlin, June 12, 1987, http://www.reagan .utexas.edu/archives/speeches/1987/061287d.htm.

86 *Hungarian frontier:* Chris Bowlby, "The Man Who Opened the Iron Curtain," BBC Radio 4, October 26, 2009, http://news.bbc.co.uk/2/hi/europe/8323140 .stm.

86 *Gorbachev did not object:* Ibid.

86 *bold red print:* Anna Husarska, "How a Partially Free Election Altered Poland," January 25, 2010, IIP Digital, U.S. Department of State, http://iipdigital .usembassy.gov/st/english/publication/2010/01/20100125173526mlenuhret0 .558952.html#axzz3bxO4zmRc.

87 *"country of their choice"*: Serge Schmemann, "Hungary Allows 7000 East Germans to Emigrate West," *New York Times*, September 11, 1989, http://www .nytimes.com/1989/09/11/world/hungary-allows-7000-east-germans-to-emigrate -west.html.

87 *embassy in Prague:* Serge Schmemann, "East Germans Line Emigré Routes, Some in Hope of Their Own Exit," *New York Times,* October 5, 1989, http://www.nytimes.com/1989/10/05/world/east-germans-line-emigre-routes-some-in-hope-of-their-own-exit.html.

87 *"onwards, immediately":* Serge Schmemann, "A Fateful Day and the East Tasted Freedom," *New York Times,* November 9, 2009, http://www.nytimes.com/2009/11/09/world/europe/09iht-wall.html?pagewanted=all.

88 *"in Russia itself":* Judt, *Postwar,* p. 632.

88 *94.5 million people:* Roberts, *A History of the English-Speaking Peoples Since 1900,* p. 386.

CHAPTER 3: DAWN OF THE AGE OF TERROR

92 *embargo on Iraq:* John-Thor Dahlburg and Jim Mann, "U.S., Soviets Ask World to Cut Off Weapons to Iraq," *Los Angeles Times,* August 4, 1990.

92 *"Cold War ended":* James A. Baker, Oral History, Miller Center, University of Virginia, 2011, http://millercenter.org/president/bush/oralhistory/james-baker-2011.

93 *world's deadliest weapons:* George J. Tenet, Porter J. Goss, Michael Hayden, John E. McLaughlin, Albert M. Calland, and Stephen R. Kappes, "Ex-CIA Directors: Interrogations Saved Lives," *Wall Street Journal,* December 10, 2014, http://www.wsj.com/articles/cia-interrogations-saved-lives-1418142644.

93 *to procure nuclear weapons:* Ibid.

94 *should conflict occur:* Secretary of Defense Dick Cheney, "Defense Strategy for the 1990s: The Regional Defense Strategy," January 1993, p. 3, http://nsarchive.gwu.edu/nukevault/ebb245/doc15.pdf.

95 *"crisis response capability":* Ibid., pp. 23–24.

95 *"to resist aggression":* Ibid.

95 *"but the prosecutors":* Andrew McCarthy, *Willful Blindness: A Memoir of the Jihad* (New York: Encounter Books, 2008), loc. 79.

96 *"the defendants":* Ibid., loc. 82.

96 *"had taken place":* Osama bin Laden, fatwa, August 23, 1996, http://www.pbs.org/newshour/updates/military-july-dec96-fatwa_1996/.

97 *seventy-five were wounded:* Michael R. Gordon and Thomas L. Friedman, "Details of U.S. Raid in Somalia: Success So Near, a Loss So Deep," *New York Times,* October 25, 1993.

97 *Somali militias:* Eric Schmitt, "Study Faults Powell Aides on Somalia," *New York Times,* October 1, 1995, http://www.nytimes.com/1995/10/01/world /study-faults-powell-aides-on-somalia.html.

97 *"keep the numbers down":* United States Senate Committee on Armed Services, "Review of the Circumstances Surrounding the Ranger Raid on October 3–4, 1993, in Mogadishu, Somalia," September 29, 1995, p. 29, https://fas.org/irp /congress/1995_rpt/mogadishu.pdf.

97 *"imagery on CNN":* Ibid., p. 31.

97 *presence in Somalia:* Ibid., p. 34.

97 *March 31, 1994:* Remarks by President Bill Clinton on the Situation in So-malia, October 7, 1993, http://www.nytimes.com/1993/10/08/world/somalia -mission-clinton-s-words-somalia-responsibilities-american-leadership.html.

98 *"became very clear":* Osama bin Laden, fatwa, August 23, 1996, http://www.pbs .org/newshour/updates/military-july-dec96-fatwa_1996/.

98 *more than five thousand were wounded:* "1998 U.S. Embassies in Africa Bomb-ings Fast Facts," CNN, October 6, 2013, http://www.cnn.com/2013/10/06 /world/africa/africa-embassy-bombings-fast-facts/.

98 *bin Laden and al Qaeda:* George Tenet, *At the Center of the Storm* (New York: HarperCollins, 2007), loc. 2044.

98 *bin Laden was involved:* Ibid., loc. 2064.

99 *"country we're aware of":* Stephen F. Hayes, "The Clinton View of Iraq-al Qaeda Ties: Connecting the Dots in 1998 but Not in 2003," *Weekly Standard,* De-cember 29–January 5, 2004.

99 *chemical weapons experts:* Ibid.

99 *Americans overseas: United States v. Usama bin Laden, et al.,* Indictment no. S(9) 98 Cr. 1023 (S.D.N.Y. 1999), http://fas.org/irp/news/1998/11/98110602_nlt.html.

101 *"someday, nuclear weapons":* Nicholas Lemann, "The Quiet Man: Dick Cheney's Discreet Rise to Unprecedented Power," *New Yorker,* May 7, 2001.

101 *"first line of defense":* Ibid.

102 *"share their fate":* President George W. Bush, Address to a Joint Session of Con-gress, September 20, 2001, http://georgewbush-whitehouse.archives.gov/news /releases/2001/09/20010920-8.html.

102 *"secret even in success":* Ibid.

102 *arrived in Afghanistan:* Gary C. Schroen, *First In: How Seven CIA Officers Opened the War on Terror in Afghanistan* (New York: Random House, 2005), loc. 1157.

102 *purchased and upgraded:* Ibid., loc. 460.

105 *"until it was too late":* President George W. Bush, Weekly Radio Address, December 17, 2005, http://georgewbushwhitehouse.archives.gov/news/releases /2005/12/20051217.html.

106 *to stop them:* Max Boot, "The Price of Liberty," *Commentary,* May 25, 2015. https://www.commentarymagazine.com/2015/05/25/the-price-of-liberty/.

106 *"identified them as such":* General Mike Hayden, Director of the NSA, Remarks at the National Press Club, January 23, 2006, https://www.press.org/speakers /transcripts-2006.

107 *back in the fight:* Jeryl Bier, "Four More Gitmo Terrorists Returned to Battlefield," *Weekly Standard,* March 6, 2014.

107 *to Syria and Iraq:* Thomas Joscelyn, "Gitmo 'Poet' Now Recruiting for Islamic State," *Weekly Standard,* November 19, 2014.

107 *wrote the* Guardian*:* Declan Walsh, "Return My Work, Says Guantánamo Poet," *Guardian,* April 3, 2006.

107 *al Qaeda operations expert:* Tenet, *At the Center of the Storm,* loc. 247.

108 *how best to attack:* George J. Tenet, Porter J. Goss, Michael Hayden, John E. McLaughlin, Albert M. Calland, and Stephen R. Kappes, "Ex-CIA Directors: Interrogations Saved Lives," *Wall Street Journal,* December 10, 2014, http://www .wsj.com/articles/cia-interrogations-saved-lives-1418142644.

109 *"inside the United States":* Central Intelligence Agency, "Khaled Sheikh Muhammad: Preeminent Source on Al-Qa'ida," July 13, 2004, http://washington post.com/wp-srv/nation/documents/Khalid_Shaykh_Muhammad.pdf.

109 *"tactics that were used":* Secretary Leon Panetta, NBC *Meet the Press,* February 2013.

110 *"before the war":* Interview with David Kay, NPR *Weekend Edition,* January 25, 2004.

111 *to do so:* Duelfer, *Comprehensive Report,* vol. 1, "Regime Strategic Intent, Key Findings," September 30, 2004, and "Realizing Saddam's Veiled WMD Intent," September 30, 2004.

112 *Iowa caucuses:* Robert M. Gates, *Duty* (New York: Knopf, 2014), p. 376.

112 *be based on fact:* This and following appeared previously in Dick Cheney and Liz Cheney, "The Truth About Iraq and Why It Matters," *Weekly Standard,* July 21, 2014.

113 *gas chambers:* Jeffrey Goldberg, "The Great Terror: In Northern Iraq, there is new evidence of Saddam Hussein's genocidal war on the Kurds—and of his possible ties to al Qaeda," *New Yorker,* March 25, 2002.

113 *"homicidal dictator pursuing WMD"*: George W. Bush, *Decision Points* (New York: Crown, 2010), loc. 5208.

114 *"re-establish Iraq's WMD programs"*: Director of Central Intelligence, National Intelligence Estimate, "Prospects for Iraq: Saddam and Beyond," December, 1993, p. vii, http://www.foia.cia.gov/docs/DOC-0001188931/DOC-000118 8931.pdf.

114 *"its nuclear weapons program"*: quoted in Charles S. Robb and Laurence H. Silberman, *The Commission on the Intelligence Capabilities of the United States Regarding Weapons of Mass Destruction, Report to the President of the United States,* March 31, 2005, part 1, p. 54, http://www.gpoaccess.gov/wmd/pdf/full_wmd _report.pdf.

114 *"the Persian Gulf region"*: quoted in Senate Select Committee on Intelligence, *Report on the U.S. Intelligence Community's Prewar Intelligence Assessments on Iraq,* July 24, 2004, p. 144, http://www.intelligence.senate.gov/108301 .pdf.

115 *"grave threat to our security"*: John Kerry, statement on the Senate Floor, October 9, 2002, http://www.freerepublic.com/focus/f-news/1240102/posts.

115 *"including al Qaeda members"*: Hillary Clinton, statement on the Senate Floor, October 10, 2002, http://www.c-span.org/video/?173141-1/senate -session.

115 *"effort led by the United States"*: Joe Biden, *Washington Post* 1998 op-ed, quoted in Michael Warren, "Reminder: Biden Supported Iraq War in 2002, October 13, 2012, http://www.weeklystandard.com/blogs/reminder-biden-supported -iraq-war-2002 654352.html.

116 *"action to prevent it"*: Jay Rockefeller, statement on the Senate Floor, October 10, 2002, http://www.c-span.org/video/?173141-1/senate-session.

116 *"weapons inspections process"*: Nancy Pelosi, statement, December 16, 1998, quoted in Mark Goldblatt, "The Final Piece of the Puzzle," *National Review,* November 15, 2007, http://www.nationalreview.com/arrticle/222830/final -piece-puzzle-mark-goldblatt.

116 "he will use them": Bill Clinton, statement on Iraq strikes, December 16, 1998, http://www.cnn.com/ALLPOLITICS/stories/1998/12/16/transcripts/clinton .html.

117 *"intelligence yield"*: General Stanley McChrystal, U.S. Army (Ret.), *My Share of the Task* (New York: Penguin, 2013), p. 146.

119 *"will not fail"*: President George W. Bush, Address to a Joint Session of Congress, September 20, 2001, http://georgewbush-whitehouse.archives.gov/news /releases/2001/09/20010920-8.html.

THE APOLOGY TOUR

123 *"secured our nation"*: Remarks by Barack Obama, St. Paul, Minnesota, June 3, 2008, http://abcnews.go.com/Politics/Vote2008/story?id=4988344.

124 *"bottom-up economic growth"*: Interview of Barack Obama by Fareed Zakaria, CNN, July 13, 2008, http://www.cnn.com/2008/POLITICS/07/13/zakaria.obama/.

124 *"land of my childhood"*: Barack Obama, *The Audacity of Hope: Thoughts on Reclaiming the American Dream* (New York: Crown, 2006), p. 329.

124 *"world's sole superpower"*: Ibid., p. 330.

124 *"corrupting effects of fear"*: Ibid., p. 337.

124 *"enormous military buildup"*: Ibid., p. 338.

124 *leaders view the world*: Ibid.

125 *closing it:* President Barack Obama, Remarks at Strasbourg Town Hall, April 3, 2009, https://www.whitehouse.gov/the-press-office/remarks-president-obama-strasbourg-town-hall.

125 *"to battle terrorism"*: Ibid., Q&A following remarks.

126 *"proliferate nuclear weapons"*: Ibid.

126 *"Greek exceptionalism"*: President Barack Obama, News Conference, Strasbourg, France, April 4, 2009, https://www.whitehouse.gov/the-press-office/news-conference-president-obama-4042009.

126 *"to do the same"*: President Barack Obama, Remarks in Prague, April 5, 2009, https://www.whitehouse.gov/the-press-office/remarks-president-barack-obama-prague-delivered.

126 *"against these missiles"*: Ibid.

126 *canceled the very missile system:* "Obama's Missile Offense," *Wall Street Journal,* September 18, 2009, http://www.wsj.com/articles/SB1000142405297020451 85045744185633466840666.

127 *"three months old"*: Major Garrett, "Obama Endures Ortega Diatribe," Fox News, April 18, 2009, http://www.foxnews.com/politics/2009/04/18/obama-endures-ortega-diatribe/.

127 *"to the Muslim world"*: President Barack Obama, Remarks in Cairo, June 4, 2009, https://www.whitehouse.gov/blog/newbeginning/transcripts/.

128 *"long-gone Cold War"*: President Barack Obama, Remarks at the United Nations General Assembly, September 23, 2009, http://www.nytimes.com/2009/09/24/us/politics/24prexy.text.html?pagewanted=all&_r=0.

129 *"is a 'non-starter'"*: "Apology Not Accepted," *Investor's Business Daily,* October 10, 2011.

129 *disavowed the plan:* Jake Tapper, "Japanese Government Nixed Idea of Obama Visiting, Apologizing for Hiroshima," ABC News, October 12, 2011, http://abcnews.go.com/blogs/politics/2011/10/japanese-government-nixed-idea-of-obama-visiting-apologizing-for-hiroshima/.

129 *bowing deeply:* Photo here: http://news.investors.com/photopopup.asp?path=ISS2c_111012.jpg&docId=587698&xmpSource=&width=3963&height=2826&caption=In+November+2009%2c+Barack+Obama+became+the+first+U.S.+president+to+bow+to+Japan%26%2339%3bs+emperor.&id=587715.

CHAPTER 4: ENDING WARS

131 *"Taliban in Afghanistan":* Senator Barack Obama, Acceptance Speech, Democratic National Convention, August 28, 2008, http://www.nytimes.com/2008/08/28/us/politics/28text-obama.html?pagewanted=all&_r=0.

131 *"IS [IS] and Iran":* Thomas E. Ricks, "Ryan Crocker on Iraq, and on Whether We Are Seeing the Arab State System Fragment," *Foreign Policy,* May 26, 2015, http://foreignpolicy.com/2015/05/26/ryan-crocker-on-iraq-and-on-whether-we-are-seeing-the-arab-state-system-fragment/.

131 *from Iraq:* Robert M. Gates, *Duty: Memoirs of a Secretary at War* (New York: Knopf, 2014), loc. 5869.

131 *enhanced interrogation program:* George J. Tenet, Porter J. Goss, Michael Hayden, John E. McLaughlin, Albert M. Calland, and Stephen R. Kappes, "Ex-CIA Directors: Interrogations Saved Lives," *Wall Street Journal,* December 10, 2014, http://www.wsj.com/articles/cia-interrogations-saved-lives-1418142644.

132 *"interrogation techniques":* Leon Panetta, *Worthy Fights* (New York: Penguin Press, 2014), p. 223.

132 *"attacking this country":* "Statement from Director Brennan on the SSCI Study on the Former Detention and Interrogation Program," Central Intelligence Agency, December 9, 2014, https://www.cia.gov/news-information/press-releases-statements/2014-press-releases-statements/statement-from-director-brennan-on-ssci-study-on-detention-interrogation-program.html; Peter Baker, "Banned Techniques Yielded 'High Value Information,' Memo Says," *New York Times,* April 21, 2009, http://www.nytimes.com/2009/04/22/us/politics/22blair.html.

132 *take this step:* Marc Thiessen, *Courting Disaster* (Washington, DC: Regnery, 2010), p. 13.

132 *release of the memos:* Panetta, *Worthy Fights,* p. 218.

133 *"how we learn":* Transcript of President Obama Remarks at the Central Intelligence Agency, April 20, 2009, https://www.cia.gov/news-information /speeches-testimony/president-obama-at-cia.html.

134 *" 'the sacred principles' ":* President Barack Obama, Remarks on National Security, National Archives, May 21, 2009, https://www.whitehouse.gov/the-press -office/remarks-president-national-security-5-21-09.

135 *"of innocent people":* Former vice president Dick Cheney, American Enterprise Institute, May 21, 2009, http://www.aei.org/publication/remarks-by-richard -b-cheney/.

136 *overpowered him:* David Ariosto and Deborah Feyerick, "Christmas Day Bomber Sentenced to Life in Prison," CNN, February 17, 2012, http://www .cnn.com/2012/02/16/justice/michigan-underwear-bomber-sentencing/.

136 *his Miranda rights:* Transcript, Robert Gibbs interview, *Fox News Sunday,* January 24, 2010, http://www.foxnews.com/story/2010/01/24/transcript-robert -gibbs-on-fns.html.

136 *"at a higher level":* Stephen F. Hayes, "System Failure: The Christmas Day Bomber Was Never Asked Specific Questions Based on the Intelligence the U.S. Government Had Already Collected on Him," *Weekly Standard,* January 21, 2010, http://www.weeklystandard.com/blogs/title-goes-here.

137 *"fully operational":* Ibid.

137 *"foment the attack":* Briefing by Homeland Security Secretary Janet Napolitano, Assistant to the President for Counterterrorism and Homeland Security John Brennan, and Press Secretary Robert Gibbs, January 7, 2010, https://www.white house.gov/the-press-office/briefing-homeland-security-secretary-napolitano -assistant-president-counterterroris.

137 *"overseas contingency operations":* Scott Wilson and Al Kamen, "Global War on Terror Is Given New Name," March 25, 2009, http://www.washingtonpost .com/wp-dyn/content/article/2009/03/24/AR2009032402818.html.

137 *"man-caused disasters":* Tim Graham, "Obamaspeak: Homeland Security Secretary Replaces 'Terrorism' with the Term 'Man-Caused Disaster,' " *Newsbusters,* March 29, 2009, http://newsbusters.org/blogs/tim-graham/2009/03/19/obama -speak-homeland-security-secretary-replaces-terrorism-term-man-caus.

137 *"isolated extremists":* Stephen F. Hayes, "An 'Isolated Extremist'? Obama Gets It Dead Wrong," *Weekly Standard,* January 18, 2010, http://www .weeklystandard.com/articles/%25E2%2580%2598isolated-extremist%25E2 %2580%2599.

137 *"workplace violence":* Michael Daly, "Nidal Hasan's Murders Termed 'Workplace Violence' by U.S.," *Daily Beast,* August 6, 2013, http://www.thedailybeast.com

/articles/2013/08/06/nidal-hasan-s-murders-termed-workplace-violence-by-u-s
.html.

138 *"deliberately, but decisively"*: Peter Baker and Thom Shanker, "Obama Meets with
Officials on Iraq, Signaling His Commitment to Ending War," *New York Times,*
January 21, 2009, http://www.nytimes.com/2009/01/22/us/politics/22prexy
.html.

138 *on which he had campaigned:* Gates, *Duty,* p. 324.

139 *"chilling effect on Iraqis"*: "U.S. Envoy Warns Against 'Precipitous' Withdrawal
from Iraq," CNN, January 22, 2009, http://www.cnn.com/2009/WORLD
/meast/01/22/iraq.withdrawal/.

139 *"devastating attacks"*: Ibid.

139 *"take in Iraq"*: Elisabeth Bumiller, "Military Planners, in Nod to Obama, Are
Preparing for a Faster Iraq Withdrawal," *New York Times,* January 14, 2009,
http://www.nytimes.com/2009/01/15/us/politics/15policy.html.

140 *America's combat operations:* Michael R. Gordon and Bernard E. Trainor, *The
Endgame: The Inside Story of the Struggle for Iraq, from George W. Bush to Barack
Obama* (New York: Pantheon Books, 2012), p. 565.

140 *"window of greatest risk"*: Ibid., loc. 11085.

140 *"organizational capacities"*: Ibid., 566.

140 *suggested by Secretary Gates:* Gates, *Duty,* pp. 324–25.

140 *50,000–55,000 troops:* Gordon and Trainor, *The Endgame,* p. 567.

141 *point at all:* Ibid.

141 *"dealt a serious blow"*: President Barack Obama, "Responsibly Ending the War
in Iraq," Remarks at Camp Lejeune, February 27, 2009, http://www.nytimes
.com/2009/02/27/us/politics/27obama-text.html?pagewanted=all.

141 *shape its future:* General Jack Keane, interview, "Leaving Iraq was an absolute
strategic failure," PBS *Frontline,* July 29, 2014, http://www.pbs.org/wgbh/pages
/frontline/iraq-war-on-terror/losing-iraq/jack-keane-leaving-iraq-was-an-abso
lute-strategic-failure/.

142 *with Iraqis himself:* Gordon and Trainor, *The Endgame,* p. 626, and Emma Sky,
The Unraveling: High Hopes and Missed Opportunities in Iraq (New York: Public
Affairs, 2015), p. 312.

142 *"or Iraq"*: Anthony Shadid, "Ambassador Leaves Iraq with Much Still Unset-
tled," *New York Times,* August 12, 2010, http://www.nytimes.com/2010/08/13
/world/middleeast/13iraq.html.

142 *"play lacrosse"*: Sky, *The Unraveling,* p. 313.

142 *"pervasive Iranian influence"*: Embassy Baghdad cable, "U/S Burns's and U/S Flournoy's meeting VP Hashemi and the IIP," May 20, 2009; quoted in Gordon and Trainor, *The Endgame,* p. 587.

142 *"growing interest in Iran"*: Ibid.

142 *"for the short term"*: Ibid.

143 *"discussions with Iran"*: Ibid.

143 *until 2020:* Tim Pearce, "Iraqi General Says Iraq Not Ready for US Pullout," Reuters, August 12, 2010, http://abcnews.go.com/International/lt-gen-babakir -zebari-iraqi-army-unable-cope/story?id=11382246.

143 *"strength of our own nation"*: President Barack Obama, Address to the Nation on the End of Combat Operations in Iraq, August 31, 2010, https://www.white house.gov/the-press-office/2010/08/31/remarks-president-address-nation-end -combat-operations-iraq.

144 *20,000 and 24,000:* Gordon and Trainor, *The Endgame,* p. 655.

144 *3,500 troops:* Ibid., p. 670.

144 *memorandum of understanding:* Ibid., loc. 13059.

144 *"our shared security"*: President Barack Obama, Remarks at Joint Press Conference with Prime Minister Maliki of Iraq, December 12, 2011, https://www .whitehouse.gov/the-press-office/2011/12/12/remarks-president-obama-and -prime-minister-al-maliki-iraq-joint-press-co.

145 *"march toward home"*: President Barack Obama, Remarks at Fort Bragg, December 14, 2011, https://www.whitehouse.gov/the-press-office/2011/12/14 /remarks-president-and-first-lady-end-war-iraq.

145 *"of the U.S. forces"*: Gordon and Trainor, *The Endgame,* p. 671.

146 *"were my decision"*: President Barack Obama, Statement on Iraq, August 9, 2014, https://www.whitehouse.gov/the-press-office/2014/08/09/statement-president -iraq.

146 *"end of the year"*: President Barack Obama, Address to the Nation on the End of Combat Operations in Iraq, August 31, 2010, https://www.whitehouse.gov /the-press-office/2010/08/31/remarks-president-address-nation-end-combat -operations-iraq.

146 *"of the Middle East"*: Obama-Romney Third Presidential Debate, October 22, 2012, http://debates.org/index.php?page=october-22-2012-the-third-obama -romney-presidential-debate.

146 *"Ending the war"*: President Barack Obama, State of the Union Address, January 24, 2012, https://www.whitehouse.gov/the-press-office/2012/01/24 /remarks-president-state-union-address.

147 *"job against the Taliban"*: Senator Barack Obama, Remarks to Veterans of Foreign Wars, August 19, 2008, http://www.washingtonpost.com/wp-dyn/content /article/2008/08/19/AR2008081901532.html.

148 *"must be achieved"*: President Barack Obama, Remarks on a New Strategy for Afghanistan, March 27, 2009, https://www.whitehouse.gov/the-press-office /remarks-president-a-new-strategy-afghanistan-and-pakistan.

148 *recommendations for resources:* McChrystal, *My Share of the Task,* p. 294.

149 *"mission failure"*: Bob Woodward, "McChrystal: More Forces or 'Mission Failure,' " *Washington Post,* September 21, 2009, http://www.washingtonpost.com /wp-dyn/content/article/2009/09/20/AR2009092002920.html.

149 *"best military advice"*: Ibid., p. 351.

149 *"needed or appropriate"*: Gates, *Duty,* p. 371.

149 *"poll numbers will be stronger"*: Ibid., p. 378.

150 *"July of 2011"*: President Barack Obama, Address to the Nation on the Way Forward in Pakistan and Afghanistan, December 1, 2009, https://www.white house.gov/the-press-office/remarks-president-address-nation-way-forward -afghanistan-and-pakistan.

150 *"about getting out"*: Gates, *Duty,* p. 378.

150 *"summer in 2012"*: President Barack Obama, Remarks on the Way Forward in Afghanistan, June 22, 2011, https://www.whitehouse.gov/the-press-office /2011/06/22/remarks-president-way-forward-afghanistan.

151 *Pakistani border:* General Jack Keane, Testimony before the United States Senate Armed Services Committee, January 27, 2015.

151 *"tide of war is receding"*: President Barack Obama, Remarks on the Way Forward in Afghanistan, June 22, 2011, https://www.whitehouse.gov/the-press -office/2011/06/22/remarks-president-way-forward-afghanistan.

151 *"It was not"*: Justin Fishel, "Obama Troop Cuts Went Beyond Largest Withdrawal Offered by Top General," Fox News, June 28, 2011, http://www.fox news.com/politics/2011/06/28/obama-troop-cuts-went-beyond-largest-withdrawal -offered-by-top-general/.

151 *beyond military ones:* See Stephen F. Hayes, "General Reveals That Obama Ignored Military's Advice on Afghanistan," *Weekly Standard,* June 28, 2011; Mark Mazetti and Scott Shane, "Petraeus Says Afghan Pullout Is Beyond What He Advised," *New York Times,* June 23, 2011; Robert Siegel, Host, "Petraeus Faces Senate Confirmation Hearing," NPR, June 23, 2011.

152 *as we've done in Iraq*: President Barack Obama, Statement on Afghanistan, May 27, 2014, https://www.whitehouse.gov/the-press-office/2014/05/27/statement-president-afghanistan.

152 *throughout the country:* Lauren McNally and Paul Bucala, "The Taliban Resurgent: Threats to Afghanistan's Security," *Institute for the Study of War,* March 2015, p. 26, http://www.understandingwar.org/report/taliban-resurgent-threats-afghanistans-security.

152 *clear the Taliban:* Ibid., p. 14.

152 *"in the community":* Ibid.

153 *"threaten our security":* Vali Nasr, *The Dispensable Nation: American Foreign Policy in Retreat* (New York: Random House, 2013), p. 14.

154 *"al Qaeda has been decimated"* Fred Lucas, "President Obama Has Touted Al Qaeda's Demise 32 Times Since the Benghazi Attacks," CNSNews.com, November 1, 2012, http://cnsnews.com/news/article/obama-touts-al-qaeda-s-demise-32-times-benghazi-attack-0.

154 *"flat out lying":* James Kitfield, "Flynn's Last Interview: Iconoclast Departs DIA with a Warning," *Breaking Defense,* August 7, 2014, http://breakingdefense.com/2014/08/flynns-last-interview-intel-iconoclast-departs-dia-with-a-warning/.

154 *"and its affiliates":* Seth G. Jones, "A Persistent Threat: The Evolution of Al Qa'ida and Other Salafi Jihadists," Rand Corporation, 2014, p. x, http://www.rand.org/pubs/research_reports/RR637.html.

155 *"10 percent":* Ibid.

155 *"mixture of groups":* Ibid., p. xi.

155 *"we knew that":* Stephen F. Hayes and Thomas Joscelyn, "How America Was Misled on al Qaeda's Demise," *Wall Street Journal,* March 5, 2015, http://www.wsj.com/articles/stephen-hayes-and-tomas-joscelyn-how-america-was-misled-on-al-qaedas-demise-1425600796.

156 *"bin Laden is dead":* President Barack Obama, Remarks Accepting the Democratic Presidential Nomination, Charlotte, North Carolina, September 6, 2012, American Presidency Project, http://www.presidency.ucsb.edu/ws/?pid=101968.

156 *"is unacceptable":* Secretary Hillary Clinton, Remarks at Andrews Air Force Base, September 14, 2012, http://insider.foxnews.com/2012/09/14/transcript-video-hillary-clinton-speaks-at-ceremony-as-bodies-of-americans-killed-in-libya-arrive-in-the-us.

157 *"grew very violent":* Ambassador Susan Rice, Remarks on September 16, 2012, appearances on *Fox News Sunday, Meet the Press, Face the Nation, This Week with*

George Stephanopoulos, CNN State of the Union, http://blogs.wsj.com/wash wire/2012/11/16/flashback-what-susan-rice-said-about-benghazi/.

157 *"common humanity":* President Barack Obama, Remarks at the United Nations General Assembly, September 25, 2012, https://www.whitehouse.gov/the-press -office/2012/09/25/remarks-president-un-general-assembly.

157 *claimed credit:* Stephen F. Hayes, "The Benghazi Talking Points and How They Were Changed to Obscure the Truth," *Weekly Standard,* May 13, 2013, http://www.weeklystandard.com/articles/benghazi-talking-points_720543.html ?page=3.

157 *Islamic militants:* Ibid.

157 *involved in the attack:* AIS Beth Jones email, September 12, 2012 http:// chaffetz.house.gov/sites/chaffetz.house.gov/files/US%20Department%20of %20State%20-%20Beth%20Jones%20emails_O.pdf.

157 *CIA station chief:* Guy Taylor, "CIA Officer Confirmed No Protests Before Misleading Benghazi Account Given," *Washington Times,* March 31, 2014, www .washingtontimes.com/news/2014/mar/31/cia-ignored-station-chief-in-libya -when-creating-t/?page=all.

157 *"prior to the attacks":* U.S. Department of State, Accountability Review Board on Benghazi, December 19, 2012, http://www.state.gov/documents/organiza tion/202446.pdf.

157 *by the CIA:* Hayes, "The Benghazi Talking Points and How They Were Changed to Obscure the Truth."

158 *"in the attacks":* Ibid.

158 *After an interagency meeting:* Ibid.

158 *should have been focused:* David Blair and Alex Spillius, "US Consulate Attack in Libya: The Warning Signs Were There in Benghazi," *Daily Telegraph,* September 12, 2012, http://www.telegraph.co.uk/news/worldnews/africaand indianocean/libya/9539148/US-consulate-attack-in-Libya-the-warning-signs -were-there-in-Benghazi.html.

159 *"difficult challenges":* Ben Rhodes email, September 14, 2012, http://www.judi cialwatch.org/document-archive/rhodes-email/.

159 *at least twenty attacks:* U.S. Department of State, Accountability Review Board on Benghazi, December 29, 2012, http://www.state.gov/documents/organization /202446.pdf.

159 *Ambassador Chris Stevens had asked:* Gregory Hicks, "Benghazi and the Smearing of Chris Stevens," *Wall Street Journal,* January 22, 2014, http://www.wsj .com/articles/SB10001424052702304302704579332732276330284.

159 *cut U.S. security staff:* Jay Solomon and Dion Nissenbaum, "Security Cut Before Libya Raid," *Wall Street Journal,* October 10, 2012, http://www.wsj.com /articles/SB10000872396390444799904578048344154761294.

159 *Libyan government had asked:* Editorial Board, "How to Help Libya's New Government," *Washington Post,* July 9, 2012, https://www.washingtonpost.com /opinions/how-to-help-libyas-new-government-succeed/2012/07/09/gJQAuhc CZW_story.html.

162 *"zero sum thinking":* Ambassador Ryan Crocker, interview, "Losing Iraq," PBS *Frontline,* http://www.pbs.org/wgbh/pages/frontline/iraq-war-on-terror/losing -iraq/transcript-66/.

162 *Abu Bakr al-Baghdadi had become the leader:* Anthony Shadid, "Iraqi Insurgent Group Names New Leaders," *New York Times,* May 16, 2010, http://atwar .blogs.nytimes.com/2010/05/16/iraqi-insurgent-group-names-new-leaders/.

162 *quickly spread:* Joe Sterling, "Da'ara, the Spark That Lit the Syrian Flame," CNN, March 1, 2012, http://www.cnn.com/2012/03/01/world/meast/syria -crisis-beginnings/.

163 *"believe he is a reformer":* Secretary of State Hillary Clinton, appearance on CBS *Face the Nation,* March 27, 2011, http://www.cbsnews.com/news/clinton-no -military-action-in-syria-for-now/.

164 *"democratic transition":* President Obama, Remarks on the Middle East and North Africa, May 19, 2011, https://www.whitehouse.gov/the-press-office /2011/05/19/remarks-president-middle-east-and-north-africa.

164 *"to step aside":* President Obama statement on Syria, August 18, 2011, https:// www.whitehouse.gov/blog/2011/08/18/president-obama-future-syria-must-be -determined-its-people-president-bashar-al-assad.

164 *"change my equation":* President Obama, Remarks to the White House Press Corps, August 20, 2012, https://www.whitehouse.gov/the-press-office/2012 /08/20/remarks-president-white-house-press-corps.

165 *"scotch any action":* Panetta, *Worthy Fights,* p. 450.

165 *"to the world":* Ibid.

165 *"believe you next time":* Amr Al-Azm, interview, "Obama at War," PBS *Frontline,* www.pbs.org/wgbh/pages/frontline/foreign-affairs-defense/obama-at-war /transcript-84/.

166 *"regional allies":* Oubai Shahbandar interview, "Obama at War," PBS *Frontline,* www.pbs.org/wgbh/pages/frontline/foreign-affairs-defense/obama-at-war/tran script-84/.

166 *"one hundred percent of their chemical weapons"*: Secretary of State John Kerry, interview, NBC *Meet the Press,* Sunday, July 20, 2014, http://www.nbcnews.com/meet-the-press/meet-press-transcript-july-20-2014-n160611.

166 *chlorine gas attacks:* Elliott Abrams, "Chlorine Warfare in Syria Continues, Unpunished," *Newsweek,* May 26, 2015, http://www.newsweek.com/chemical-warfare-syria-continues-unpunished-335592.

166 *intelligence reports:* Former secretary of defense Leon Panetta, interview, and former ambassador James Jeffrey, interview, "Rise of ISIS," PBS *Frontline,* October 28, 2014, http://www.pbs.org/wgbh/pages/frontline/iraq-war-on-terror/rise-of-isis/transcript-70/.

167 *"jayvee team":* David Remnick, "Going the Distance, On and off the road with Barack Obama," *New Yorker,* January 27, 2014, http: //www.newyorker.com/magazine/2014/01/27/going-the-distance-remnick?currentPage=all.

167 *"stretched across territory":* Ibid.

167 *"interpretation of Islam":* Graeme Wood, "What ISIS Really Wants," *Atlantic,* March 2015, http://www.theatlantic.com/features/archive/2015/02/what-isis-really-wants/384980/.

168 *"would order it":* Remarks by President Obama at G20 Press Conference, November 16, 2014, https://www.whitehouse.gov/the-press-office/2014/11/16/remarks-president-obama-g20-press-conference-november-16-2014.

169 *"not defeat ISIS":* General Jack Keane, Testimony, U.S. Senate Committee on Armed Services, May 21, 2015.

170 *"deluding ourselves":* Ambassador Ryan Crocker, "Islamic State Is Getting Stronger and It's Targeting America," *Wall Street Journal,* September 8, 2014, http://www.wsj.com/articles/ryan-crocker-islamic-state-is-getting-stronger-and-its-targeting-america-1410218507.

170 *"price of war":* President Harry S. Truman, Remarks to a Joint Session of Congress, "Special Message to the Congress on the Threat to the Freedom of Europe," March 17, 1948.

CHAPTER 5: APPEASING ADVERSARIES

172 *handed over the briefcase:* Gordon Corera, *Shopping for Bombs: Nuclear Proliferation, Global Insecurity, and the Rise and Fall of the A. Q. Khan Network* (New York: Oxford University Press, 2006), pp. 59–63.

172 *weapons-grade levels:* David Albright and Andrea Stricker, "Iran's Nuclear Program," Iran Primer, U.S. Institute for Peace, http://iranprimer.usip.org/resource/irans-nuclear-program.

172 *Tehran Research Reactor:* Arms Control Association, "Timeline of Nuclear Diplomacy with Iran," p. 1, https://www.armscontrol.org/factsheet/Timeline-of
-Nuclear-Diplomacy-With-Iran.

172 *world has now signed:* United Nations Office for Disarmament Affairs, "Treaty
on the Non-Proliferation of Nuclear Weapons (NPT)," http://www.un.org
/disarmament/WMD/Nuclear/NPT.shtml.

172 *safeguards agreement:* https://www.iaea.org/sites/default/files/publications
/documents/infcircs/1974/infcirc214.pdf.

173 *share of the Iranian economy:* Emanuele Ottolenghi, *The Pasdaran: Inside Iran's
Islamic Revolutionary Guard Corps* (Washington, DC: FDD Press, 2011),
p. 1.

173 *American casualties:* Kimberly Kagan, *The Surge: A Military History* (New York:
Encounter Books, 2009), pp. 160–61.

174 *Geneva nuclear talks:* U.S. Department of Defense, "Progress Toward Security
and Stability in Afghanistan," October 2014, p. 98, http://freebeacon.com/wp
-content/uploads/2014/11/afghanistan-security-stability_201410.pdf.

174 *across the Middle East:* Lieutenant General Michael T. Flynn, USA (Ret.), Testimony, Joint Foreign Affairs and HASC Subcommittees, June 10, 2015.

174 *secret nuclear facilities:* Alireza Jafarzadeh, Remarks on New Information on Top
Secret Projects of the Iranian Regime's Nuclear Program, August 14, 2002, http?//
www.iranwatch.org/library/ncn-new-information-top-secret-nuclear-projects
-8-14-02.

174 *room for 50,000:* Albright and Stricker, "Iran's Nuclear Program," p. 4.

175 *matter of weeks:* Matthew Kroenig, *A Time to Attack: The Looming Iranian Nuclear Threat* (New York: Palgrave Macmillan, 2014), p. 62.

175 *"equipment in Isfahan":* Prime Minister Netanyahu, Speech to the UN General
Assembly, October 1, 2013, http://www.timesofisrael.com/full-text-netanyahus
-2013-speech-to-the-un-general-assembly/.

175 *broke the IAEA seals on:* "Iran Breaks Seals at Nuclear Plant," CNN, August 10,
2005, http://www.cnn.com/2005/WORLD/europe/08/10/iran.iaea.1350/.

176 *at Natanz:* "Iran Breaks Seals at Nuclear Sites," BBC, January 10, 2006, http://
news.bbc.co.uk/2/hi/middle_east/4597738.stm.

176 *resolution 1696:* http://www.un.org/press/en//2006/sc8792.doc.htm.

177 *most often in New York:* Juan C. Zarate, *Treasury's War: The Unleashing of a New
Era of Financial Warfare* (New York: PublicAffairs, 2013), p. 26.

177 *"a death sentence":* "A Fearful Number," *Economist,* June 5, 2015, http://www
.economist.com/news/finance-and-economics/21653673-bank-rejects-american
-accusations-it-abetted-financial-crime-fearful.

177 *four resolutions:* Jason Starr, "The U.N. Resolutions," Iran Primer, United States Institute of Peace, http://iranprimer.usip.org/resource/un-resolutions.

178 *that very bank:* Zarate, *Treasury's War,* pp. 300–301.

178 *"raise suspicions":* Ibid., p. 301.

178 *to Iranian businesses:* Undersecretary for Terrorism and Financial Intelligence Stuart Levey, U.S. Department of the Treasury, Testimony, Senate Committee on Finance, April 1, 2008, http://www.treasury.gov/press-center/press-releases /Pages/hp898.aspx.

178 *terrorist-financing institution:* U.S. Department of the Treasury, "Treasury Cuts Iran's Bank Saderat Off from U.S. Financial System," September 8, 2006, http://www.treasury.gov/press-center/press-releases/Pages/hp87.aspx.

178 *Bank Sepah:* U.S. Department of the Treasury, "Iran's Bank Sepah Designated by Treasury Sepah Facilitating Iran's Weapons Program," January 9, 2007, http://www.treasury.gov/press-center/press-releases/Pages/hp219.aspx.

178 *Bank Mellat:* U.S. Department of the Treasury, "Treasury Designates Iranian State-Owned Bank for Facilitating Iran's Proliferation Activities," May 17, 2011, http://www.treasury.gov/press-center/press-releases/Pages/tg1178 .aspx.

179 *Bank Melli:* Zarate, *Treasury's War,* p. 304.

179 *as did the Chinese:* Robin Wright, "Stuart Levey's War," *New York Times,* October 31, 2008, http://www.nytimes.com/2008/11/02/magazine/02IRAN-t.html ?pagewanted=all.

179 *IRGC and Iran's Ministry of Defense:* Zarate, *Treasury's War,* p. 307.

179 *work isolating Iran on hold:* Ibid., p. 324.

179 *"we were the problem":* Vice President Joe Biden, Remarks at the Rabbinical Assembly Convention, May 8, 2012, http://politicalticker.blogs.cnn.com/2012 /05/08/biden-defends-iran-stance-we-were-the-problem/.

180 *was overrun:* Gates, *Duty,* p. 178.

180 *Madeleine Albright apologized:* Kenneth Pollack, *The Persian Puzzle: Deciphering the Twenty-Five Year Conflict Between Iran and America* (New York: Random House, 2004), loc. 190.

180 *"nation any good":* Ibid., loc. 219.

181 *holiday of Nowruz:* President Barack Obama, Videotaped Remarks in Celebration of Nowruz, March 20, 2009, https://www.whitehouse.gov/the_press_office /VIDEOTAPED-REMARKS-BY-THE-PRESIDENT-IN-CELEBRATION-OF -NOWRUZ/.

181 *"Death to America"*: Stephen F. Hayes, "Iran Responds: 'Death to America,' " *Weekly Standard*, March 21, 2009.

182 *sent a letter:* "Exclusive: U.S. Contacted Iran's Ayatollah Before Election," *Washington Times*, June 24, 2009, http://www.washingtontimes.com/news /2009/jun/24/us-contacted-irans-ayatollah-before-election/print/.

182 *62.6 percent of the vote:* Thomas Erdbrink, "Ahmadinejad Re-elected in Iran as Demonstrators Protest Results," *Washington Post*, June 14, 2009, http:// www.washingtonpost.com/wp-dyn/content/article/2009/06/13/AR20090613 00627.html.

182 *in jeopardy:* Ryan Lizza, "The Consequentialist: How the Arab Spring Remade Obama's Foreign Policy," *New Yorker*, May 2, 2011, http://www.newyorker.com /magazine/2011/05/02/the-consequentalist.

182 *outside Qom:* Karen DeYoung and Michael D. Shear, "U.S., Allies Say Iran Has Secret Nuclear Facility," *Washington Post*, September 26, 2009, http:// www.washingtonpost.com/wp-dyn/content/article/2009/09/25/AR20090925 00289.html.

182 *"a nuclear expert":* Ibid.

183 *ending the round of negotiations:* Nasr, *Dispensable Nation*, p. 118.

183 *remained on hold:* Zarate, *Treasury's War*, pp. 329–30.

183 *set of sanctions on Iran:* Joel Winton, "Rewriting History: The Real Hillary Record on Iran Sanctions," *Weekly Standard*, June 9, 2014, http://www.weekly standard.com/keyword/Joel-Winton.

183 *Steinberg sent a letter:* Ron Kampeas, "Obama and Kerry Slowing Iran Sanctions Legislation Push," *Jewish Journal*, December 15, 2009, http://www.jewishjournal .com/iran/article/obama_and_kerry_slowing_iran_sanctions_legislation_push _20091215.

184 *"crippling sanctions":* David Lerman, "Senators Call for Crippling Sanctions on Iran Central Bank," *Bloomberg Business*, August 9, 2011, http://www.bloom berg.com/news/articles/2011-08-09/senators-call-for-crippling-sanctions-on -iran-central-bank.

184 *between the United States and Iran:* Hillary Rodham Clinton, *Hard Choices* (New York: Simon & Schuster, 2014), loc. 7142.

185 *"threw them a lifeline":* Authors' meeting with senior government official in the Middle East, April 2014.

185 *secret meetings:* Associated Press, "How a Series of Secret Meetings Between U.S. and Iran Led to Historic Deal," November 25, 2013, PBS *Newshour*,

The Rundown blog, http://www.pbs.org/newshour/rundown/how-a-series-of
-secret-meetings-between-us-and-iran-led-to-historic-agreement/.

185 *began in mid-2011:* Associated Press, "How a Series of Secret Meetings Between
U.S. and Iran Led to Historic Deal," November 25, 2013, PBS *Newshour,* The
Rundown blog, http://www.pbs.org/newshour/rundown/how-a-series-of-secret
-meetings-between-us-and-iran-led-to-historic-agreement/.

185 *Oman in July 2012:* Clinton, *Hard Choices,* loc. 7518.

185 *continue to enrich:* Michael Doran, "Obama's Secret Iran Strategy," *Mosaic,*
February 2, 2015, http://mosaicmagazine.com/essay/2015/02/obamas-secret
-iran-strategy/.

186 *Assad or his forces:* Jay Solomon and Carol E. Lee, "Obama Wrote Secret Letter
to Iran's Khamenei About Fighting Islamic State," *Wall Street Journal,* November 6, 2014, http://www.wsj.com/articles/obama-wrote-secret-letter-to-irans
-khamenei-about-fighting-islamic-state-1415295291.

188 *months to delay:* Hillel Fradkin and Lewis Libby, "Iran Inspections in 24 Days?
Not Even Close," *Wall Street Journal,* July 21, 2015, http://www.wsj.com
/articles/Iran-inspections-in-24-days-not-even-close-1437521911.

190 *"the anticipated agreement":* Dr. Robert Joseph, Testimony, House Committee
on Foreign Affairs, Subcommittee on the Middle East and North Africa, June
10, 2015.

190 *non-nuclear purposes:* Secretary Jack Lew, Remarks at Washington Institute
for Near East Policy, April 29, 2015, http://www.washingtoninstitute.org
/policy-analysis/view/remarks-of-treasury-secretary-jacob-j.-lew.

191 *refrain from reimposing:* Robert Satloff, "What's Really Wrong with the Iran
Deal," *New York Daily News,* July 14, 2015, http://www.nydailynews.com
/opinion/robert-satloff-wrong-iran-nuclear-deal-article-1.2292264.

192 *"border of Jordan":* Doran, "Obama's Secret Iran Strategy."

195 *fix the label:* Hillary Rodham Clinton, *Hard Choices* (New York: Simon &
Schuster, 2014), p. 206.

196 *"other had to lose":* President Barack Obama, Remarks at the New Economic
School, Moscow, July 2009.

197 *"theory of the world":* David Remnick, "Watching the Eclipse," *New Yorker,* August 11, 2014.

197 *"even the EU today":* Open Letter to the Obama Administration from Central
and Eastern Europe, July 15, 2009, http://wyborcza.pl/1,98817,6825987,An
_Open_Letter_to_the_Obama_Administration_from_Central.html.

198 *installations in Poland:* Megan K. Stack, "Poles Indignant That U.S. Altered Missile-Shield Plans," *Los Angeles Times,* September 29, 2009.

199 *"false sense of security":* Bret Stephens, "The Meltdown," *Commentary,* September 1, 2014.

199 *"more flexibility":* J. David Goodman, "Microphone Captures a Candid Obama," *New York Times,* March 26, 2012, http://www.nytimes.com/2012/03/27/us /politics/obama-caught-on-microphone-telling-medvedev-of-flexibility.html? _r=0.

199 *so strenuously opposed:* David M. Herszenhorn and Michael Gordon, "U.S. Cancels Part of Missile Defense that Russia Opposed," *New York Times,* March 16, 2013, http://www.nytimes.com/2013/03/17/world/europe/with-eye-on-north -korea-us-cancels-missile-defense-russia-opposed.html.

200 *Snowden to Moscow:* Isabel Gorst and Joby Warrick, "Snowden Leaves Moscow Airport to Live in Russia," *Washington Post,* August 1, 2013, http://www .washingtonpost.com/world/europe/snowden-leaves-moscow-airport-to-live -in-russia/2013/08/01/2f2d1aba-faa9-11e2-a369-d1954abcb7e3_story.html.

200 *Whether Snowden was a Russian operative:* See, for example, Edward Lucas, *The Snowden Operation: Inside the West's Greatest Intelligence Disaster* (Kindle Single), Amazon Digital Services, Inc., January 23, 2014.

200 *He "called in":* Lukas I. Alpert, "Snowden Appears on Putin Call-in Show," *Wall Street Journal,* April 17, 2014, http://www.wsj.com/articles/SB100014240527 02304311204579507422585333620.

200 *New START as a "serious step":* Michael D. Shear, "Obama, Medvedev Sign Treaty To Reduce Nuclear Weapons," *Washington Post,* April 8, 2010, http://www.wash ingtonpost.com/wp-dyn/content/article/2010/04/08/AR2010040801677.html ?sid=ST2010040801040.

200 *"bolster our national security":* Secretary of State Hillary Clinton, Remarks at United States Institute of Peace, October 21, 2009, http://www.usip.org/sites /default/files/resources/clinton_usip_remarks.pdf.

201 *"more weapons deployed":* Baker Spring, "Disarm Now, Ask Questions Later: Obama's Nuclear Weapons Policy," Heritage Foundation Backgrounder, No. 2826, July 11, 2013.

201 *than the United States:* Robert Joseph, Eric Edelman, and Rebeccah Heinrichs, "After You, Mr. Putin," *National Review,* March 4, 2015.

202 *cheating in November 2012:* Josh Rogin, "U.S. Knew Russia Violated Intermediate-Range Nuclear Forces Treaty," *Daily Beast,* November 26, 2013.

202 *"needs to take place"*: Stephen F. Hayes, "Obama's Fantasy-Based Foreign Policy," *Weekly Standard,* March 17, 2014, http://www.weeklystandard.com/articles /obama-s-fantasy-based-foreign-policy_784266.html.

203 *"separatist fighters"*: Michael Weiss and James Miller, "New Putin Invasion Coming This Summer," *Daily Beast,* May 17, 2015.

204 *"precisely nothing"*: Eric Edelman, "Confronting Putin's Invasion: It Can—and Must—Be Done," *Weekly Standard,* March 17, 2014.

CHAPTER 6: DISARMING AMERICA

207 *"freedom and peace"*: Remarks by President Ronald Reagan, "Address to the Nation on Defense and National Security," March 23, 1983, http://www.reagan .utexas.edu/archives/speeches/1983/32383d.htm.

207 *"ready to defend"*: Remarks prepared for delivery by President John F. Kennedy, Dallas Citizens Council, Trade Mart, Dallas, Texas, November 22, 1963, http://www.jfklibrary.org/Asset-Viewer/Archives/JFKPOF-048-022.aspx.

207 *"world freedom"*: Ibid.

208 *"United States of America"*: William J. Perry, John P. Abizaid, et al., "Ensuring a Strong Defense for the Future: The National Defense Panel Review of the 2014 Quadrennial Defense Review," July 31, 2014, p. vii.

208 *to do so:* President Barack Obama, Press Room Remarks, August 28, 2014, https://www.whitehouse.gov/the-press-office/2014/08/28/statement-president; President Barack Obama, Press Conference after G-7 Summit, Krun, Germany, June 8, 2015, https://www.whitehouse.gov/the-press-office/2015/06/08 /remarks-president-obama-press-conference-after-g7-summit.

208 *"nation's deficit problems"*: Secretary of Defense Robert Gates press conference, August 9, 2010, http://www.washingtonpost.com/wp-dyn/content/article /2010/08/11/AR2010081105285.html.

209 *"of higher value"*: Gates, *Duty,* p. 316.

209 *"January 6, 2011"*: Secretary of Defense Robert Gates and Chairman of the Joint Chiefs Robert Mullen, press briefing, January 6, 2011, http://www .defense.gov/transcripts/transcript.aspx?transcriptid=4747.

209 *had already proposed:* Editorial Board, "Mr. Obama's Defense Cuts," *Washington Post,* April 20, 2011, http://www.washingtonpost.com/opinions/mr-obamas -defense-cuts/2011/04/20/AFlMqNEE_story.html.

209 *"politically convenient"*: Gates, *Duty,* p. 464.

210 *of government spending:* Representative Buck McKeon, Chairman, House Armed Services Committee, "Putting 50% of Sequester Cuts on Defense's 17% Is Bad," Letter to the Editor, *Wall Street Journal,* December 4, 2013.

210 *239-year history:* John T. Bennett, "Military Chiefs Warn Anew About Sequester Cuts," *DefenseNews,* February 2, 2015, http://www.defensenews.com/story /defense/policy-budget/congress/2015/01/28/sequestration-military-isis-budget /22462259/.

210 *"current and projected operations":* General Mark A. Welsh, III, Chief of Staff, United States Air Force, Testimony, United States Senate Armed Services Committee, January 28, 2014, http://www.armed-services.senate.gov/imo/media /doc/Welch_01-28-15.pdf.

211 *"in many years":* Chris Jennewein, "CNO Says Budget Cuts Leave Navy at 'Lowest Point' in Years," *Times of San Diego,* March 5, 2015, http://timesof sandiego.com/military/2015/03/05/cno-says-budget-cuts-leave-navy-at-lowest -point-in-years/.

211 *at risk unnecessarily:* Nick Simeone, "Sequester Degrades Navy, Marine Corps Readiness, Officials Say," U.S. Department of Defense, DoD News, February 26, 2015, http://www.defense.gov/news/newsarticle.aspx?id=128259.

211 *since before World War II:* Dan Lamothe, "Army Details How It Will Cut to Its Smallest Size Since Before World War II," *Washington Post,* July 9, 2015, http:// www.washingtonpost.com/news/checkpoint/wp/2015/07/09/army-details-how -it-will-cut-to-its-smallest-size-since-before-world-war-ii/.

211 *no carrrier presence:* David Larter, "Navy to Pull Carrier from Central Command This Fall," *Navy Times,* June 5, 2015, http://www.navytimes.com/story /military/2015/06/05/navy-pulls-carrier-centcom-islamic-state-group-presence /28554047/.

211 *"cuts to $937 billion":* National Defense Panel Review of the 2014 Quadrennial Defense Review, p. 29, http://www.usip.org/sites/default/files/Ensuring-a -Strong-U.S.-Defense-for-the-Future-NDP-Review-of-the-QDR_0.pdf.

212 *"to our posture":* General Raymond T. Odierno, Chief of Staff, United States Army, Testimony, United States Senate Committee on Armed Services, January 28, 2015.

212 *"Second World War":* Former secretary of state Henry A. Kissinger, Testimony, United States Senate Committee on Armed Services, January 29, 2015.

213 *"increasingly dangerous world":* Former undersecretary of defense for policy Michèle Flournoy, Testimony, United States Senate Committee on Armed Services, February 10, 2015.

213 *"national security strategy"*: National Defense Panel Review of the 2014 Quadrennial Defense Review, p. 23.

214 *"second region"*: President Barack Obama, Defense Strategic Guidance, January 2012, p. 4, http://www.defense.gov/news/Defense_Strategic_Guidance.pdf.

214 *"stability operations"*: Ibid., p. 6.

214 *"end today's wars"*: Ibid., cover letter.

215 *"in our capabilities"*: The Honorable Mac Thornberry, Chairman, House Armed Services Committee, letter to the Honorable Tom Price, M.D., Chairman, House Budget Committee, February 21, 2015.

216 *"currently have fielded"*: Undersecretary of Defense for Acquisition, Technology, and Logistics Frank Kendall, Testimony, U.S. House of Representatives Committee on Armed Services, "A Case for Reform: Improving DOD's Ability to Respond to the Pace of Technological Change," January 28, 2015.

216 *"very uncomfortable"*: General Martin Dempsey, Chairman of the Joint Chiefs of Staff, interview, *Fox News Sunday,* January 12, 2015, http://www.atlanticcouncil.org/blogs/natosource/dempsey-cyber-is-the-only-domain-in-which-us-has-peer-competitors.

216 *"to any country"*: Robert Joseph, "Second to One," *National Review,* July 2, 2012, http://www.nationalreview.com/article/304310/second-one-robert-g-joseph.

217 *nuclear force structure:* Former undersecretary of defense for policy Eric Edelman, Testimony, U.S. Senate Committee on Foreign Relations, "The New START Treaty Benefits and Risks," June 24, 2010.

217 *America's deterrence capability:* Ibid.

217 *already below 700:* Ibid.

217 *defense interceptors:* Former undersecretary of state for arms control and international security Robert Joseph, Testimony, U.S. Senate Committee on Foreign Relations, "The New START Treaty Benefits and Risks," June 24, 2010.

217 *"no way, no how"*: Undersecretary of State for Arms Control and International Security Ellen Tauscher, Special Press Briefing, March 29, 2010, http://www.state.gov/r/pa/prs/ps/2010/03/139176.htm.

217 *language in the treaty:* Robert Joseph testimony, June 24, 2010.

217 *"current and planned"*: U.S. Department of State, Bureau of Verification, Compliance, and Implementation, "Ballistic Missile Defense and New START Treaty," Fact Sheet, April 21, 2010, http://www.state.gov/t/avc/rls/140624.htm.

218 *existing warheads:* Ibid.

218 *"new military capabilities"*: 2010 Nuclear Posture Review, U.S. Department of Defense, April 2010, p. xiv, http://www.defense.gov/npr/docs/2010%20 Nuclear%20Posture%20Review%20Report.pdf.

218 *"nuclear postures"*: President Barack Obama, Remarks at the Brandenburg Gate, Berlin, Germany, June 19, 2013, https://www.whitehouse.gov/the-press -office/2013/06/19/remarks-president-obama-brandenburg-gate-berlin -germany.

218 *5,000 kilometers:* Treaty Between the United States and the USSR on Elimina- tion of Their Intermediate-Range and Shorter-Range Missiles (INF), http:// www.state.gov/t/avc/trty/102360.htm.

219 *"will pay a terrible price"*: Michael Anton, "Our Nuclear Posture: Under the Obama Administration? Supine," *Weekly Standard,* April 19, 2010, http:// www.weeklystandard.com/print/articles/our-nuclear-posture?page=2.

221 *"top priority"*: President Barack Obama, Remarks to the Australian Parlia- ment, November 17, 2011, https://www.whitehouse.gov/the-press-office/2011 /11/17/remarks-president-obama-australian-parliament.

221 *"it can't happen"*: Zachary Fryer-Briggs, "DOD Official: Asia Pivot 'Can't Hap- pen' Due to Budget Pressures," *DefenseNews,* March 4, 2014, http://archive .defensenews.com/article/20140304/DEFREG02/303040022/DoD-Official -Asia-Pivot-Can-t-Happen-Due-Budget-Pressures.

221 *"can and will continue"*: Ibid.

221 *by double digits:* U.S.-China Economic and Security Review Commission, "2014 Report to Congress," November 2014, p. 11, http://origin.www.uscc.gov /sites/default/files/annual_reports/Executive%20Summary.pdf.

222 *"maneuverable warheads"*: Ibid.

222 *hypersonic missile:* Bill Gertz, "China Conducts Fourth Test of Wu-14 Strike Ve- hicle," *Washington Free Beacon,* June 11, 2015, http://freebeacon.com/national -security/china-conducts-fourth-test-of-wu-14-strike-vehicle/.

222 *"U.S. and allied vessels"*: Bill Gertz, "ONI Reveals Massive Chinese Naval Buildup," *Washington Free Beacon,* April 10, 2015, http://freebeacon.com /national-security/oni-reveals-massive-chinese-naval-buildup/.

222 *the Indian Ocean:* Ibid.

222 *by 2020:* U.S.-China Economic and Security Review Commission, "2014 Re- port to Congress," p. 12, http://origin.www.uscc.gov/sites/default/files/annual _reports/Executive%20Summary.pdf.

222 *bolster these claims:* Gordon Lubold and Adam Entous, "U.S. Says Beijing Is Building Up South China Sea Islands," *Wall Street Journal,* May 9, 2015 http:// www.wsj.com/articles/u-s-says-beijing-building-up-south-china-sea-islands -1431109387.

222 *two thousand acres:* Ibid.

222 *U.S. military flights:* "U.S. Warns China Not To Challenge Military Flights Over South China Sea," *FoxNews.com,* May 22, 2015, http://www.foxnews .com/politics/2015/05/22/us-warns-china-not-to-challenge-military-flights over-south-china-sea/.

223 *drone force:* Zachary Keck, "China Is Building 42,000 Military Drones: Should America Worry?" *National Interest,* May 10, 2015, http://nationalinterest.org /blog/the-buzz/china-building-42000-military-drones-should-america-worry -12856.

223 *jamming communications:* Bill Gertz, "Chinese Military Using Jamming Against U.S. Drones," *Washington Free Beacon,* May 22, 2015, http://freebeacon .com/national-security/chinese-military-using-jamming-against-u-s-drones /print/.

223 *rocket-propelled sea mines:* Michael Pillsbury, *The Hundred-Year Marathon: China's Secret Strategy to Replace America as the Global Superpower* (New York: Henry Holt, 2015), p. 154.

223 *tactical high-energy laser weapons:* Ibid.

223 *"weakest point":* Ibid., p. 138.

223 *of twenty years:* Ibid., p. 154.

223 *U.S. private sector:* Ellen Nakashima, "Confidential Report Lists US Weapons Systems Designs Compromised by Chinese Cyberspies," *Washington Post,* May 27, 2013, http://www.washingtonpost.com/world/national-security/confidential -report-lists-us-weapons-system-designs-compromised-by-chinese-cyberspies /2013/05/27/a42c3e1c-c2dd-11e2-8c3b-0b5e9247e8ca_story.html.

223 *Twenty-two million people:* General Michael Hayden, "Why Can't We Play This Game?" *Cipher Brief,* June 24, 2015, http://www.thecipherbrief.com/articles /why-cant-we-play-game.

224 *"and their tools":* Ibid.

224 *"country in the world":* Pillsbury, *The Hundred-Year Marathon,* p. 151.

225 *"freedom of action":* David R. Sands, "New Russia-China Alliance Latest Diplo- matic, Strategic Blow to Obama," *Washington Times,* April 30, 2015, http://www .washingtontimes.com/news/2015/apr/30/china-russia-alliance-challenges-us -western-domina/?page=all.

225 *"might more accurately be called"*: Bret Stephens, "The Meltdown," *Commentary,* September 1, 2014, https://www.commentarymagazine.com/article/the-melt down/.

226 *"eating the seed corn"*: Former undersecretary of defense for policy Eric Edelman, Testimony, Senate Armed Services Committee, February 10, 2015.

227 *"live on our knees"*: President Franklin D. Roosevelt, "Message to the Special Convocation of the University of Oxford," June 19, 1941, American Presidency Project, http://www.presidency.ucsb.edu/ws/?pid=16131.

227 *"but first"*: President John F. Kennedy, Remarks at Breakfast of the Fort Worth Chamber of Commerce, November 22, 1963, American Presidency Project, http://www.presidency.ucsb.edu/ws/?pid=9538.

CHAPTER 7: RESTORING AMERICAN POWER

231 *"welfare of this nation"*: President Harry S. Truman, Address to a Joint Session of Congress, March 12, 1947, http://avalon.law.yale.edu/20th_century/trudoc.asp.

231 *"success of liberty"*: President John F. Kennedy, Inaugural Address, January 20, 1961, http://www.jfklibrary.org/Asset-Viewer/BqXIEM9F4024ntFl7SVAjA .aspx.

233 *"No foe in the field"*: General Jim Mattis (Ret.), Testimony, Senate Armed Services Committee, January 27, 2015.

233 *$661 billion:* Department of Defense FY2012 Budget Proposal, February 14, 2011, http://www.defense.gov/home/features/2011/0211_fiscalbudget/SUM MARY_OF_THE_DOD_FISCAL_2012_BUDGET_PROPOSAL_with_Charts _Updated_1710_02.14.2011.pdf.

234 *"shortchanges innovation"*: Ibid., p. 4.

235 *"undue emphasis on budgetary constraints"*: National Defense Panel Review of the 2014 Quadrennial Defense Review, p. 3, http://www.usip.org/sites/default /files/Ensuring-a-Strong-U.S.-Defense-for-the-Future-NDP-Review-of-the-QDR _0.pdf.

235 *"directed-energy weapons"*: Ibid., pp. 40–45.

235 *left ourselves vulnerable:* General Michael Hayden, "Why Can't We Play This Game?" *Cipher Brief,* June 24, 2015, http://www.thecipherbrief.com/articles /why-cant-we-play-game.

236 *nation's electric grid:* Henry F. Cooper and Peter Vincent Pry, "The Threat to Melt the Electtric Grid," *Wall Street Journal,* April 30, 2015, http://www.wsj .com/articles/the-threat-to-melt-the-electric-grid-1430436815.

238 *"all else rests"*: Mark Helprin, "Indefensible Defense," *National Review,* June 11, 2015.

238 *sixty vetted candidates:* Austin Wright and Philip Ewing, "Ash Carter's Unwelcome News: only 60 Syrian rebels fit for training, Politico, July 7, 2015, http:// www.politico.com/story/2015/07/ash-carter-syrian-rebel-training-119812.html.

238 *near-term requirements:* General Jack Keane, Testimony, Senate Armed Services Committee, January 27, 2015.

238 *Thousands of advisors:* Jack Keane and Danielle Pletka, "An American-Led Coalition Can Defeat ISIS," *Wall Street Journal,* August 24, 2014, http://www .wsj.com/articles/jack-keane-and-danielle-pletka-an-american-led-coalition-can -defeat-isis-in-iraq-1408919270.

240 *25 percent fewer surge forces:* Ibid.

240 *prevent those attacks:* General Mike Hayden, Remarks at National Press Club, January 23, 2006, https://www.press.org/speakers/transcripts-2006.

241 *recruiter for ISIS:* Thomas Joscelyn, "Gitmo Poet Now Recruiting for Islamic State," *Weekly Standard,* November 19, 2014, http://www.weeklystandard .com/blogs/gitmo-poet-now-recruiting-islamic-state_819587.html#.

242 *"successful regional power":* President Obama, Interview, NPR, December 29, 2014, http://www.npr.org/2014/12/29/372485968/transcript-president-obamas -full-npr-interview.

242 *"threat to our security":* Secretary of Defense Dick Cheney, "Defense Strategy for the 1990s," January 1993, p. 8, http://www.informationclearinghouse.info /pdf/naarpr_Defense.pdf.

244 *took force off the table:* Tamar Pileggi, "Obama: There Is No Military Option to Stop Iran," *The Times of Israel,* June 1, 2015, http://www.timesofisrael.com /obama-a-deal-only-way-to-stop-iran-no-military-option.

244 *"make more concessions":* "Obama's False Iran Choice," *Wall Street Journal,* July 15, 2015, http://www.wsj.com/articles/obamas-false-iran-choice-1437001404.

253 *"ballistic-missile attack":* Robert Joseph and Eric Edelman, "Here's the Difference Between How Obama and Reagan Handled Nuke Negotiations," *National Review,* April 3, 2015.

254 *protect us from attack:* Ibid.

INDEX